Elegant Design
A Designer's Guide to Harnessing Aesthetics

LUCA IANDOLI
GIUSEPPE ZOLLO

BLOOMSBURY VISUAL ARTS

LONDON • NEW YORK • OXFORD • NEW DELHI • SYDNEY

Bloomsbury Publishing Plc
50 Bedford Square, London, WC1B 3DP, UK
1385 Broadway, New York, NY 10018, USA
29 Earlsfort Terrace, Dublin 2, Ireland

BLOOMSBURY, BLOOMSBURY VISUAL ARTS and the Diana
logo are trademarks of Bloomsbury Publishing Plc

First published in Great Britain 2022
Copyright © Bloomsbury, 2022

Cover design by Louise Dugdale
Cover image: Lazar El Lissitzky - *Kestnermappe Proun, Rob. Levnis and
Chapman GmbH Hannover-5* / The Artchives / Alamy Stock Photo

Library of Congress Cataloging-in-Publication Data
Names: Iandoli, Luca, 1972- author. | Zollo, Giuseppe, author.
Title: Elegant design : a designer's guide to harnessing
aesthetics / Luca Iandoli and Giuseppe Zollo.
Description: London ; New York : Bloomsbury Visual Arts, 2022. |
Includes bibliographical references and index.
Identifiers: LCCN 2021040842 (print) | LCCN 2021040843 (ebook) |
ISBN 9781350174269 (paperback) | ISBN 9781350177451 (hardback) |
ISBN 9781350174276 (epub) | ISBN 9781350174283 (pdf)
Subjects: LCSH: Design--Philosophy. | Aesthetics.
Classification: LCC NK1505 .I15 2022 (print) | LCC NK1505 (ebook) | DDC 174--dc23
LC record available at https://lccn.loc.gov/2021040842
LC ebook record available at https://lccn.loc.gov/2021040843

ISBN: HB: 978-1-3501-7745-1
PB: 978-1-3501-7426-9
ePDF: 978-1-3501-7428-3
eBook: 978-1-3501-7427-6

Typeset by Lachina Creative, Inc.
Printed and bound in India

To find out more about our authors and books visit
www.bloomsbury.com and sign up for our newsletters.

CONTENTS

INTRODUCTION

It seems that perfection is reached not when there is nothing left to add, but when there is nothing left to take away.

Antoine de Saint-Exupery

The age of aesthetics

In 1952, the Museum of Modern Art in New York hosted an exhibition titled *Olivetti: Design in Industry*. Like IBM, Olivetti had started as a typewriter (Fig. 0.1a and 0.1b) and mechanical calculator manufacturer (Fig. 0.1c) and would soon evolve into a digital company able to develop Programma 101, the first commercial desktop computer in history (Fig. 0.1d)[1]. The MOMA curators' motivations in organizing this exhibition included the intention to 'encourage our industries in the battle for good, integrated design by illustrating the excellence of the Olivetti program' (MOMA 1952: 1). The MOMA bulletin article introducing the exhibition reports a description of some of the Olivetti products on display (MOMA, 1952):

> The Lexicon 80 Office Typewriter is the most beautiful of the Olivetti machines. The blank metal envelope in the hands of a sensitive designer has become a piece of sculpture. There is a precision in the balance of planes, in the relationship of curved to flat surfaces, and in the modeling and bold jutting-out of the large handle which moves the carriage. The dip and rise of the hood, tightly fitting over the mechanical parts, enlivens the front plane without interrupting its smooth descent to the keys . . . *By this means, a look of order and simplicity is achieved* [. . .]

In the Lettera 22 Portable Typewriter, which is light in weight and compact in shape for ease of transportation and storage, the designer has preserved more clearly the appearance of a box. This appearance is enhanced by a subtle integration of parts. Here the uniform putty-beige colour is punctuated by a most effective accent—one single tabulator key of brightest red. *The keys themselves are modeled like shallow bowls, a shape inviting both to the eye and to the finger* [. . .]

[The Printing Calculator's] ridged back indicates that the metal envelope not only covers but also follows closely the interior arrangement of mechanical parts. A thin line created by the joining of the hood to the body cuts across the smoothly flowing sculptural indentation at the back. The keyboard on the gently slanting front section is a black-rimmed white field, with keys and levers in black, white, and red. *The keyboard arrangement, evaluated for color, shape, and organization of space within a limited field, is an abstract composition which enlivens the entire design.*

Olivetti was among the first companies to understand that product aesthetic was not only a feature to please the senses, but also a fundamental design choice to lower the barrier between technology and its users[2]. Simple, elegant design is instrumental to confer to

(a)

(c)

(b)

(d)

FIGURE 0.1 Olivetti office machines.
(a) Olivetti Lexikon 80 (case design by Marcello Nizzoli, 1949); (b) Olivetti Lettera 22 (case design by Marcello Nizzoli, 1950); (c) Divisumma 14 (case design by Marcello Nizzoli, 1948); (d) Olivetti Programma 101 (case design by Mario Bellini, 1965)

products 'a look of order and simplicity', to generate forms that are inviting and 'suggestive of their functions', and to arrange elements of a system following artistic criteria to 'facilitate understanding and information processing'. Olivetti was also the first company to understand the power of beautiful design in communication, in the design of the workplace environment and human-centred management practices (Iandoli 2021a, 2021b).

Later, other successful companies followed this idea of combining beauty and technology. Apple comes immediately to mind (Gelernter 1998), but nowadays simple and elegant design has become much more widespread. The Sony PlayStation 4 console comes as a sleek, black monolith (Fig. 0.2a) characterized by the apparent absence of complicated controls. The Bose SoundLink Mini portable speaker (and similar products developed by other speaker companies, such as Bang and Olufsen or JBL) adopts design solutions aimed at removing or hiding unnecessary complexity while embedding sophisticated audio technology into a pleasurable box characterized by rounded edges; smooth, high-quality materials; and a monochromatic, no-frills appearance. All these examples show that the pursuit of simplicity and elegance in design has been rediscovered in the development of consumer products that are supposed to be just as aesthetically pleasant as they are usable for consumers.

A similar trend is in place in management studies and practice. Theories of organizational simplification aimed at eliminating unnecessary complexity in business through streamlined organizational design are receiving increasing attention[3]. Design thinking has become a pervasive problem-solving discipline that is based on a humanistic view that puts users, and the way they understand the world, at the centre of every design attempt (Brown and Katz 2019). And focus on design is turning into impressive business figures: After analyzing two million pieces of financial data and 100,000 design

(a)

FIGURE 0.2
(a) Sony PlayStation 4; (b) Bose SoundLink Mini. Both products are examples of how tech companies are trying hard to beautify technology, in these cases by hiding complexity through streamlined and minimalistic design.

(b)

'actions' for 300 public companies over a five-year period, McKinsey (2018) found that those with the strongest commitment to design and the most adept execution of design principles had 32 percent more revenue and 56 percent more total returns to shareholders.

Why is this happening? What does complexity have to do with beauty? How can aesthetically pleasing design help manage this trade-off? Finally, how can we create a complex design that otherwise looks nice, feels nice, and is highly usable and useful? These are the main questions this book addresses.

Beauty and complexity

On the one hand, beauty is not just ornamental or contemplative. On the other, beautiful objects do not necessarily have an immediate practical use. So, what function, if any, will attractive design serve? In this book, we will argue it can help users and designers to deal with complexity.

To understand the relationship between complexity and beauty, let's consider the impact of digital technologies on our lives. Digital technologies make it easier than ever to embed more information and intelligence into products and services. About 50 percent[4] of the cost of an automobile will be based on its electronics by 2030; it was 1 percent in the 1950s, 10 percent in the 1980s, 35% in the 2010s. It will only increase with the development of electric and self-driving cars.

An executive working for Domino's, who was a guest speaker in one of our classes, told us during the break: 'People think we are a pizza company; in reality, we are an information technology company.' He was alluding to the sophisticated technology with which Domino's digitalizes the experience of ordering and delivering food and capitalizing on the massive amount of analytics that pizza ordering makes available.

These are just two examples from quite traditional industries showing how digitalization changes the production and fruition of goods and services in all the economic sectors[5]. While digital technologies empower our experience in many ways, this empowerment comes with a price: *information overload.*

Proper delivery and digital information organization become of the utmost importance, not only for data scientists and app developers but for virtually everybody. Anytime we deliver or collect data through digital media, the relationship between what we want to communicate (content) and how to visually arrange this content (format) becomes even more crucial than it is in nondigital media. For instance, consider the level of editorial curation that Instagram heavy users adopt when posting a picture.

Indeed, increasing competition makes beautiful design a differentiation factor, but there is more than that.

The vast amount of information we are bombarded with, or actively look for, makes us more informed and knowledgeable – and more aware of what we do not know. This awareness makes the world appear complex and makes us anxious. Because simple and useful design is tough to create, average designers react by overshooting complexity and stuffing our devices (and our personal lives) with more features, layers, functionalities, structures and gears. The waste that results from overdesigning – in terms of materials, time, money, frustration and environmental damage – is huge and no longer sustainable.

This book will argue that aesthetic thinking can be an excellent resource to help users cope with complexity and guide designers to achieve elegant solutions while eliminating waste.

Beauty will save the world, once again – this time, from complexity.

FIGURE 0.3 *A Lady Writing a Letter* (Vermeer, c. 1665). The lady seems distracted by someone or something, but at the same time focused and thoughtful. We don't know if she is gazing into space or observing a person. The painting's ambiguity is the primary source of aesthetic pleasure.

Elegant design

Recent findings in neuroscience (Kandel 2016; Ramachandran 2012; Zeki 2011) consistently show that the understanding and the enjoyment of artistic work derives from our ability to identify and appreciate non-obvious patterns, and that, when this appreciation takes place, our brains feel pleasure. This research also shows that appreciation of order appears to be a constant that transcends local and subjective variations of what is supposed to be aesthetically pleasant in different cultures and different people (Dutton 2009). Neuroscientists argue that if our brain has developed this universal ability and an associated pleasure-inducing reward system, it means that aesthetic thinking has played an essential role in our evolution as a species (Hoffman 2019; Prum 2017).

Survival requires the mastering of two antithetic basic instincts (Berghman and Hellert 2017). On the one hand, we want to minimize the risks deriving from exposure to novel, unknown situations. On the other, we are excited to discover new opportunities that may be accessible if we engage in risky exploration. This dual thinking is ubiquitous in our decisions: Should we accept a new job? Should we wear more unconventional attire at the event we are planning to attend? Should we try that new dish?

This book will argue that *aesthetics is a fundamental driver behind most human choices*. No, I won't accept the new job because it doesn't *feel* like the right thing to do at this stage of my life. Yes, I will wear that eccentric outfit because it better *fits* with the social event I will attend. Yes, I will try the new dish because it *looks* good. 'Feeling right', 'better fit' and 'good looking' are examples of aesthetic decision criteria. Aesthetic reasoning involves filtering information and making decisions through these types of aesthetic criteria.

Aesthetic reasoning works pretty well because aesthetic judgment contains useful knowledge that has been accumulated and validated through evolution (reproduction and survival), culture (is it socially desirable?) and personal experience (did it work in the past?).

The good news is that aesthetic decision-making is a skill, and as such, we can learn it. To acquire a new skill, we need two tools: first, a method and, second, one or more metrics – the evaluation criteria to assess whether we are doing well.

This book offers both. The method consists of the mastery of eight design heuristics, a set of principles for the organization of visual information. The metric measures how efficiently a design helps users absorb new information (effective complexity).

THE METHOD: EIGHT DESIGN HEURISTICS TO SIMPLIFY AND COMPLEXIFY OUR DESIGN

Honing our aesthetic judgment requires time and energy. It turns out that artistic work's production and fruition are effective means to help with this task. To illustrate this point, we can resort to an example taken from the world of visual art, something we will continuously do in this book.

In *A Lady Writing a Letter* (Fig. 0.3), Johannes Vermeer portrays an unknown woman sitting at her desk while composing a note for someone. She appears to be very focused and thoughtful, and her suspended gesture and her beautiful spacious forehead, slightly bent forward and turned towards the observer, introduce an element of perplexity. We are unable to determine whether the woman is staring into the empty space to organize her thoughts or whether she has been distracted or interrupted by someone or something. Who is she writing to? Why is she wearing an elegant dress with fur lapels? Was she perhaps waiting for a visitor, who interrupted or startled her while she was writing?

Surprisingly, the painting's ambiguity is not disturbing; on the contrary, it is the primary source of aesthetic pleasure. The feelings we experience in front of this painting result from the competition between two critical information processing modes. On the one hand, our search for plausible answers pushes us to look for different angles (*search for variety*). On the other, our brain tries to match what we see with what we already know (*search for unity*). We will finally settle on an old or new answer, and that match will generate some amount of aesthetic pleasure.

Excellent artistic works, especially those appreciated by both the broad public and the much more restricted circle of professional critics, are generally characterized by a remarkable mix of conventional and surprising elements. The traditional elements are there to position the representation in a familiar context that helps us recognize the scene (a lady writing a letter while sitting at a desk). The surprise elements are there to violate these expectations and to give us the shiver of novelty (the gesture, the forehead turned to the side, the reflective gaze, the fancy clothes). Back to our survival strategy: Conventions support safety and cautiousness, surprise nurtures discovery. Art offers a form of playful simulation, so we are more likely to risk innovative interpretations here than we are in reality. For instance, we are more likely to fantasize about the content of the letter the lady is writing than to assume she is only putting together a to do list.

This book shows that this intuitive dual thinking (search for variety versus search for unity) can be applied more systematically through eight fundamental design heuristics, four supporting each mode. We define these heuristics as compositional strategies because they can help designers achieve given design objectives by arranging design elements in different configurations. Here is a short description of each strategy.

Strategies in the search for unity

1. SUBTRACT DETAILS: Artists create some abridged version of reality by reducing an experience's complexity to a subset of relevant entities.
2. DEVELOP SYMMETRY: In art as in nature, symmetry allows our cognitive system to generate complex forms more efficiently through hierarchies, focal points, distances, directions and visual weights.
3. GROUP: Cluster similar objects into logical, spatial or narrative categories.
4. SPLIT: Organize and navigate complexity across a hierarchy of information layers.

Strategies in the search for variety

5. USE THE POWER OF THE CENTRE:
Create a dominant visual centre using colours,
shapes, lines and visual weights to guide the
observer's understanding of the deep structure
of the composition.

6. EMPHASIZE: The goal of this strategy is
the deliberate distortion of some detail or
significant feature.

7. REMIX: Break down and reconnect elements
in new, unexpected combinations.

8. CONTRAST AND BALANCE: Create
tension and equilibrium among the elements
of a composition to stimulate emotions.

We will describe each strategy and its
application in a dedicated chapter.

THE METRIC: WHEN IS GOOD 'GOOD ENOUGH'? EFFECTIVE COMPLEXITY

We mentioned that aesthetic pleasure is related to
the perception of order. But what kind of order
do we look for? And how much order do we need?
Confirming the trade-off between the search for
variety and search for unity, cognitive science
research shows that we prefer combinations of
familiar and novel stimuli (Berlyne 1970; Reber
et al. 2004). Conversely, situations in which either
the 'familiar' or the 'novel' prevail tend to both be
unpleasant, although for different reasons. When
the arrangement of elements in a composition
is too predictable and obvious, we experience
boredom; when we have to deal with too much
novelty, we feel overwhelmed and confused. Thus,
order is acceptable as long as it is not trivial,
whereas novelty is welcome as long as we can
handle it.

Think of any artistic performance or situation
calling for aesthetic judgment. A story needs
to have some recognizable structure and some
surprise elements that are not easily predictable.
Very conservative attire is anonymous, but a
very eccentric outfit can be too loud. A new job
proposal needs to offer us some fresh and exciting
career prospects, but we want to make sure it
falls in the professional domain and skillset we
can master.

So, how do we measure the ideal mix
of familiarity and novelty in an aesthetic
arrangement? Help comes from a discipline one
would not expect to contribute to this discussion
(again, some surprise is always welcome):
complexity science. Murray Gell-Mann, the
American physicist who received the 1969 Nobel
Prize in physics for his work on elementary
particle theory, defines effective complexity as the
shortest description of the perceived regularities
in a system (Gell-Mann and Lloyd 1996). He also
provides a mathematical formulation, but that is
hard to operationalize. This academic definition
suggests a powerful and intuitive concept of
efficiency in human understanding based on
compressing information. How can we express
the most by saying the least? If we have to venture
into a more straightforward, simplified formula,
we could say that:

$$\text{effective complexity} = \frac{\text{meaning}}{\text{information}}$$

Art comes to the rescue, as always. Think of
beautiful poetry or great literature. If you are
a superb poet such as Pablo Neruda, you can
express how much you love someone with the
following verse: 'I want to do with you what
spring does with the cherry trees' (Neruda, *Every
Day You Play*).

Otherwise, you can just say, 'I love you' (precious, but quite boring). You can also write a very long and complicated love letter to express what loving someone means to you (maybe exhaustive, but unnecessarily complicated). What Neruda does, instead, through the careful choice of words and a beautiful visual metaphor, is to express the consequences of love for the loved one with the parsimony of signs.

Think now about products. Aren't the best products those which fulfil this equation? When the interface is too complicated, users must process too much information to figure out what they can do with that product. If it's too simple, the product will be easy to use, but quite disappointing in terms of performance.

These two extreme cases show us that there is good complexity and bad complexity. As the well-known designer Donald Norman (2016) points out, 'We need some complexity'. What we call a simple interface is actually an effectively complex interface.

The relationship between complexity and aesthetic judgment is intriguing and is the angle from which we explore aesthetic thinking and its implications for design in this book.

Our theory is summarized in Fig. 0.4. The strategies in the search for variety can add excitement to our design. Still, when novelty exceeds the threshold that users can tolerate, it creates too much entropy, and excitement turns into confusion. To reduce confusion, we can search for unity, typically by reducing entropy through the removal of information and functionalities. However, if we exceed in this direction, the design becomes dull, boring and underperforming. The process unfolds through a trial-and-error approach, via multiple attempts to simplify or complicate the design, searching

for the sweet spot where effective complexity and aesthetic pleasure peak.

This method of work is particularly visible in the process of artistic creation. A good work of art typically requires painstaking experimentation and production of multiple iterations of intermediate drafts before an artist gets to the point at which a superior composition is achieved. Great artists pack information into visual representations that are powerful in communicating a message. We think that designers face essentially the same challenge, and for these reasons, our pedagogy in this book will be based on learning how great artists achieve effective complexity.

Achieving effective complexity is essential for the design of tools and interfaces able to facilitate users' information processing. However, determining the right amount of complexity users can and want to absorb is not an easy task because it depends on many factors, such as the users' cognitive skills, manual dexterity, purposes,

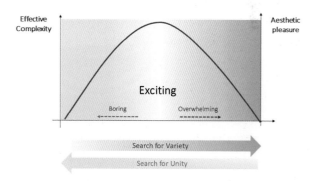

FIGURE 0.4
Design strategies to achieve effective complexity and maximize aesthetic pleasure through the right mix of surprise (searching for variety) and familiarity (searching for unity).

motivations, and the situational circumstances in which the design will be used. Given the high number of elements involved and their variability, it is practically impossible to define the criteria that a best solution must meet. However, we are all able to appreciate whether one object appears less complicated than another. Take, for example, the two smartwatches in Fig. 0.5 (a recent version of the Samsung Galaxy and one of the first smartwatches launched by Timex in the late 1990s Datalink series).

The Galaxy appears much simpler than the Datalink. The Datalink showcases a screen in which information is distributed across five horizontal arrays. The dial is surrounded by labels indicating additional functions, and the ring bears five buttons. On the contrary, the Galaxy is an empty space waiting to be filled. The minimalist design of its dial hides the functional richness,

which is relegated to the smartphone app through which the watch can be managed and controlled, a common design solution today. Thus, while the Datalink exhibits all its functional richness on the surface, the Galaxy allocates this complexity across a few layers: a surface level that suggests ease and immediacy of use, and hidden layers accessible through a companion device and ad hoc software application. The Galaxy makes its complexity available to its users, but it does not force them to face it if they do not want to or do not have the skills to handle it. The Galaxy's organization across layers also introduces some level of graduality that can help users to explore this additional complexity with small and incremental efforts. It is worth noting that contemporary smartwatches tend to look more like traditional wristwatches than their early models did.

Today this design has become dominant for smartwatches. Following the disappointing sales of the first smartwatches, manufacturers learned they had to balance two different design approaches to respond to opposite needs, as illustrated in Fig. 0.4. On one hand, a smartwatch had to provide the additional, surprising functionalities that customers expected from sophisticated digital technology (search for variety). On the other hand, it was necessary to reduce the information overload that came with the added complexity to realize a product of immediate understanding and more familiar shape (search for unity). This example shows how the pursuit of effective complexity can take place through a trial-and-error process in which designers strive to achieve the delicate balance between familiarity and novelty, the 'known' and the 'unknown', the expected and the surprising, the old and the new.

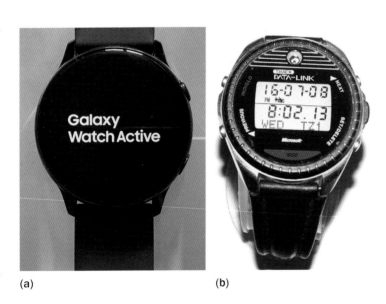

(a)   (b)

FIGURE 0.5
Watches with different design philosophies: (a) Samsung Galaxy Watch (b) Timex Datalink Model 150.

How this book is designed

Think of the last time you had to solve a problem and came up with an unsatisfying solution. Think of how you represented the problem and how this representation led you to critical design decisions and an execution plan. Finally, consider the outcome and whether your customers were happy about it. If they were not, it was for either one of the following reasons: 1) the design was too simple to capture the actual complexity of their problem; 2) the design was too complex for their problem. *In either case, the complexity of the solution did not match the complexity of the problem*. It was the likely result of an inadequate understanding of the problem and/or insufficient experimentation with design alternatives exhibiting different complexity levels.

Think now at what you could have done better. First, did you fail because your solution was too innovative? Or because you underestimated the novelty of the problem and tried to adapt a known solution that ultimately did not work?

The next step is to apply some of the strategies we described above. Did you include too many irrelevant or redundant parts? Did your design lack symmetry? Could you have clustered functions and components in a more streamlined organization? Was your design too flat, and you missed the opportunity to emphasize what mattered? Would a better organization of functions and parts across levels have made salient information more understandable and accessible to users?

It is possible to develop similar diagnostic questions for each of the eight strategies and visualize an alternative design of the solution. We are confident enough to anticipate that you can already see some benefits in applying the working method we propose in this book.

The structure of the book reflects this intuitive approach through which we handle and tame complexity in everyday decisions and choices via aesthetic reasoning.

After two initial chapters that introduce readers to aesthetic reasoning basics, we will present each strategy in a dedicated chapter and report examples of its applications in visual arts and design.

Each 'strategy' chapter has the same structure. We start with an opening story to illustrate how the design strategy works in a narrative and suggestive fashion. Then we offer detailed examples from art and design to illustrate the successful application of the strategy in question. In the final part of the chapter, we report key findings from research in cognitive and brain science, providing empirical support and sound theory for why the strategy works from the perceptual and psychological points of view.

Each chapter comes with a wrap-up table summarizing the key points and their implications for designers. A set of exercises fully described on the book's website provides opportunities to put these principles into practice. We have organized these exercises into four groups, following a learning-by-doing pedagogy. In this approach, the first and second types of activities are about learning from examples: 'Case study' and 'Anatomy of a masterpiece'. The third type of exercise, 'The Art of noticing'[6], helps train observation skills. The fourth one is to 'Design exercise' via creative design exercises.

Designing for information *and* meaning

Each chapter comes with many images selected from well-known artworks and design examples. We cherrypicked these images to convey how design heuristics are applied and how they function.

Most of the artwork we present has been selected from classics in pre-contemporary western art. A trivial reason behind this choice is that this is the type of art we are most familiar with and know well. Another reason is that, for the purposes of this book, we consider the analysis of non-figurative art, such as abstract art, less effective.

Our choices by no means intend to indicate the superiority of certain beauty canons, aesthetic cultural traditions, or artistic and design schools, or to imply any value judgement on figurative versus non-figurative, formal versus informal or western versus non-western art. If anything, in this book we strive to identify universal cognitive and perceptual mechanisms that transcend local aesthetic preferences developed in a given time, space and culture. For this reason, whenever possible, we have included comparative visual examples from various aesthetic traditions to prove that the design heuristics presented in this book have been applied and work across culture and time.

With this, we do not intend to deny that aesthetic values and preferences are strongly influenced by many context-specific factors and are exalted or criticized through the social, political and power games occurring between different social groups, elites and classes. However, the analysis of these factors will typically lie outside of the scope of this book.

We argue that there are two fundamentally different but highly complementary design mindsets: designing for information and designing for meaning. Traditionally, design for information refers to packaging information properly to augment aesthetic pleasure and usability, while design for meaning prioritizes sensing what users want, like and need at a deeper level; how they make sense of a design; and how they interpret it.

Of course, it is impossible to separate information from meaning in such an academic way, but in practice designers can prioritize either one and take the other for granted (or even ignore it).

We agree that great design is primarily innovation in meaning and that great designers tend to function more as social antennas than usability engineers. So, it may sound like a contradiction that, in this ideal continuum, our book sits more on the information design side of the spectrum. However, what we suggest here is that our design strategies and metrics can be used beyond optimizing information processing by working as actionable tools that readers can use to dissect their visual experience, break the status quo and get inspired towards the development of creative solutions. We will insist that this analytical experience is not contemplation but requires emotional and cinematic interaction with an object and with users, awareness of how the users' eyes move when exploring an image, how their bodies react, and how they and we feel when we analyze a visual experience. Our method, then, is a call to action to reconstruct this experience in different and better ways.

The design strategies we illustrate in this book will not tell designers what they can, must, or should express but rather *how they can express it better*. However, in pushing them to find better ways to say what they want to say, our heuristics will help designers to revisit, re-examine and possibly reinvent the message. Finally, our design strategies can be used metaphorically, beyond the material layout of information, and thus, in the realm of meaning. For instance, can we use the 'grouping' strategy to build a new narrative about what the design is or does? Does our 'emphasize' strategy work in a given cultural context? What kind of storytelling do we enable when we 'split' information in a certain way?

It is then important for us to clarify right here, at the beginning of our journey, that while the suggested design heuristics have been traditionally applied in the pursue of the canonical 'good form', this is not the spirit with which we use them in this book. We agree that canons are in question in today's world, that they appear inadequate to grasp the continuous remixing of shapes and content that an information society subjects us to. As a result, most of us feel as we are in a condition of permanent flux in which little space is left for the stable meanings of academic beauty and traditional aesthetic canons. However, we feel that a way to understand and cope with this complexity and the transiency of the digital life is to resort to effective cognitive analytical tools that can help us to navigate this complexity, *figure* that out (literally), and recon-*figure* it to serve our purposes. As the scientific method invented during Newton's time is still a valid tool to understand and assess non-Newtonian physics, as the Greek myths are still so powerful in representing and understanding human psychology and cognition even in the age of neuroimaging, so we believe that the fundamental cognitive laws that regulate perception and understanding are still useful in the new aesthetic of the digital age.

When it comes to the choice of design examples, we have tried to achieve a good mix between classics and more contemporary examples, erring perhaps towards the classic side of the spectrum. The reason is simple: Classic iconic design has stood the test of time as opposed to something that was very cool at some point but that then is rapidly forgotten. In other words, we think we can learn more design lessons from the Xerox/Apple/Windows good old desktop interface than from Second Life (we hope you remember it[7]).

We honestly admit that sometimes we chose products and brands that for various reasons, including our personal biography, are dear to us. After all, we think that one characteristic that regularly surfaces from good designs is that their users end up developing some form of affection, if not love, for them. We hope we will be able to leverage such affection and love to convey our message as clearly and as enjoyably as possible throughout these examples and the book.

Online resources to accompany this book are available
at http://www.bloomsburyonlineresources.com/elegant-design.
If you experience any problems, please contact Bloomsbury at: onlineresources@bloomsbury.com

1 The Simplifying Machine

ABSTRACT

How do we make sense of our experience? Understanding is the result of the integration of two cognitive processes, one specialized in processing sensory information and the other connecting this information to pre-existing knowledge. Our brain projects what we know already on our immediate experience and tends to be biased towards the confirmation of our pre-existing expectations. In this way, we simplify the complexity of sensory data by summarizing our experience into information patterns that are easy to recognize and recall. Understanding how the simplifying power of our brain works is a key factor to grasp some fundamental properties of how humans reason aesthetically and what implications this has for designers.

KEYWORDS

experience

pattern recognition

confirmation bias

simplification

complexification

emotion

reason

At eight, I was Raphael. It took me a whole lifetime to paint like a child

Pablo Picasso (quoted in Marina Picasso 2001: 182)

Impressions

The Museum of Modern Art in New York is one of the top museums in the world for modern art. Every year, between 2 and 3 million visitors crowd the 53rd Street museum building. Toward which paintings do people gravitate during peak times? You can regularly find that Impressionist paintings attract most of the public, particularly masterpieces of the calibre of Van Gogh's *Starry Night* or the giant Monet water lilies. Why is Impressionist art so attractive to modern museumgoers?

The French critic Louis Leroy (1874) coined the term 'Impressionism' to disparage Monet's *Impression Sunrise* (Fig. 1.1): 'Impression!' he wrote, 'Wallpaper in its embryonic state is more finished!' Leroy couldn't imagine that the unfinished, incomplete and fleeting images of quiet landscapes, bustling city scenes or simple still life subjects portrayed in Impressionist paintings would be so exciting and pleasant for us.

Is there a reason why we love unfinished representations and prefer them to more accurate renderings? Why, for instance, would many

FIGURE 1.1 *Sunrise Impression* (Claude Monet, 1872).
The only fairly defined element is the orange red sun. Everything else blurs in the morning fog. The eye wanders around the painting without encountering barriers.

more people prefer to hang in their homes a reproduction of an Impressionist painting, such as Berthe Morisot's *The Dining Room* (Fig. 1.3), instead of the beautiful portrait of Catharine Lorillard Wolfe by Alexandre Cabanel (Fig. 1.2)? Cultural conditioning and personal taste aside, isn't it a paradox that a picture with less information is perceived as more exciting and perhaps even more informative?

To solve this paradox, we need to look at what happens in our brains when observing these works.

Simple minds

One of the Impressionist artists' objectives was to get rid of traditional academic painting conventions in order to revert to a simpler representation of everyday scenes, based on the honest recording of emotions and perceptions through a new, unconditioned observation of reality.

As challenging, exciting and innovative as their artistic intent was, the Impressionists' hypothesis was wrong. Our brain receives something like 10 million bits per second through the eyes, but

FIGURE 1.2 *Catharine Lorillard Wolfe* (Alexandre Cabanel, 1876).
The precision of the details invites the observer to take an analytical look: to highlight and classify details as a scientist at work.

FIGURE 1.3 *The Dining Room* (Berthe Morisot, 1875).
The observer is captured by the dance of colours, the natural pose in an everyday fleeting moment.

it eventually processes only a small fraction of it (University of Pennsylvania 2006)[8]. This means that a significant part of this data flow is discarded as irrelevant noise. How do we filter salient information from such a huge amount of data? How do we make sense of the complex and sometimes contradictory evidence that hits our senses?

Humans tend naturally to organize experience into more abstract categories that are representative of broader classes of events or objects. For instance, we store behaviour routines in the form of scripts that we recall every time we identify specific clues in a situation, as when we go to a restaurant and order a meal (Schank and Albelson 1977; Schank 1991). Every dining experience is different, but we categorize this experience under a 'going to the restaurant script' that works most of the time: enter, wait to be seated, read the menu, order, eat, pay, and tip. We can also think of these higher-level categories as summaries or compressed data.

Cognitive psychologists and behavioural economists have identified other examples of how our mind simplifies reality, such as using stereotypes to predict other people's behaviour, the role of first impressions in judgment formation, or the disproportionate importance we assign to more salient and recent information in making decisions. Most of the research in behavioural decision making has shown how often these simplification attempts lead us astray and make our choice prone to manipulation (Kahneman (2011)).

Other researchers have demonstrated instead that, in everyday life, these simplification strategies are most of the time very effective in helping us to make 'good enough' decisions in real-world situations that are quite far from the abstract experimental setting used by behavioural

psychologists in academic research (Goldstein and Gigerenzer 2002)[9]. For instance, only humans are particularly good at compressing text and other types of complex contents into compact syntheses we call summaries, an ability that is still unparalleled even by the most advanced artificial intelligence (Knight 2017) – at the time of this writing, at least!

It's also important to observe that the ability to summarize experience is not just cold selection and archival of features, as would happen in a computer database. Studies on human memory show that our brain constantly recreates recollections of past events and that the act of remembering is actually ex-post reconstruction and recoding of our past experience so that we can relate it to the present situation or needs[10]. That's why, if we tell a story multiple times, it will be slightly different every time and why we don't remember correctly the Instagram logo (give it a try without checking your phone). We have to recreate these memories anytime we recall them.

Instagram, one of the leading social media platforms on the market for image sharing, decided recently to redesign its logo. In the process of creating the new logo, the lead designer Ian Spalter had the idea to ask his collaborators to draw the Instagram logo as they remembered it. It turned out that most of them were not able to draw the logo in an accurate fashion, despite the fact that active Instagram users tap on that icon on their smartphones dozens of times per day. Invariably though, the large majority of the team remembered only some key elements of the old logo (Fig. 1.4a), which turned out to be the lens, the viewfinder, and the rainbow.

It makes sense: If we think of a camera, we instinctively picture a lens attached to a viewfinder. The rainbow was a peculiar graphic element that symbolized what was a distinctive

(a)   (b)

FIGURE 1.4 Old and new Instagram logos.
The new logo reduces the image to just a few easy-to-remember essentials. The user is free to infer the app's functional characteristics. Displaying them in plain sight, as the old logo did, is an unnecessary complication.

feature of Instagram, the use of filters through which users could recreate in digital pictures the nostalgic allure of 70s and 80s colour photography. Thus, Spalter decided to redesign the logo by adopting an abstraction strategy[11], incorporating into the new design only the graphic features that its users found more representative and meaningful (Fig. 1.4b).

The attempt to understand reality by removing unnecessary complexity, via abstraction and compression in the Instagram example, is clearly an effective cognitive strategy. Less obvious is how the mind simplifies, how much information we filter versus which details we discard, how we perform such selection, and how we maintain these simplified representations in our memory for later reuse or recall. More importantly, how do we make sure that our simplified representations of the world are 'good enough'?

What you see is what you get? understanding as pattern recognition

All we need to recognize the Instagram logo is to know some of its most memorable features. The same also applies to face recognition: Instead of cataloguing faces based on a long list of specific details (after all, every face is special in its own way), our brain mainly relies on a few data points and key metrics, such as the distance between the eyes and between the nose and the mouth (Fig. 1.5). Once our brain knows these rules and tricks, it can instruct our eyes on how to look at faces by pointing our gaze to the right spots in order to collect only the necessary data points.

If understanding is about filtering and retaining salient information – as well as about maintaining and occasionally updating mental

FIGURE 1.5 Eye movement tracking.
Reproduction of the eye movements tracking of a photograph with both eyes as detected through an eye-tracking device; lines represent eye movements called *saccades*.

representations in order to reuse them quickly and efficiently when needed – our brain must have ways to be selective and to perform this selection in a good way.

Since the selection of stimuli cannot be arbitrary, the mind cannot be a clean slate, despite the Impressionists' effort to silence our pre-existing expectations and knowledge of reality. Later studies on human vision have showed that our brain possesses different areas: Some specialize in processing sensory information and others in connecting this information to pre-existing knowledge. Studies on subjects who had brain injuries that affected the connections between these areas showed that these patients were unable to recognize even familiar forms even though their eyes and visual nervous systems were intact[13]. If this connection is severed in our brains, we are not able to recognize the faces of our beloved ones or most everyday objects. This is clear evidence that *we see what we know*.

Gestalt psychologists were among the first to understand that vision is a process that starts from the brain and not from the eyes[14]. They used optical illusions to show that we may end up seeing things that are not real; in fact, we think we see what we see, but the image we visualize is only in our brain and not in reality.

Let's observe the picture in Fig. 1.6. What do you see? Chances are that you see a square, as most people do, but in fact there is no square in the picture, just four little Pac-Mans. (In fact, there is no Pac-Man, either; we recognize the shape if we know the videogame context. That shape most likely does not make any sense to you if you have not played videogames from the 80s.)

Gestalt psychologists explained this and other optical illusions using a set of principles, later known as Gestalt's laws, that appear to guide our perception. These principles are rather abstract and general, so much so that we can apply them to interpret images in virtually any situation. Artists, architects and photographers have derived from these laws image composition principles that are widely taught and applied in their professional practice (Freeman 2007). For instance, the principle of closure is at work with the square in Fig. 1.6: When an object is incomplete, but the ways to complete it are suggested in the picture, our mind cannot help but fill the blanks and create a closed representation.

In our classes, some people have been creative enough to see in Fig. 1.6 a sort of lunar vehicle, in which the Pac-Mans are movable wheels while the square is the cockpit. This apparent over-interpretation of an otherwise quite simple geometric shape is explained by another Gestalt principle: the law of common destiny, according to which objects that are in proximity and somehow connected should move together.

What is astonishing in Gestalt theory is not only the fact that these scientists anticipated by several decades what neuroscience would have discovered later thanks to the availability of sophisticated brain imaging technology, but that

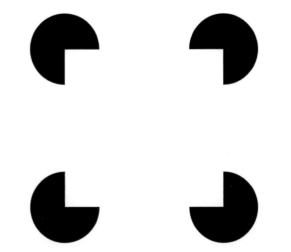

FIGURE 1.6 Optical illusion of a square.
Most people observing this picture would see a square emerging form the empty space of this abstract figure. Of course, the square is only in our mind.

the laws configure our vision as a very dynamic, almost narrative device. We see things clustering, connecting, closing, and moving together because our brain builds a story through a cinematic interpretation of the image. That's why vision is so important for creativity, and that's why in visual art most of the artist's effort is directed towards the creation of the illusion of tensions, movements and dynamism.

After decades of research in psychology, cognitive sciences and neurobiology, there is now wide consensus that the human brain is an amazing simplifying machine. Simplification is the product of the anticipation in our brain of what could or should happen. We project what we know on reality, and we are biased towards the confirmation of our pre-existing expectations. Such a feed-forward rationality makes sense from the evolutionary point of view: the human species is likely better off using quick and dirty cognitive routines to scan the environment, anticipate potential threats and act accordingly, rather than

investigating reality, computing the probability of all possible scenarios, and then making a normatively correct choice. Rational assessment of choice alternatives makes sense in the lab and for the advancement of science, but it does not help us to be responsive and fast in the many micro decisions that need to be made on the spot everyday (apparently a few hundred just in order to eat[15]).

What the anticipatory brain does is to match mental models to reality and look for the best possible match. This matching process can be so frequent and repetitive that in many cases we perform it almost unconsciously; it happens in the process of habit formation. When our brain settles on a possible match, how does it know that's the best possible guess? Somewhat surprisingly, cognitive scientists have shown that human decision-making is much less rational and much more emotional than most people think. In other words, we know we are right when it *feels* right.

The joy of guessing: ambiguity and emotions in understanding

In an interview for the popular podcast *TED Radio Hour*, the NPR anchor Guy Raz asked Toni Fadell, one of the Apple iPod designers and the founder of NEST, a leading company in home automation, what explains why some products really took off, like the iPod, but other perfectly designed MP3 players like Microsoft Zune didn't.

Fadell (2016) replies:

So this is a thing that I've been wrestling with [my entire] career. And I think I figured it out. And what you always have to look at is when you design something, there are two halves to design, just like there's two halves to your brain – the emotional part and the rational part. If you want people to truly adopt your product . . . it has to have an emotional component, you know, something that grabs you . . . unlocks that curiosity that says there's something cool here. It also needs to rationally work. There's got to be a good reason why I'm doing it. Is it for saving money? Is it for saving time? Is it going to be more convenient for me? And you need to separate your features into both the rational features that cause people to want to buy it and the emotional features that get people off their duff to actually buy it.

Fadell points out to something that as consumers we have at least occasionally experienced: the excitement that comes from interacting with truly exceptional products. It could be the elegant simplicity of the NEST thermostat[16], the sleek design of the iPhone and the smoothness of its mobile interface, the amazing sound portability experience of the Sony Walkman, or the cruising comfort of a Mercedes. Customers enjoy indulging in sensory interaction with these 'pet' products because their design is conducive to the creation of this type of physical as well as emotional relationship. Fadell rightly points out that this excitement is due to a mix of the rational and the emotional thinking and to the product's ability to excite both in our brain[17].

The deep connection between emotions and rational thinking has been demonstrated in cognitive psychology and neuroscience, starting from the seminal work of Damasio (1994). The neuroscientist argues that the dichotomy between cold/rational and hot/emotional thinking is false, and that any human decision is the product of a tight cooperation between the emotional and rational brain.

The cooperation between the rational and the emotional thinking is even more visible when pattern recognition is not driven by an immediate urge or other practical purpose, as happens in contemplation of art.

The role of aesthetic pleasure in understanding

Between 2012 and 2014, Johannes Vermeer's famous panting, *Girl with a Pearl Earring* (Fig. 1.7), was on one of the longest and most acclaimed traveling art exhibitions ever. Why this painting, also nicknamed the 'Mona Lisa of the north', is the source of such fascination and followership is not clear.

There is something enigmatic in this work that attracts our attention. A large part of it is in the expression and the pose of the girl; Vermeer captured a fugacious instant in the eyes of the character, in her gracious and elusive expression. She was perhaps delivering a message that only the master could decipher or, more likely, just capture the ephemeral essence of.

The painting raises more questions the more we interrogate it. Who was the girl? What was her connection with the painter? It's unlikely that a girl with modest attire could have owned a valuable pearl earring; who gave it to her? Was it a gift from the artist or just an object she was asked to wear for the portrait[18]? Was there a sentimental relationship between the artist and his model? Why is she wearing a blue turban?

We do not know which interpretation is correct. We argue that the success of the painting is its ambiguity: The viewer can project multiple meanings, each building a different but legitimate narrative. Even better, some of the opposite interpretations that come to mind could co-exist in this character, and those contradictions would make the subject even more intriguing.

Ambiguous images exercise a strange fascination on our brain. Our anticipatory brain tries to interpret this painting by projecting the expression of the girl over some existing meaning or stereotypes, but we do not find only one. Multiple interpretations are possible, and our mind contemplates and evaluates

FIGURE 1.7 *Girl with a Pearl Earring* (Vermeer, 1665).
The ambiguity of the expression on the girl's face raises a variety of questions; this is key for the emotional involvement of the observer.

which one is the most plausible in a fascinating dance of possibilities. If we cannot settle on a simple solution, then we enjoy the multiplicity. Ambiguity, at least when it comes to disinterested artistic contemplation, is not a source of concern but of aesthetic pleasure.

How does the mind handle and resolve ambiguity? In simple, trivial, everyday patterns, such as a recognition task (for instance, when we are at the grocery store to buy fruit and we pick up the apples with a better look and feel), ambiguity is resolved easily because the stimulus is mapped onto a unique and readily available representation (in this case, of what a good apple is supposed to look and feel like). The match is found; it's satisfying, and the problem is solved in a fraction of a second.

In other cases, resolving ambiguity is not easy. Multiple solutions are available, and straightforward choice criteria are not. The ambiguity of the stimulus asks for extra effort from our brain and pushes our mind to engage in discovery and learning. Learning does not only require effort but also generates anxiety (Schein 2002), so our brain requires a significant reward to compensate for this fatigue.

In simple cases, an extrinsic reward is readily available (we know we chose a good apple after we taste it and find it sweet and crunchy). But in many and more important decisions, we do not have the luxury of repeatable empirical testing and immediate feedback. Our primate ancestors were often given only one chance in many life-or-death choices, such as eating a fruit that could poison them or anticipating whether a predator had the intention to attack.

Non-repeatable choice is even more common in more complex societies. Napoleon could not afford to experiment in the battle of Austerlitz; he had to recognize potential patterns in the enemy troop's deployment and attack strategy and sense

which were the most adequate countermeasures, based on his previous experience. Or think of the effects of laws and policies on your everyday decisions. Or consider simple, but critical, individual choices: Should I take that job? Should I marry that girl? Who should I vote for? Which is the right design for a new product? In all these cases, there is no simple test to run or, even if a test is technically possible, it might be just too late for its outcomes to reverse the decision. So, we need to rely on other ways to know whether we are on the right track before the results are fully in.

Back to Vermeer's painting: The presence of multiple patterns, all equally intriguing and plausible, all telling us something about the mystery of the girl portrayed in the painting, amplifies the pleasure of discovery during the process of discovery itself. It has been argued, in fact, that one of the functions of art is to provide a safe mental space in which we can play with pattern recognition and refine our ability to observe and map reality into creative alternative representations without taking any chances (Tooby and Cosmides 2001: 6–27). In the end, there is no right or wrong in the way we look at a painting in the sense that there will be no consequences if our interpretation is inaccurate or plainly wrong. Art can help us to create an artificial world in which we can run experiments to refine our ability to simulate possible worlds and imagine the future by envisioning alternative courses of action.

Maybe the girl with the earring was just a servant who occasionally posed for a painter, or maybe she was a fictional character inspired by some real person – Vermeer's daughter, according to some art scholars. We will possibly never know, but how entertaining and pleasant is to build stories that unfold as parallel potential worlds around this mysterious portrait. We enjoy the variety and surprise that the best stories allow us to discover without hurting ourselves or anyone else. Learning without the pain of learning is probably the secret mix behind aesthetic pleasure. Great art can trigger this sort of reverse-engineered creativity because artists wisely infused *some* complexity in simple representations people could easily relate to.[19]

Too good to be true

The Instagram logo and Vermeer's *Girl with a Pearl Earring* provide some insights into how our brain separates relevant information chunks from the noise embedded in the incessant flow of sensory data.

However, when we push too much on the simplification pedal, our understanding of the world can end up being less effective as well as less pleasurable. It can be less effective because the application of readily available stereotypes or categories can make us blind to novel and meaningful data. It is less pleasurable because the quick recognition of a known fact or the experiencing of an instant reward will not trigger any meaningful surprise or discovery. The same applies to art and design: Mediocre artists and designers simplify in the wrong way when they over-apply conformist aesthetic canons and representational conventions that make their artifacts predictably boring. This predictability can be comforting and feel safe, but it is hardly perceived as novel and exciting.

So, the quest for comforting simplification has to be balanced by some other process that prevents our aesthetic choices from ending up trivial.

Of course, we can also err in the opposite direction: when we push too hard on the 'complexify' pedal, we are adding unnecessary complexity to problems that could be solved with a simpler approach. This happens, for instance, when we overthink a problem and ignore our gut feelings. The suppression of instinct and emotions leads toward decisional paralysis by making us blind to the spontaneous activation of patterns that would trigger fluid and effective behaviour. This is particularly evident in behaviours based on manual ability or developed by repeated exposure. Reading is a case in point: Reflect upon how you read while you are reading; quite likely, you will find that your reading experience will become more awkward and less fast, fluid, and pleasurable.

The key point we make in this book is that the cognitive strategies through which our brain perceives art and beauty can teach us a few things about how we understand and resolve complexity in design. We will show that understanding how much complexity our design should have is a critical, if not *the* critical, decision for a designer. More specifically, we will apply this analogy to design by drawing inspiration from how artists experiment with more or less complicated representations of their subjects. We will show that good design is the product of a similar extensive experimentation in which the cognitive pendulum moves back and forth between simplification and complexification until a sweet spot is reached in which designers provide their users with 'just enough' complexity. In the next chapter, we define this ideal amount of complexity as *effective complexity* and show that the oscillation between simplification and complexification can be tracked, analyzed, and even measured, thanks to insights from complexity theory in a surprisingly short circuit with art, design, and brain science.

PUTTING IDEAS INTO PRACTICE

Key takeaways for this chapter

LESSON LEARNED	DESIGN IMPLICATIONS
Non-finite: Individuals tend to appreciate underspecified, incomplete visual representations. On one hand, this reflects the preference toward simple renderings; on the other hand, our brain seems to enjoy the act of filling the gap, provided that just enough information is provided.	• Do not hyper-specify your design; let the users do the task of filling the gaps. Less is better; choose a focal element and suggest potential connections.
Pattern recognition: Human understanding is driven by pattern recognition. We project known mental models over the information we receive from the environment and tend to find patterns in the data that match our expectations.	• Build patterns in your design that are respectful of the patterns that your users are familiar with, can understand or can autonomously discover. If you do not possess enough knowledge, spend enough time observing prospective users while they interact with your prototype or a competing design and discuss with them.
Ambiguity and the joy of guessing: It turns out that users can appreciate some level of ambiguity if they can resolve it with little effort and discover new information or patterns. When this happens, our brain rewards us with pleasure-inducing hormones.	• Create designs users are intrigued by. Facilitate users' autonomous discovery. Build interaction patterns that lead toward 'predictable' surprises.

Creativity lab

The full description of each exercise is available on the book companion website: http://www.bloomsburyonlineresources.com/elegant-design

1.1 Case study: the design of the Instagram logo
Learn how to use abstraction from how Ian Spalter created the Instagram logo.

1.2 Anatomy of a masterpiece: the non-finite in Cezanne and Turner
Learn how great art masters such as Turner and Cezanne use non-finite, pattern-making and suggestive details, leading to pleasurable and surprising discoveries.

1.3 The art of noticing: take an icon walk
Learn how to design an effective icon.

1.4 Design exercise: create an icon
Exploit the power of simplifying by following Pablo Picasso's drawing of a bull, sketching a minimalistic representation of an animal of your choice.

2 Elegance as Effective Complexity

ABSTRACT

The previous chapter showed that pattern recognition is a key ability of our brain. However, how do we choose and why do we prefer specific patterns? Aesthetic criteria drive our choices, and emotions play a crucial role in determining those criteria. We illustrate this aspect by analyzing how artists make aesthetic choices in their works through multiple iterations and painstaking experimentation while being guided by their "emotional" brain. This process helps artists deliver complex and novel messages that are highly meaningful and surprisingly easy to process. We refer to this effective complexity as *elegance* and show that users experience aesthetic pleasure when this good complexity is made available in a design. This chapter briefly presents eight fundamental design heuristics to achieve elegance through effective complexity, each of which will be presented in detail in subsequent chapters of this book.

KEYWORDS

emotion

creativity

complexity

aesthetics

composition

aesthetic pleasure

elegance

Now thy pleasure take for guide
Dante Alighieri (*The Divine Comedy*, Pur. XXVII)

There is no recipe for creativity

After receiving three Michelin stars, the Italian chef Alfonso Iaccarino became a member of world-class chefs' most exclusive elite. What got him such a prestigious recognition was his ability to transform the ordinary act of eating into an aesthetic experience that involves all our senses: the taste and smell, obviously, but also the sound created by the food texture, and the sights and tactile stimulation of the soft tablecloths and finely designed plates and cutlery.

We met Alfonso at his resort (named Don Alfonso 1890 after his grandfather), on the Sorrento coast in Italy, on a beautiful bright morning during a torrid and hazy summer. Our ambitious aim was to discuss how his creative process unfolds to understand what makes it unique and successful. He welcomed us with lemonade made with freshly squeezed lemons from his estate in Punta Campanella in front of Capri Island, where he sources most of the ingredients for his dishes. We sat in the resort's garden and started the interview by asking Alfonso to discuss one of his most successful dishes, such as the spaghetti with mackerel breadcrumbs, pine nuts and caramelized onions on turnip sauce (Fig. 2.1), and to describe the process through which he created that recipe.

Alfonso meandered excitedly and ended up talking primarily about the ingredients. We had the impression he was deflecting our question, so we tried to put him back on track. 'A recipe?' he asked. 'Just a useful writing exercise, but a recipe is not a plate.' Ingredients, rather than recipes, are the starting and arrival points for Alfonso's creative process. Here is how he describes this process:

FIGURE 2.1 Spaghetti with mackerel, breadcrumbs, pine nuts and caramelized onions on turnip sauce. The essence of each of chef Alfonso Iaccarino's creations is a subtle system of tensions that he creates through the juxtaposition and matching of the ingredients.

Every ingredient in a plate has a role based on its essence. This essence must be, first of all, respected and enhanced in combination with the other ingredients. My creativity originates from the raw matter. For instance, I spend considerable time in just smelling a tomato harvested from my garden. Next, I wonder how I can bring the feeling of well-being that the scent gives me to the table. I believe that eventually, my dishes reflect how I breathe the land where I was born and raised.

Alfonso was adamant in admitting that he cannot create anything if he does not trust the ingredients, their genuine character and specificity, thus identifying an intriguing link between creativity and integrity. He described a meditation triggered by a particular tomato he tasted in the early morning in his estate in Punta Campanella, and wandered into his encyclopaedic knowledge about how tomatoes are (or should be) cultivated and harvested. His attitude recalled Flaubert's advice to his pupil, the young Maupassant, at the beginning of his writing career (cited in Steegmuller 1949: 60):

> In every experience, there is something that remains not fully understood, because we fall into the habit of remembering, every time we use our eyes, what others before us have thought about what we are observing. [But] Even the most insignificant object has something unknown. It's up to us to find out. To describe a burning fire or a tree on a plain, we must remain before that fire or that tree as long as they do not resemble any other fire or tree.

Alfonso defines his total immersion as 'seizing the soul of an ingredient', a soul that should be brought to light, expressed in all its lushness, and defended from globalization's threats, which suppress diversity in favour of economies of scale and other business advantages.

However, the discovery of the ingredient's essence is just the beginning. Alfonso remarked that what follows next is a struggle to articulate his 'tomato experience' in a language made of flavours, smells, textures, and colours. The knowledge of produce and condiments, the cooking skills and science, the stubbornness in tirelessly recombining ingredients through dozens of experiments and enduring the weight of the (many) failures, all come into play.

However, Alfonso glided over these aspects, which he considered just technicalities, parts of a protocol that his heart knows before his mind. Instead, he talked about his enthusiasm for letting the mind wander – and the sudden *a-ha* moment

after so much thinking. He praised the virtue of patience and the joy of experimenting with, for instance, dozens of different types of peppers, until he finally 'stumbles' into his final creations, some of which we had the privilege to taste right away when, after the long interview, he told us: 'I hope you have planned to stop for lunch.'

The hidden workflow of the creative process

Alfonso Iaccarino's creative process can be described through three key steps:

1. Demarcating a cognitive *and* emotional space in which a process of discovery can unfold;
2. Discovering resources through constraints;
3. Identifying interactions between the ingredients as dynamic tensions.

Furthermore, Alfonso makes it very clear that his creativity is spurred from what is available to him at a certain moment in a given situation. For instance, a missing ingredient may offer an opportunity to experiment with a new constraint. The recognition of situational opportunities and constraints is an essential requirement for the creative process, which ultimately is an adaptive process.

Finally, good design is about good composition. Good composition is the artistic arrangements of information into a coherent whole that is more than the sum of its parts.

Alfonso achieves this result by identifying and exploiting a system of tensions among the ingredients. His objective is to boost an ingredient's potential, something he elusively defines as the ingredient's essence. One of his methods consists of reframing his quest as a tension between opposites. The tension provides a baseline against which differences can be more finely appreciated, very much like an image on the forefront stands out against a suitable background.

Alfonso masterfully exploits this contrast by combining sweet with salty flavours or velvety with grainy textures. By emphasizing and tempering flavours simultaneously, Alfonso eventually builds a network of tensional relationships between opposite sensations that his customers can explore when eating his dishes. The result of all this emotion and sensory-driven mind-wandering is aesthetic pleasure.

How does it feel? the role of emotions in the aesthetic experience

What Alfonso does with his culinary art is to build an aesthetic experience for his clients. Aesthetics is generally associated with art and perception of beauty, but its meaning is wider. The word comes from the ancient Greek term αἰσθητικός (aisthetikos), which means 'sensitive' or 'sentient', and the corresponding verb in Greek means 'to perceive', 'to feel'. So, an aesthetic experience pertains primarily to what we perceive and how we judge and value it.

Neuroscience research has shown that perception is a highly complex process requiring a smooth and complex coupling between mental states and sensory data flow (Leder et al. 2004). Another key finding is that emotions critically drive perception: Our brains analyze sensory input by using affective criteria and emotional response to filter information and determine meaningful action (Damasio 1999).

Emotions are involved in perception in two main ways (Marković 2012). First, positive feedback is generated by recognizing an

anticipated regularity; for instance, when we expect to see a familiar shape and find a match between what we expect to see and what we see. We called this feeling the *joy of guessing* in chapter 1. Second, our brain enjoys finding connections between events and assembling them into meaningful narratives through which we either make sense of what is happening or project anticipations over what is going to happen. We call this the *joy of forecasting*.

The role of emotions in our thinking and decision-making can be experienced through somatic markers such as muscle twitching, increased blood pressure, heart rate, sweating and trembling, usually accompanied by more intense brain activity (Damasio and Carvalho 2013). Such markers are body signals that our brain takes into consideration to mobilize our attention towards the most appropriate course of action, as in 'fight or fly' decisions. This process takes place through a continuous dialogue between emotion and reason. However, we tend to underplay emotions in favour of 'rational', cold thinking.

Of course, feeling that something is right does not guarantee it is, but more often than we might suspect, it is the recognition of a pattern that triggers an emotional spike. In the end, as we mentioned in chapter 1, accuracy depends on the quality of one's previous experience and learning, but the critical role of the emotional test is evident.

These aesthetic mechanisms operate intensely in visual perception, and neuroscientists have investigated them in studies on art perception (Ramachandran 2012; Zeki 2011).

An essential ability of our visual system is to integrate a critical set of visual clues, such as colour, motion, shapes, distance and speed, into mental images of the world. Given the massive amount of raw data that our eyes capture and our need to be highly responsive to visual stimuli, vision is more about confirming pre-existing assumptions than neutral absorption of sensory input. Some of these assumptions come as simple rules (Gigerenzer 2007); for example: 'close objects appear larger than faraway ones', or 'lighting comes from above', or 'shadows are always darker'.

Visual artists apply these rules consistently. Giotto revolutionized painting in the Middle Age by applying an intuitive perspective for the first time to create a sense of depth and make the scene more realistic (Fig. 2.2).

Modern artists have deliberately circumvented conventions to communicate the sense of cognitive discomfort resulting from violating the rules. In his proto-Cubist painting titled

The Pavers, Umberto Boccioni represents the pavers' movements through a puzzle of geometric tiles that convey the idea of frenetic busyness (Fig. 2.3).

In her sculptures and architectural works (Fig. 2.4a), Zaha Hadid questions the more conventional use of straight lines and instead exploits the dynamic power of curves to challenge the force of gravity so much so that her buildings seem to float in the space, much like clouds, or emerge from the ground as organic formations. Similar examples can be found in other masters of organic architecture, such as in Gaudi's oblique pillars in Parc Guell, Barcelona (Fig. 2.4b).

Analyzing how the brain perceives a work of art is crucial to understanding how we deal with these aesthetic paradoxes and develop abstract concepts by integrating rational and emotional thought. Samir Zeki (2011) is one of the pioneers

FIGURE 2.2 *The Adoration of the Magi* (Giotto di Bondone, 1320 ca.).
Giotto shows the difficulty of mastering the rules of perspective in drawing the roof of the hut. The result is the creation of an indefinite space, halfway between the realistic space of the daily experience and the metaphysical space of an otherworldly event.

FIGURE 2.3 *The Pavers*, (Umberto Boccioni, 1914).
The painting's subject is the movement, portrayed as a geometry of gestures broken down into fragments that the observer has to put back together.

FIGURE 2.4A
In this sculpture created by Zaha Hadid (2016) for the Sotheby's Beyond Limits Monumental Outdoor Sculpture Show at Chatsworth House (UK), the monumental mushroom-shaped monoliths surprise us in their ability to defy gravity

FIGURE 2.4B
Antoni Gaudi designed this oblique arched pillar to support the roadway viaduct in Parc Guell, Barcelona (1900), challenging the convention that pillars have to be vertical and straight and creating forms that resemble the shape of natural caves and tree trunks.

in the study of how our mind perceives beauty. His research shows that the understanding of how the visual brain works and of its capability to appreciate works of art are fundamental to shedding light on how the human mind understands and makes sense of reality.

Zeki (2011) argues that we see to know the world. The ability to select and classify relevant information is possible because vision is an active process that is driven by the brain and not by the stimuli we receive from the environment. It is a three-step process that we will refer to with the term *sense-making*:

1. Isolate salient informational features;
2. Compare them with pre-existing mental models;
3. Resolve ambiguity by confirming or revising our expectations.

According to Zeki (2011), artists – and great artists, in particular – are very effective in this process. The artist's objective is to isolate the essential in what she sees, often through prolonged observation of an object and painstaking refinements that lead to an 'elegant' representation. This process is akin to what Alfonso Iaccarino does in the preparation of his dishes when he captures and exalt the essence of an ingredient. It is a two-way process, looking for an optimal match between the forms in the brain and the sensory information, between abstraction and perception. But how does this experimentation take place? And how do artists know when to stop?

When is it 'good enough'? aesthetic pleasure and effective complexity

One does not need to be an artist to engage in some creative task. We are, in fact, creative anytime we arrange elements into some aesthetically pleasant configuration. Suppose you have to compose an email: In this case, it is the arrangement of the words that matters, and we instinctively know that some versions are more effective than others. Let's make the case that we are writing a message through which we want to persuade someone to do something, for instance, to invite someone we like on a date. We know that a very blunt and straightforward text just asking someone out would not be nice; so, we try to embellish it such that the message is still conveyed, but in a more pleasant way. The first draft, though, looks too lengthy and has lost its spontaneity. In other words, it is too complicated, so we need to go back to cut out unnecessary material. Then we do a little bit of wordsmithing so that the new version looks better. Quite likely, there will be a few iterations and drafts until we think the message seems 'good enough'.

We argue that this process of adding and removing information to make the message more expressive is akin to what artists do. When our chef Alfonso Iaccarino experiments with his dishes, he makes his recipe more or less complex by adding and removing ingredients. The difference between a Michelin-starred chef and someone who likes to cook a good recipe at home is that, for a start, Iaccarino can rely on his state-of-the-art knowledge and exclusive culinary experience to nurture his creativity. Second, he doesn't settle for merely 'good enough' but actively searches for an optimal arrangement to maximize aesthetic pleasure. While our everyday designs in persuasive emails or in home cooking may be inferior to what a master would create, we argue that the process of creation and the search for the right amount of complexity takes place following a similar dynamic.

The above examples show that an effective arrangement is one that delivers some complexity that the observers can process in a surprisingly effortless way. The idea that it is possible to package meaning into some optimal composition has surfaced in fields as diverse as design, art critique, psychology, fiction, and complexity science. In his book *Living with Complexity*,

Donald Norman (2016) states that we need *some* complexity: when the design of a product is too simple, it is predictable and boring; when it is too complicated, it creates anxiety and confusion. Berlyne (1970) offered systematic evidence to back this observation, showing that subjects in his experiments tended to experience higher aesthetic pleasure when exposed to intermediately complex stimuli. The art critic Roland Barthes argued that 'Art does not acknowledge the existence of noise . . . It is a pure system: there are no wasted units' (Barthes and Duisit 1975: 245). Antoine de Saint-Exupery said that perfection is attained not when there is nothing more to add, but when there is nothing more to remove (1970).

The Nobel Prize physicist Murray Gell-Mann has proposed a metric he termed *effective complexity* to capture this intuitive idea (Gell-Mann and Lloyd, 1996). Effective complexity is the length of a compact description of an entity's identified regularities. Gell-Man argues that the total information in a system is equal to its effective complexity plus a "noise" component:

Total information = effective complexity + noise

Effective complexity is, then, the ideal amount of information we need to understand the meaning of something. A design that is too complicated contains too much information, which generates the perception that some of it is irrelevant noise. One that is too trivial has *negative* noise – that is, it misses information that could make it more exciting, understandable and useful. This book will argue that great artists and designers create zero-noise solutions – and that we can learn from them how to achieve this level of ideal complexity.

However, it is important to clarify right away that there is no such a thing as an objective amount of complexity that fits everybody's need. The design of the organization of a workspace can offer an interesting example of how the type and amount of desired complexity can be highly subjective and can vary across different users. In his cult novel, *The Zen and the Art of Motorcycle Maintenance*, Robert Pirsig identifies two types of mechanics, based on how they organize their workspace. In the workshop of a mechanic of the 'photographic mind school' tools and parts are scattered and cluttered; nevertheless, the mechanic can 'put his [or her] hand on any tool in this mess without having to think about where it is' (2005: 100). The designs of the makers' carts that are increasingly common in school labs and maker spaces are based on the other school of organization, the one that requires tools and parts to be arranged in a complex but rationally ordered classification system. Note, however, how the cart's design is based on a modular structure that can accommodate different ways of arranging these elements to match the way different individuals prefer to organize information.

Strategies for effective complexity

How do masters achieve effective complexity? Recent research in neuroscience shows that artists resort, deliberately or unconsciously, to a set of universal rules that have been likely selected by evolution to improve our pattern recognition skills (Ramachandran 2012). We can apply these rules by trial and error to achieve an optimal level of 'noise' in a design through two fundamental thinking modes. Following Berghman and Hekkert (2017), we refer to them as the search for unity and the search for variety (Fig. 2.6).

The search for unity mode is the most intuitive. As we described in the first chapter, our brain is a formidable simplifying machine: empirical stimuli are mapped onto known, simple mental models that we can easily understand and process. The search for unity relies mainly on eliminating details and reducing noise by subtraction and aggregation.

FIGURE 2.5 A maker's cart in a lab at Rowan University (2018).
Makers' carts provide a modular design to accommodate different ways users want to organize the complexity of their workspace.

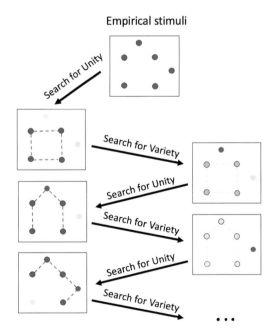

FIGURE 2.6 Search for unity and search for variety to pursue effective complexity.
Effective complexity is the result of a trial and error process in which designers combines opposite strategies aimed at minimizing noise.

However, in a novel or unusual situation, a search for unity will deliver oversimplified, trivial understanding. Thus, we need to search for variety to 'complexify' our experience and develop more articulated mental representations. Of course, if we err on the variety side, our interpretations will be too noisy and unnecessarily complex.

Our brain alternates between these two thinking modes to discover existing or unexpected regularities. This dual thinking is at work in creative thinking and design, through a mix of divergent versus convergent reasoning, as exemplified in the double diamond process proposed by the British Design Council (2016) and based on Banathy's work (1996) (Fig. 2.7).

We explore more complex possibilities through divergent reasoning, while convergent reasoning helps us focus on viable solutions. What the dualism of divergence-convergence does not tell us is when to stop. The answer to this question is: when an adequate level of complexity is achieved.

In other words, in creative problem-solving, we look for effectively complex representations by trial and error. The difference between great artists and most of us is that the artists are trained and exceptionally skilled at achieving

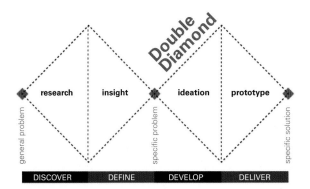

FIGURE 2.7
The double-diamond design process combines divergent and convergent thinking. The first part of the diamond serves the purpose of understanding different ways to describe and articulate a problem, while the second part helps us to explore the variety of possible solutions.

high levels of effective complexity. Those outstanding achievements are the product of long apprenticeships, hard work, research and endless experimentation.

However, the good news is that by surveying work in neuro-aesthetics, Gestalt psychology, and design theory, we have identified eight compositional strategies to achieve a higher level of effective complexity. We briefly introduce these design strategies in the following section. In the rest of this book, we will dedicate a chapter to present each strategy and its applications in art, management and design.

STRATEGIES IN THE SEARCH FOR UNITY: REDUCE NOISE

Strategy 1. Subtract details. The fundamental idea behind this strategy is that artists and designers should suggest rather than describe reality. They can do so by reducing a complex system to a few powerfully expressive elements. Good examples are Cezanne's seemingly coarse landscapes (Fig. 3.4), Delaunay's Cubist city scenes (Fig. 3.5) and the evanescent haze in Turner's works (Fig. 3.3).

Strategy 2. Develop symmetry. Symmetry allows our brain to generate complex shapes in a more efficient way, by using only half of the information. Symmetry helps to identify hierarchy, focal points, distances and directions. In Middle Age and early Renaissance paintings with traditional religious subjects, symmetry is typically used to remind us of divine order, hierarchy and the centrality of the holy subject or event (Fig. 4.3).

Strategy 3. Group. As discovered by Gestalt psychology, groups provide order by similarity, vicinity, closure and segregation or by suggesting common destiny. Our brain identifies some common trait or feature shared by different elements to cluster them into a category, as Leonardo does to create the animated and upset reactions of Jesus' disciples in his *Last Supper* (Fig. 5.1).

Strategy 4. Split. Complex information needs to be displayed at different levels. For instance, contrasting foreground with background helps us to focus on a particular level of the image. Encapsulating details into a larger structure guides the eye from the general to the particular and vice versa, as in *The Little Street* by Vermeer, in which the building's façade opens 'down' to more detailed interior scenes (Fig. 6.5).

STRATEGIES IN THE SEARCH FOR VARIETY: INCREASE ENTROPY

Strategy 5. Use the power of the centre. This strategy is about the creation of one or few dominant visual centres by using colours and lines to guide the eye toward particular points, as happens in Van Gogh's *Starry Night* (Fig. 7.3) in which the vortexes help our gaze meander across the beauty and the anguish of the night sky.

Strategy 6. Emphasize. This strategy consists of the deliberate attempt to celebrate diversity or exceptionality, e.g. by rejecting realistic proportions as in the elongated necks of the ladies portrayed by Amedeo Modigliani (Fig. 8.4).

Strategy 7. Remix. This strategy is about the disassembling and reconnecting of elements into new combinations to deliver novel meaning as in Dali's paintings of dreams, where elements and parts of objects and animals are reassembled to create fantastic and impossible creatures (Fig. 9.10).

Strategy 8. Contrast and balance. This strategy works by juxtaposing elements that are supposed to be in some relationship using colour, shapes, or composition. Examples are the use of dark and bright tones to separate light from shadow, the association of complementary colours, the spatial arrangement of shapes and elements around some direction to balance their visual weight. Degas' ballerinas (Fig. 10.4) offer beautiful examples of how balance can be achieved through contrast.

The necessity of art

Research in cognitive psychology and neuroscience is giving a deeper meaning to why we enjoy art and why art exists in the first place (Zeki 2011). First, art can teach us how to achieve effective complexity through the optimal arrangement of the elements in a composition. In masterpieces, all the elements and their relationships are necessary (Barthes and Duisit 1975). We can hardly remove a single note from a Mozart sonata, or a brushstroke from a Velasquez painting, without making it less exceptional.

Second, a work of art activates numerous neuronal populations in our brain, synchronizing them in a sort of cerebral choreography. The neurons' dance can occasionally induce aesthetic ecstasy, manifesting as dizziness, tremors, crying and sweating. This is sometimes called 'Stendhal's Syndrome' after the writer who described it (Stendhal in Stanska 2017):

> Absorbed in the contemplation of sublime beauty . . . I reached the point where one encounters celestial sensations . . . Everything spoke so vividly to my soul. Ah, if I could only forget. I had palpitations of the heart.

Human beings have leveraged art to stimulate and develop fundamental cognitive skills; we use it as a laboratory to perform imaginary experiments in a safe environment, in which failure will do no harm to us or other people.

The understanding of how artists induce aesthetic pleasure helps us to develop the design skills that organize information to achieve effective complexity. It can also teach designers how to better integrate rational and emotional responses to achieve an adequate balance between technical performance and psychological arousal.

In this book, we propose that a way to accomplish these results is to train our mind to alternate between the opposite thinking modes of the search for unity and the search for variety by applying their associated design strategies that will be presented in the following chapters.

PUTTING IDEAS INTO PRACTICE

Key takeaways for this chapter

LESSON LEARNED	DESIGN IMPLICATIONS
Rationality and emotions: Human reasoning is the result of the interplay between the rational and the emotional brain. Emotional thinking is fast and tacit while rational thinking is slow and articulate. Understanding requires both emotional validation (feels good) and analytical assessment (understanding how and why it works).	• Assess your design from both the emotional and the functional points of view. Understand how emotional and technical aspects of the design positively interact or negatively interfere. Identify the design features that are associated with certain emotional responses.
Design as composition: Composition is an essential part of good design. Good composition requires us to arrange and combine parts into a coherent, consistent and meaningful whole.	• Identify and play with opposites. Offer emotional hints to users. Create meaningful connections among the elements of a design.
Effective complexity: The pursuit of simplicity in design is misleading; what users are looking for is the right amount of complexity (effective complexity). Aesthetic pleasure tends to be higher for designs characterized by intermediate levels of complexity, where intermediate is relative to the target users' ability and will to process and absorb complexity. Effective complexity is achieved by trial and error by adding information when the design seems 'too simple' and by removing it when the design seems 'too complicated'.	• Effective simplicity is actually effective complexity; do not be afraid to add complexity to your design. Create multiple design iterations characterized by different levels of complexity by adding and removing information (alternate the search for unity and the search for variety).

Creativity lab

The full description of each exercise is available on the book companion website: http://www.bloomsburyonlineresources.com/elegant-design

2.1 Case study: emotional design

Learn how to read a product from the emotional point of view. Follow the instructions to perform a comparison of different design alternatives using the framework proposed by Don Norman in his 2004 book, *Emotional Design*.

2.2 Anatomy of a masterpiece: emotional tension in Caravaggio

Learn how Caravaggio creates compositions able to trigger emotional tensions.

2.3 The art of noticing: let's have coffee!

Learn how to observe users' emotional responses in a live situation and to map those reactions towards the design details that may be the cause of such responses.

2.4 Design exercise: a primer on photographic composition

Create more powerful images by mastering Gestalt composition principles in a picture-taking exercise.

2.5 Design exercise: detect and iconize emotions

Learn to understand human emotions by reading facial expressions, a fundamental skill for empathy, through the design of an emotion.

3 Subtract Details

ABSTRACT

This chapter presents the design strategy of subtraction. More effective and meaningful designs can be created by thoughtfully eliminating superfluous information. With many examples of this strategy being applied in art and design, the chapter illustrates three reasons this strategy works and what it accomplishes. First, subtraction supports fast information processing through information compression. Second, it helps designers to focus on what matters in the situations in which a design will be used. Finally, simple and even incomplete representations are suggestive and liberate users' imaginations.

KEYWORDS

abstraction

abstract art

Cubism

information compression

imagination

minimalism

simplicity

Numquam ponenda est pluralitas sine necessitate [Plurality ought never be posited without necessity]

William of Occam

(quoted in Lombard, 1150 (ca.): dist. 27, qu. 2)

The art of concision

The train went on up the track out of sight, around one of the hills of burnt timber. Nick sat down on the bundle of canvas and bedding the baggage man had pitched out of the door of the baggage car. There was no town, nothing but the rails and the burned-over country. The thirteen saloons that had lined the one street of Seney had not left a trace. The foundations of the Mansion House hotel stuck up above the ground. The stone was chipped and split by the fire. It was all that was left of the town of Seney. Even the surface had been burned off the ground.

Ernest Hemingway (*Big Two-Hearted River*, 1922)

This excerpt is the opening of one of Ernest Hemingway's well-known short stories, *Big Two-Hearted River*. This passage is an excellent example of the writing style that made Hemingway famous. The text is deliberately devoid of plot and action, most sentences are very compact and include only one proposition, and punctuation is limited to the essential. The whole text appears as a collection of sharp images that follow each other as in a movie scene. Narration by precise visual imagery through clear, blunt language was one core rule of Imaginism, a literary movement born in England in the early 1920s. Hemingway encountered these ideas through Ezra Pound, one of his writing masters.

This dry, sharp writing style was also, in part, the result of Hemingway's work as a reporter. In his first job as a journalist at the Kansas *City Star*, he had to adhere to the newspaper's writing style recommendation, a set of rules that later Hemingway credited as the best he had ever learned for writing. Such rules included: 'Use short sentences', 'Use short first paragraphs', 'Use vigorous English', 'Be positive, not negative', and 'Eliminate every superfluous word'.

Hemingway's minimalist prose was the result of countless revisions and constant editing. In an interview he released to the *Paris Review* (Plimpton 1958), he declared that he rewrote the ending of *Farewell to Arms* thirty-nine times before he was satisfied. The interviewer asked whether there was some technical problem there that had stumped him. To which Hemingway replied, 'Getting the words right.'

We argue that to achieve the artistic results that his readers and literary critics enjoy, Hemingway worked by subtraction. Still, as he implies in his interview, removal was not just aimed at eliminating redundancy and irrelevant materials but consisted of chiselling the text to increase its expressive power. Hemingway's prose is flawless because he achieves semantic efficiency: say the most and say it right with the fewest words possible. This seems somehow paradoxical: How do we increase meaning by eliminating information?

The answer to this question, according to Hemingway at least, is that well-crafted concision leads to highly evocative mental imagery. Most sentences in *Big Two-Hearted River* entail rich visuals that can create each scene with fantastic precision in the reader's mind, so much so that this 'fishing story' appears to be familiar even to readers who have no experience at all with fishing. By inspiring his writing with the visual innovations of Cezanne's works, Hemingway could focus on the main image while leaving details out or keeping only some of them on the background.

Evocation and focus can be powerful mechanisms to support our understanding.

They are at the core of our first strategy: Subtract details. Through several other examples from art, science, and management, we will show how we can resolve complexity by subtraction. More specifically, we will show that good subtraction is an effective form of information compression, which our brain routinely employs to represent and make sense of reality.

The case for abstraction

While art history books commemorate outstanding and innovative artistic production, they say little of the conventional art that even famous artists had to produce to make a living. Typically, this production included portraits. In addition, early modern tourists traveling across Southern Europe to rediscover classic art and archaeology in what was nicknamed 'the Grand Tour' would buy as souvenirs idyllic landscape pictures (called *vedute* in Italian) of marinas, panoramas, or 'picturesque' rural scenes.

No wonder then that artists' prowess was assessed in terms of their ability to reproduce or embellish reality in a technically flawless way.

The invention of photography changed the art world forever. It was undoubtedly unsettling for conventional artists, but it was a stimulus for more innovative minds to find alternative artistic creation paths rather than just imitating life. Thanks to the demand for souvenirs for elite travellers, Joseph Mallord William Turner started to explore the beauty of the haze and mist of ports and marine landscapes, one of his customers' favourite subjects. Figs. 3.1, 3.2 and 3.3 show a comparison between Turner's more academic early work, rather conventional marinas, and his more mature style, in which details are almost entirely lost in the terrifying character of a snowstorm at sea (Fig. 3.3).

In part, the rise of abstract art was a result of this departure from the dogma of loyalty in artistic representation. One of the most important artistic currents in abstract art, Cubism, paradoxically was born out of the most realistic attempts to represent reality: Impressionism. Monet's brush strokes aimed at capturing nuances of light in *plein air* to reproduce the way human vision supposedly worked. This evolved into geometric shapes as Cezanne started to realize that vision is about constructing rather than scanning reality. Whatever we see is the result of this construction, an analytical projection of elementary mental shapes. Cezanne's brush strokes are perceptual quanta, colourful geometric tiles that our brain projects on reality to understand form and volume (Fig. 3.4).

Cubist painters such as George Braque and Pablo Picasso brought this idea to its extreme consequences. Natural forms gradually disintegrated into the aggregation of basic geometric units, or 'cubes', as the French critic Louis Vauxcelles named them after seeing the landscapes Braque had painted in 1908 at L'Estaque, with an apparent reference to Cezanne's work (Rewald 2004). Robert Delaunay applied these ideas to represent the urban landscape as in his *Ville de Paris* (Fig. 3.5).

The early Cubist works were still realistic enough that the subject could be recognized. The details were stripped down, shapes were reduced to their elementary geometric counterparts, such as cubes and pyramids, and curved lines almost disappeared. In later works, Cubists apply the same principles with more intensity to subjects other than landscape, such as human figures and still life. Their art departs from any attempt to represent reality by using the deliberate distortion produced by multiple vanishing points, creating inconsistent points of view. It is the birth of abstract art.

FIGURE 3.1 *Calais Pier* (William Turner, 1801).
The stormy sea appears to be the main subject on the foreground with its waves and white foam, but the artist still lingers in describing the many details of the pier and the sailors' figures.

FIGURE 3.2 *The Wreck of a Transport Ship* (William Turner, 1810).
The stormy sea here occupies half the painting. Its liquid chaos demolishes and sucks up all forms. There is no proportion between the forces of nature and the desperate resistance of men and things.

FIGURE 3.3 *Snow Storm Steam-Boat off a Harbour's Mouth* (William Turner, 1842).
Sea and sky are totally mixed up by the storm. The artist renders this chaotic sensory experience by focusing on light and dark masses of colour without any consideration for detailed forms.

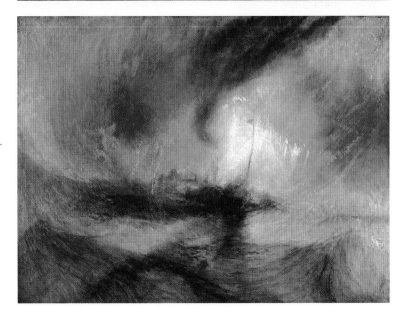

FIGURE 3.4 *Mount St. Lazaire* (Paul Cezanne, 1902–06).
Cezanne assumed that our understanding of reality is based on elementary units that must be reassembled into meaningful unity. He realizes these units through sharp brushstrokes of colours while disregarding the drawing of contours and leaving to the observer's eyes and brain the task of integrating these units into higher level forms.

FIGURE 3.5 *Ville de Paris* (Delaunay, 1912).
The world represented by Delaunay is the world of memory, where things seen reappear like coloured fragments without any need for spatial and temporal order. Cezanne's units have become basic geometric shapes, 'cubes', units of sense that can be reassembled without necessarily paying respect to conventions and the laws of perspective.

Pablo Picasso was one of the most prominent representatives of Cubism. During a visit to an exhibition on African art at the Trocadero in Paris, he was particularly impressed by African masks. The nineteenth-century Fang mask in Fig. 3.6a is likely similar to the ones that Picasso saw. Far from looking like a real human face, the mask is nevertheless forcefully expressive. All the most essential details appear as simple geometric shapes: triangles for the mouth and the nose, diamonds for the eyes, and an oblong oval for the face's shape. Picasso assembled these very same elementary shapes in the women he portrayed in one of his most famous works, *Les Demoiselles d'Avignon* (Fig. 3.6b).

By bringing Cezanne's intuition to its extreme consequences, Cubists wanted to exalt the constructed nature of perception, representing how our mind projects known shapes on reality and creates meaning. Not surprisingly, this projection is dynamic, continually flickering and evolving; the use of conflicting perspectives, which is a key style characteristic of Cubism, aims to represent movement and the constant questioning that our brain engages with when trying to make sense of complex and unstable images. We can keep this in mind so that the next time we have the opportunity to admire these paintings, we move around the works to look at them from all possible angles.

One of the key lessons of Cubist art is about the limitations and wonders of human perception. Our memory is not able to store an image as it happens for a digital picture. Instead, seeing consists of the hard work of remixing and reassembling simple shapes together to capture the fleeting nature of physical reality.

Other artistic movements and masters have advanced this idea further by experimenting

FIGURE 3.6A Fang or Makina (Oseba) people, Ngil Mask, River Mbini (Rio Muni), nineteenth century. African masks show that the construction of a face according to classical proportions is only a cultural construction. We rarely see a still face. We see faces from lateral views and subject to continuous movements.

FIGURE 3.6B Study for *Les Demoiselles d'Avignon*, Pablo Picasso (1907). Eyes, nose and mouth is all we need to identify a face. In fact, a well-known face is only the mental integration of all the times we have observed the eyes, nose and mouth of a certain individual from the most varied points of view.

with different techniques and concepts. Futurists have used a similar analytical and geometric approach to represent the movement, energy and speed of the new machines, such as trains and cars. Mark Rothko has gone beyond geometry to focus on coloured bands' nuances to capture the shades of fundamental human emotions. Joan Mirò experimented with simple shapes and primary colours to focus on the development of the most basic form in art, the line; his later works, consisting of only one irregular, naked line crossing a large white canvas, communicate the obsession of the artist trying to understand how we draw what we draw, what guides our hand, where intention stops, and when action seems to take a life on its own.

Most abstract artworks have in common the attempt to understand complexity by recognizing essential patterns: identify basic elements and rules, project them selectively on sensory inputs and information flow, focus all the attention on this filtered reality, and forget about the rest. It is important to remark that subtraction is only one possible way to achieve abstraction. Islamic art avoids the representation of realistic subjects for religious reasons. Arab-Andalusian artists used abstract representations for decorations that are all but minimalistic, such as in the use of tessellation (Fig. 3.7). Assembling tiles of different shapes and colours creates beautiful and complex patterns that are easy to understand once the observer has identified the essential pattern that is endlessly repeated to generate the whole representation.

Subtracting the obvious, adding the meaningful

Achieving beauty by subtraction is effective. The use of simple modules that can be rearranged in many ways makes it easier for the viewer to understand complexity. It also

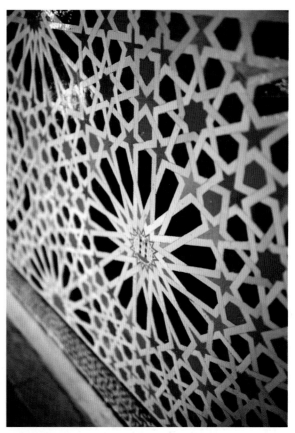

FIGURE 3.7 The Mexuar in Nasrid Palaces at the Alhambra, palace and fortress complex located in Granada, Andalusia, Spain. Islamic décor is abstract but not minimalist. Nevertheless, we are able to understand its intricacy once we identify the basic pattern that is endlessly repeated to generate the mosaic.

makes our experience pleasurable because it leads to discovering the primary forms that can create order in the world. A caveat, though: Simplification is not about just removing details, but about understanding which simple elements we need to support meaningful and even complex tasks.

Not surprisingly, designers have been increasingly adopting a similar approach to design products that are increasingly simple but whose simplicity gets along with increased technological sophistication and enjoyment.

(a)   (b)

FIGURE 3.8
The pursuit of simplicity through minimalist design and easy to use/assemble/operate products is increasingly associated with aesthetically pleasant design in consumer products: (a) the iPod Nano shuffle; (b) the Ikea Billy bookshelf designed by Boerje Lindgren.

In recent years there has been a growing interest in the pursuit of simplicity. Apple's obsession with the 'insanely simple' is well known (Segall 2013): It was the constant pursuit of making sophisticated technology simpler and more user friendly that determined the success of Apple bestsellers, such as the iMac, the iPod, and the iPhone. The iPod Nano shuffle (Fig. 3.8a) came as a piece of white plastic with the essential navigation wheels and without any screen, button, light or decor. More recently, this trend has become dominant across diverse product categories. Think of Ikea furniture, such as the Besta line or the Billy bookshelf, with their clean and minimalistic designs (Fig. 3.8b) or think back to consumer electronics such as the Sony PS4 and the Bose speakers presented in the introduction of this book (Fig. 0.2).

The disappearance of the interface in digital products is becoming even more conspicuous with the growth in popularity of voice-controlled personal assistants, such as the Amazon Echo or Google Home. The artificial intelligence technology on which these solutions are based is embedded into smart speakers characterized by elementary geometric shapes; neutral colours, such as white or grey; smooth surfaces and absence of visible controls (Fig. 3.9). After all, why would you need an interface if you can effectively interact with a device solely by voice-activated commands?

Contemporary design, and perhaps good design in general, tends to be minimalist. The LC4 chaise longue designed by Le Corbusier (Fig. 3.10) or Alvar Aalto Paimio armchair (Fig. 3.11) are characterized by no-frills designs that mirror the

FIGURE 3.9 Amazon Echo speaker.
AI-enabled smart speakers come in abstract shapes
characterized by extremely regular geometry, neutral
aspect, and absence of buttons and other controls.
Some versions, such as the Amazon Echo in this
picture, contrast the dullness of their extremely simple
shape with accents such as the backlight at the base
or the virtual digital clock.

FIGURE 3.10 Perriand's LC4 chaise longue (1928).
Le Corbusier called the chaise longue a 'rest machine'
to emphasize its essentiality and the extreme attention
to functionality.

FIGURE 3.11 Alvar Aalto Paimio armchair (1931–32).
The chair was designed for a tuberculosis sanatorium.
The angle of the back was intended to help sitters
breathe more easily. The chair has the presence of
a sculpture and at the same time the lightness of a
friendly object.

silhouette of a human body at rest and second its
movements in a very natural way.

One criterion to evaluate the effectiveness of
an interface is its full transparency to the user.
Great interfaces disappear from the cognitive and
sometimes even the user's visual field because they
make it natural to interact with a device.

An outstanding example of a ghost interface is
the Google search bar. If you travel in time back to
the early nineties when the Internet was emerging
as the new and global mass communication
infrastructure, search engines were very different
from what we are used to now. The market leaders
of the time, such as Altavista, looked more like web
portals, very crowded web pages covered with news,
ads, and a lot of information clogging the whole
screen, in the midst of which you could barely see
what you were looking for: the search bar.

Of course, the main reason we prefer Google, Bing, and the like is that they have better search algorithms, but Google's innovation was not limited to the platform's back-end. Google founders understood that searching among the massive information available on the Internet was all about relevance and minimization of users' cognitive efforts. Accordingly, they designed a search algorithm, Google PageRank, driven by relevance instead of other search mechanisms, such as word matching or semantic analysis. Sites linking to my sites must be relevant, and that's all I need to know. Consistently, Google designers stripped down the home page to the bare minimum: a search bar with the multicoloured Google logo on the top and two buttons at the bottom ('Search' and 'I'm feeling lucky'). It was a bold and revolutionary move that made Google the first real new media of the Internet era. Google applied this philosophy to advertising, following the basic idea that ads should be shown when they are relevant to the user's search context. Google business is based on this principle: Minimize the information that has to be delivered to maximize its relevance for the customers.

In his book, *The Laws of Simplicity*, John Maeda (2006), the Director of the prestigious Rhode Island School of Design, states that achieving simplicity is about removing the obvious and adding the meaningful. He suggests ten laws to accomplish this objective in design. The rule that sits at the top of Maeda's Decalogue is about reducing complexity through 'thoughtful reduction': when in doubt, remove, but be careful about what you remove. Reduction must be thoughtful because it requires endless experimentation to identify what matters. The iPod's minimalist interface made this device stand out among the crowded MP3 reader market. Apple designers did not invent the portable MP3 reader; they just figured out how to make it usable and enjoyable. With two basic movements, click and rotate, everybody can navigate the richest music catalogue. Like Braque and Picasso, Apple designers found the basic units of meaning that users could recombine in multiple ways to generate complexity through simplicity.

Small talks

Allegedly, when a cabinet member asked former US President Woodrow Wilson about the amount of time he spent preparing speeches, he replied: 'It depends. If I am to speak ten minutes, I need a week for preparation; if fifteen minutes, three days; if half an hour, two days; if an hour, I am ready now.'

Why do we need to spend so much time to convey less? It's not just because sometimes we have to stick with limited time constraints for our presentations. It's because we know that short, well-crafted messages are more effective. Why is that?

For one, severe constraints on the length of a text provide unsuspected opportunities for creativity. Both western and eastern poetry has been playing this brevity game extensively. Japanese haikus are poems that consist of three lines: The first and last lines of a haiku have five syllables; the middle line has seven syllables. Here is an example:

First autumn morning
the mirror I stare into
shows my father's face.

Murakami Kijo, 1923

The English translation requires bending a little bit of the constraint on the number of syllables. Still, it does not detract from the beauty of these three verses and their ability to evoke in our mind a profound narrative that resonates so well with the way we experience how time goes. Western poetry is rich in short formats too. For instance, the sonnet, allegedly invented by Jacopo da Lentini in the thirteenth century, is composed of fourteen verses arranged in two quatrains followed by two triplets that rhyme according to the schema *abba abba cde cde*. Using chained triplets formed by lines of eleven syllables with this rhyming rule, Dante Alighieri wrote the *Divine Comedy*, an all-time literary masterpiece composed of three books (*Inferno*, *Purgatory*, and *Paradise*), each divided into thirty-three parts called Canti.

These constraints force poets to compress information while maximizing the meaning that information is supposed to deliver.

The other reason short texts work is related to the limitation of our working memory. In a well-known study, Miller (1956) showed that the number of objects the average human can hold in working memory at a given time is equal to seven, plus or minus two. Neuroscience research subsequently confirmed Miller's conclusions about the limitation of our short-term memory (Alvarez and Cavanagh 2004).

The love of short statements is at the base of Twitter's success, the well-known microblog platform that limits every message's length (early Tweets were no more than 140 characters; more recently the limit was doubled). According to Twitter's inventors, the 140-character limitation was sufficient to answer the question: What are you doing now? The limit originates from the 160-character limitation of the mobile phone texts.

The story goes that in 1986 a German engineer, Friedhelm Hillebrand, at the time the chairman of the non-voice services committee within the Global System for Mobile Communications (GSM), came up with this number (Milian 2009). After some unsystematic research, he observed that the average number of characters used in media such as postcards or telex was 160. GSM technology had to be tweaked a little bit to accommodate the additional 32 characters Hillebrand was asking for over the 128 supported by the available GSM free bandwidth. It was a Nokia engineer Matti Makkonen that developed the first commercial application of the SMS technology. Text messaging success was as spectacular as much as it was totally unexpected. This service quickly became the most important source of revenue for mobile carriers, anticipating that customers were more interested in transmitting data than voice over their phones. Text messaging was then abandoned by users in favour of online chat apps, such as Whatsapp, Snapchat, and Messenger. Still, these platforms just repurposed the SMS technology and format to serve multimedia communication in the digital age.

The science of brevity

Cognitive psychology and brain science provide abundant evidence of our brain's inclination to handle complexity by subtraction. Let's look at some research findings that confirm this tendency.

Studies in behavioural economics show that we tend to use simple cognitive heuristics when making a choice instead of engaging with systematic data collection and probabilistic inference. Most of these heuristics are based on the selective subtraction of information that is not considered relevant. Consider the following example. Read the individual profile reported below and then guess the most likely option regarding what this person does or likes among a limited set of alternatives (example adapted from Piattelli Palmarini 1996):

> Luigi is 34 years old. He is smart but not very creative, likes routine, and does not have a very active lifestyle. In school, he was good at math but did not like humanities. Which is the most likely option among the following:
>
> A- Luigi is a doctor and likes playing poker
>
> B- Luigi is an architect
>
> C- Luigi is an accountant
>
> D- Luigi plays jazz music
>
> E- Luigi likes windsurfing
>
> F- Luigi is a journalist
>
> G- Luigi is an accountant and enjoys playing chess
>
> H- Luigi enjoys hiking

When we reproduce this experiment in our classes, we obtain diverse answers. While students each provide a different rationale for their guesses, none says that they used probability calculus to answer. For instance, students do not ask us data such as the base frequency (i.e. the possibility of picking up an architect in a random population) and do not apply Bayes' theorem (even the students who know this theorem). Instead, they use simple mental models by eliminating any randomness or details that do not conform to information retrieved from direct experience (do I know someone fitting that profile?) or via learned stereotypes (the nerdy student). For instance, some people guess that option G is more likely than C because G better fits the nerdy student

stereotype. Probability theory, however, explicitly forbids this result (the probability of a joint event is always less than or equal to the likelihood of each event occurring alone).

While mental models built by subtraction can introduce biases in our decisions, they work reasonably well in many situations because such heuristics are the result of thousands of years of adaptation. Gerd Gigerenzer, the Director of the Center for Adaptive Behavior and Cognition (ABC) at the Max Planck Institute for Human Development, argues that judgments based on gut feelings and intuition are the result of the applications of simple rules (Gigerenzer 2007) forged by natural selection that allow us to make effective decisions when time and data are limited.

In everyday life, we know that our ability to solve a problem depends on how we frame the problem, and we tend to build minimalistic frames that can accommodate as many as examples as possible.

A good interpretative frame must be minimalistic because it should help us to take into account only the variables that matter. Marketing research consistently shows that customers' choices are typically determined by a very limited set of criteria, even for complex products. According to a study on cars (Hirsh et al. 2003), all decision factors boil down to only two: the cost of ownership and the perceived quality. Nevertheless, when we buy a car, we spend considerable time assessing several attributes that, ultimately, will not have any impact on our satisfaction.

An additional reason minimalistic representations are useful comes from studies in neuro-aesthetics. These findings are quite surprising because they show a less intuitive advantage of designing by subtraction: Minimalist design can trigger our imagination.

For instance, experiments show that people tend to prefer realistic to abstract paintings (Aviv 2014). Based on what we described in the first chapter of this book, this result is not surprising (see the joy of forecasting): Representations of known landscapes or other familiar subjects are more likely to activate the dopamine rewards circuit because they easily relate to something we already know. However, other studies showed that individuals enjoyed abstract representations, as well, but in a different way. The data showed that different types of paintings activated different parts of our brain (Kawabata and Zeki 2004). Specifically, while realistic paintings triggered distinct but confined parts of the brain depending on the type of subject (landscape or portrait, for example), abstract works stimulated brain activity in a larger number of brain regions.

The enjoyment of abstract painting probably derives by the fact that this type of art allows for unconstrained exploration (the joy of guessing; see chapter 1). By stripping realistic details from their images, abstract artists removed constraints and limits to the observer's imagination. This freedom enables us to mentally wander across the painting, project multiple representations, and possibly discover unanticipated meanings. The joy of guessing is more intense than the joy of forecasting because it entails novelty and surprise.

Thus, almost paradoxically, subtracting details can free our minds and challenge our imagination. It is maybe this the reason why very young kids enjoy playing with toys with stylized shapes. Obviously, a toddler's cognitive skills are not sufficiently developed to play chess, but why, as Piaget (1964) demonstrated, do deduction and mathematical skills develop quite late in kids, only in their teenage years? Natural evolution may have determined our ability to imagine to be more fundamental than logic.

PUTTING IDEAS INTO PRACTICE

Key takeaways for this chapter

LESSON LEARNED	DESIGN IMPLICATIONS
Semantic efficiency/compression: Subtraction is not just aimed at eliminating irrelevant materials; it also helps in effectively compressing information in a design to increase its expressive power. This design strategy is fundamental to achieving semantic efficiency: communicate the most with minimum information.	• Work by subtraction: Question the necessity of each element of your design in the most rigorous way. • Eliminate distractions: Identify what is impossible to remove. • Better to be sorry than safe: When in doubt, remove it! (You can always add it back.)
The power of context: Things exist in a context and their meaning and use change across different contexts. Not all the details of an object are important in each situation: to make an object relevant in a given context, we have to strip or ignore all the details that do not matter (if a chair is used as a ladder, in that context the armrests are not relevant).	• To someone with a hammer, the whole world is a nail (and the opposite is true as well: if you need to drive a nail, the entire world can be a hammer). Identify essential user needs and map them over essential product features and functions. Repurpose design.
The joy of discovering: Simplification is generative; the lack of details favors creative thinking and unconstrained exploration more than the mere recognition of known forms does (compare with the joy of guessing in chapter 1). Well-crafted concision can lead to highly evocative mental imagery.	• The value of emptiness: Do not cram your design; leave space for thinking and exploring. • Assess the evocative power of your design: What does it communicate beyond the obvious? How much? How well? • Redundancy: Eliminate what users can easily deduce by themselves. • What is missing now that should not be missed? Time to add it back!

Creativity lab

The full description of each exercise is available on the book companion website:
http://www.bloomsburyonlineresources.com/elegant-design

3.1 Case study: the LC4 chaise longue

Understand how to apply the 'subtract details' design strategy through the analysis of the design of this iconic piece of furniture.

3.2 Anatomy of a masterpiece: the power of abstraction

Learn how artists develop and apply a few powerful abstract ideas to represent complex concepts, such as representation of three-dimensional space on a plane.

3.3 The art of noticing: creativity is in the context

Capture the essential design features of a product through a creative exercise in which you are required to imagine as many as possible alternative uses for a common object.

3.4 Design exercise: parsimony of signs

Practice the art of creating complex visuals by using a very limited set of parts with a Tangram puzzle.

4 Develop Symmetry

ABSTRACT

Symmetry is present everywhere in the physical world.
In this chapter, we show that this is the case because
symmetry meets the criteria of cost-effectiveness, efficiency,
stability and balance. The ability to recognize symmetry is
hardwired in our brains. Neolithic decorations of artifacts
show how our ancestors created abstract symmetric order
in their visual representations. We illustrate how to leverage
symmetry to stabilize meaning and build bridges between
different knowledge domains. Thanks to the stability and
information efficiency obtained by symmetry, humans
apply it to many spheres of human action. On the social
level, people's symmetry is linked to ideas of fairness,
justice, balance and neutrality. Symmetry in art and
design is a source of enjoyment, as symmetry preserves
unity while helping us to recognize individual parts and
their connections.

KEYWORDS

natural forms

minimum energy

knowledge organization

abstract thinking

social stability

fairness

balance

*We might like to turn the idea around and think
that the true explanation of the near symmetry of
nature is this: that God made the laws only nearly
symmetrical so that we should not be jealous of
His perfection!*

Richard Feynman (1963)

Blood, sweat and tears: what goes up, can't go down

During the middle of the fourteenth century, Europe was devasted by one of the deadliest epidemics ever recorded in history of humankind. The Black Death, as the plague was later infamously dubbed, had arrived in Europe in 1347 from the Middle East, probably carried by a fleet of twelve Genoese caravels docked at the Sicilian port of Messina. From the coasts of Sicily, the disease diffused throughout the whole continent by traveling along the dense network of trade routes that had already made Europe a highly integrated economic system in those days. At the end of 1353, when the epidemic lost its strength, anything between a quarter and a half of the European population was swept from the face of Earth and the structure of European economy and society changed forever (Kelly 2005).

Medical science in the Middle Age was very different from today's medical practice, which is based on rigorous scientific protocols and government regulation. As mandated by the best academic practices of the time, the works of the ancient Greek Philosophers and Savants formed the cornerstone of any academic discipline, and medicine was no exception. Hippocrates was the undiscussed authority in the field of medicine. He developed the 'four fluids' theory, according to which the human body was the host of four fundamental liquids: blood, black bile, yellow bile, phlegm (Wallis 2010). According to the theory, individual health depends on the right proportion in the human body of these fluids, while a deficiency or an excess of any of them produces an unhealthy imbalance, leading to pain and illness.

Why four? The answer, in the eyes of medieval academics, was obvious: four is the key number for the physical world. There are four elements,

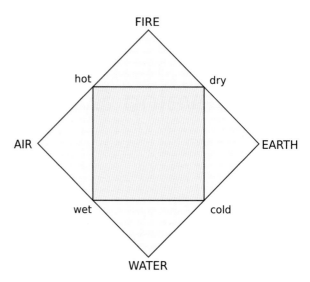

FIGURE 4.1 The four elements and their qualities. Natural phenomena in ancient Greek physics are explained in terms of the seductive force of symmetrical oppositions.

according to Empedocles and Aristotle: earth, air, water and fire, to which the fundamental qualities of matter (i.e. hot, cold, wet and dry) are associated. More specifically, earth is cold and dry, fire is hot and dry, water is humid and cold, while air is humid and warm, as illustrated in the diagram in Fig. 4.1.

If the whole material world is subject to these constraints, medieval doctors reasoned, human health is no exception. In fact, the black bile is cold and dry, the yellow bile is hot and dry, the phlegm is moist and cold, and the blood is moist and warm.

This theory could be used to explain any disease in terms of the rupture of the symmetry between the elements, as induced by some external cause. Among the four elements, air had a place of honour when it came to illness development, because breathing put the body liquids in connection with the environment. In the summer of 1348, the doctors of the medical school of

Paris had no doubt: the cause of the plague was to be searched in unhealthy air. But what had infected the air of all Europe everywhere and at the same time? Which natural causes could have generated a phenomenon of such magnitude? The most prestigious science of that age, astrology, was there to help to solve this dilemma.

The medical school of Paris stated that the first cause of this plague was an exceptional celestial configuration that occurred on 20 March 1345, exactly one hour after midday, when there was a conjunction of three planets in the constellation of the Aquarium. This unusual planetary alignment caused a contamination of the air: Jupiter 'being moist and warm, extracts the vapors infected from the Earth', while Mars, 'being excessively hot and dry, inflames them'. The harmful, heated vapors penetrate human hearts, contaminate the blood, and turn body liquids into poisonous substances. The contagion was then favoured by the winds that would spread this harmful air throughout Europe (Wallis 2010: 414–419).

This explanation of the plague was tremendously seductive in the eyes of the wise men of that age. Its charm was due to the many pairs of symmetries that perfectly matched one another. Symmetry provided a unique ordering principle through which it was possible to read and interpret the world; perhaps in incorrect ways, as the story shows, but ones that can make a lot of sense.

A shortcut to balance: symmetry in art

Ambrogio Lorenzetti has left us one of the most powerful artistic representations of the art of good government. His fresco, realized between 1338 and 1340 in the medieval city hall of Siena (Italy), represents the daily life of a Middle Age city guided by virtuous politics (Fig. 4.2). A central role is played by the allegory of justice, represented by a young woman (top left corner) who, guided by the divine Wisdom, holds a scale on whose plates two angels distribute rewards or

FIGURE 4.2 *Allegory of the Good Government* (Ambrogio Lorenzetti, 1338–1340).
In virtually every culture, symmetry is associated with the values of fairness, justice, power, order and stability. On the left side symmetry is associated to equity in rewards and punishment. On the right symmetry refers to the balance of virtues.

punishment. A rope departing from divine justice connects all the righteous citizens (bottom of the painting) who commit to live in concord (from Latin *cum corda*, meaning literally with a rope, a metaphor indicating the need for establishing social ties driven by mutual respect and common good). The idea, of Aristotelian origin, is that justice, like the other ethical virtues, is based on equidistance from excesses of any sign. In this view, the distinctive aspects of justice are equilibrium, neutrality and moderation (Frugoni 2019).

The metaphor of the balanced scale evokes symmetry from many points of view: the equality of all human beings in front of the law, the proportions of merits and rewards, crimes and punishments, damage and compensation. Justice brings equity into society by rebalancing the perverse effects caused by individual excesses that tear apart virtuous human relationships.

While symmetrical representations were common in Medieval and Renaissance art as a way to represent divine order (Fig. 4.3), the use of symmetry as a compositional strategy is pervasive throughout the whole history of art (Enquist and Arak 1994; Gombrich 1979; Hodgson 2011; Tyler 2000; Weyl 2015) and across different human cultures (Figs. 4.4). In the Native American totem pole, symmetry in the composition recalls the symmetry of the human body across vertical and horizontal dimensions, while in the Hindu tantric tradition, the abstract symmetry of yantras is used to stimulate meditation as well as to decorate floors in temples and shrines.

In modern and contemporary art, the use of symmetry is deliberately questioned, as in abstract Expressionism, or reimagined in original or problematic ways. Mondrian's lattices are intriguing because they offer symmetries that are continually interrupted (Fig. 4.5). Rothko's canvases are built on a horizontal symmetry based

on layers of colours (Fig. 4.6). When symmetry is brought to the extreme consequences, we get a blank, empty canvas, as in the work bluntly titled *White Painting* by Robert Rauschenberg, in which absolute uniformity makes it possible to choose any direction as an axis of symmetry.

To find the first surviving examples of symmetry in figurative art, we must look at Neolithic artifacts (Fig. 4.7). The geometric patterns typical of this art reflect an ability to organize the composition using abstract conceptual schemes. The regular arrangement of spirals, lines, diamonds and the like are evidence of the ability to create visuals through the imposition of order.

FIGURE 4.3 Symmetry in Renaissance painting, Pala di San Bernardino, Lorenzo Lotto (1521).
Symmetry gives order and balance to the composition and at the same time gives a dominant role to the centre, typically a holy subject in Medieval and early Renaissance paintings.

**FIGURES 4.4
Symmetry as an aesthetic
canon in many cultures.**
Human preference for
symmetrical representations
is evident in many
different and separate
cultural traditions. On
the left, an example from
Native American art,
the *K'alyaan* Totem Pole at
Sitka National Historical
Park (Alaska, USA) to
commemorate the lives lost
in the 1804 Battle of Sitka.
On the right, a Hindu Sri
Yantra with correct traditional
colours from a silkscreen
print made in 1974 at the
Tantra Research Institute in
Oakland, California.

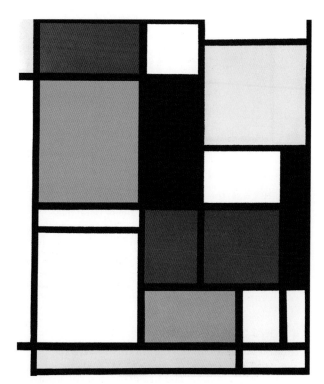

FIGURE 4.5 Symmetry in modern abstract art –
Tableau II by Piet Mondrian (1921–25).
The interruption of symmetries generates instability
in the composition and produces the impression of a
continuous movement.

FIGURE 4.6 Symmetry in modern abstract art –
(Mark Rothko, 1957).
A skilful play between symmetries and asymmetries of
large colour surfaces creates an emotional space in
which to immerse yourself.

FIGURE 4.7 Symmetry in prehistoric art – cone-shaped vase with geometric decoration ca. BCE 4500–4100 (Iran). Abstract signs indicate a conquest of the human mind: emancipation from the tyranny of the visible and ability to reason with ideal forms.

Understanding symmetry requires the ability to abstract our thinking from the immediacy of perception and feelings. Abstracting requires two basic operations: first, to isolate the object from the background; second, to assume a point of view. Consider, for example, the human body. Our body is not perfectly symmetric, and the perception of its symmetry can be problematic when we observe a real figure from one of its sides or in movement. However, once we mentally visualize an ideal human figure, as Leonardo da Vinci did with his Homo Quadratus, we will be able to capture ideal body symmetry as well as, in contrast, the little imperfections and asymmetries of the body of a real person.

Even more complex is the recognition of symmetry in a scene. To appreciate the symmetry of a scene we have to turn the scene into a unitary object. This can be done by imposing a frame that cuts out the scene from its background (Arnheim 1965). The frame creates invisible medians and diagonals around which elements in the composition acquire visual weights, roles, and meanings as part of a system of perceptive and cognitive tensions (Fig. 4.8). The symmetry

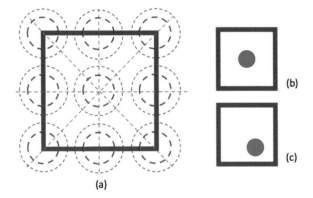

FIGURES 4.8 The force field of a square.
(a) Symmetries of a square and visual force field created by focal points; (b) circle in a stable position as forces are symmetric; (c) circle in un unstable position as forces are asymmetric.

imposed by the frame thus becomes one of the fundamental means to create this system of tensions (the other one is the use of visual centres, as we will discuss in chapter 7).

The imposition of an abstract order on everyday experience has a considerable advantage over the fluid mind. The abstract mind is better at manipulating and connecting concepts and at generating more complex representations (Hofstadter and Sander 2013). Thanks to this artificial stability, obtained through abstraction, human beings began to build their own artificial world and apply it to other spheres of human action (Harari 2012).

Symmetry as social game

As in visual arts, symmetry can provide a system of tensions around which social relationships can be built, constrained and managed to create order and equilibrium in otherwise chaotic, unbridled social interaction. The breaking of social symmetry can liberate the energy that is restrained by these tensions.

Think of the physical layout in which you had your latest meeting. If it was a lecture or keynote speech, the speaker was probably talking to an audience from a podium. The vertical symmetry of this layout reflects the hierarchical relationship between the speaker and listeners, and it comes along with a vertical communication process in which interruptions are not allowed outside of occasional questions that will be accepted and answered at the time set by the speaker. In a brainstorming meeting, the setting tends to be more horizontal with people sitting in a circle: horizontal layouts communicate that frequent interaction and interruptions are not only allowed but desired. The increasing use of movable furniture in classrooms helps to disrupt the symmetry of traditional, mono-directional teaching – or at least to alternate it with more collaborative sessions based on layouts favouring peer-to-peer exchange and teamwork (Fig. 4.9).

FIGURE 4.9 Redesigned classroom with moveable furniture at Monterrey Institute of Technology and Higher Education, Mexico City.
The simple act of rearranging furniture in a classroom opens to a new set of ways to exchange information that disrupts the vertical symmetry based on the hierarchy of teacher-speaker and pupil-listener.

A totally symmetrical setting can create a social dynamic in which participants feel like they are equal and open, as, for instance, when they sit in a circle of chairs. This is the option chosen by Alcoholics Anonymous to emphasize the need to open yourself to the group and listen from them without any mediation (Baldwin and Linnea 2010).

The circular symmetry can be easily broken by the addition of a special chair in a central position in which some higher status participant is supposed to sit. In some cultures, you will notice that people may tend to spread around this seat in a hierarchical fashion, with the more important participants sitting closer to the leader and the ones who oppose the leader sitting on the other side of the circle. Interestingly, people tend to stick with these rules even when they are not openly enforced.

Social relationships have their own dynamics and cannot be crystallized into rigid systems. The failure of bureaucracy to accomplish the freezing of these relationships along the only patterns that are allowed by explicit rules and procedures is a telling example of this impossibility. Rather, in groups and organizations, explicit procedures cohabit with implicit rules of the social game that, again, are characterized by an alternative level of symmetry that counteracts the dominant, explicit one. If the group is too hierarchical, its members develop informal ways to compensate for this excess of verticality. If it is too egalitarian, informal leadership and authority will emerge (Smith and Berg 1987; Hansen et al. 2007; Iandoli and Zollo 2007; Michellone and Zollo 2000; Schneider and Sommers 2006).

In complex ecosystems, such as the rainforest, it's this circular, lose-win-lose symmetry that eventually guarantees that no species will dominate the others, so much so that when an external perturbation breaks the existing equilibrium, it will create a temporary unfair advantage for the dominant species that eventually will backfire by threatening the existence of the whole ecosystem (just look at the catastrophic impact of anthropogenic environmental changes around you, if you need examples).

Equity is an important requirement in human interaction. A simple test shows the enormous role played by the perception of symmetry in social relations when it is perceived in terms of fairness.

The following task is proposed to participants in the test: You have the chance to get a $100 bonus from your company. You have to share this money with another colleague, taken at random, making him or her an offer of free money. The following rule is in place: If your colleague accepts the proposed amount, you keep the rest; otherwise, if the offer is rejected, nobody gets money. We have carried out this test countless times in university classrooms and training courses for company employees, each time with the same result. According to traditional economic explanations, the duo should settle quickly on a $99 to $1 deal because $1 is obviously better than nothing and the first participant must offer at least $1 to maximize profit. However, most duos end up with a 50/50 settlement. This happens because individuals prefer fairness over profit maximization as decision-making criterion. According to anthropologists, this criterion has been selected over time by evolution because fairness and reciprocity helps a group to increase its cohesion, which in turns leads to greater chance of survival in a hostile environment (Tracer 2003; Strang et al. 2015).

A practical way to increase cohesion and offset the excess of rational/opportunistic behaviour is to promote volunteering. In every group we can find a mix of defectors and cooperators. Volunteering has the effect of mitigating the advantages of defectors, giving rise to a society where cooperators, defectors and volunteers coexist. This is because the circular symmetry defectors-cooperators-volunteers has the effect of levelling the playing field for all the parties involved (Semmann et al. 2003).

Symmetry can be seen at work in other social domains, including politics, government and management. Montesquieu's balance of powers is at the foundation of liberal democracies (Montesquieu 1748). Weber (2015) makes symmetry the key principle of order for the proper functioning of any organization. In Taylor's *The Principles of Scientific Management* (1911), symmetry reigns everywhere: each worker can be replaced by another, workloads need to be balanced, all workers are equally subject to company policies and rules.

The science of symmetry

The term 'symmetrical' derives from the combination of two words from the ancient Greek: 'syn', which means 'same', and 'metric', meaning 'measure'; hence, the 'same measure'. This word expresses an ideal of order and equilibrium that is achieved through proper arrangement of parts in a well-balanced unity[20].

But why is symmetry so powerful in ordering our intentions and perceptions? Why is symmetry so closely connected to our ideas of knowledge, order, beauty, balance, fairness, predictability? What is the relationship between symmetry in the human body, in social dynamics, or in architecture? And why do we associate the concept of symmetry with the feelings of balance, solidity and power?

The answer to all these questions is simple yet powerful: Symmetry helps us build identity from distinct parts. If we trace a plane that cuts the human body vertically into two sides and turn one part over the other, the two parts roughly coincide. This reflection establishes an identity. If we rotate a star by a fifth of a circle, we do not notice any change. Symmetry exists only by virtue of a movement that restores the initial form; its secret is in the way this movement takes us back to identity and unity. It's almost a paradox: The aim of each movement should be to reach a final state

that is different from the initial one. Symmetric movements instead lead us back to the starting point, showing us the secret identity of the world (Golubitsky and Stewart 1992).

It took about twenty-four centuries to understand that we had to look at movement to unveil the mathematical structure of symmetry. Those years separated Pythagoras from Evariste Galois, a young mathematician who shortly before a deadly duel on 31 May 1832 wrote a fundamental essay on symmetry (Galois et al. 1976). The mathematical theory of groups was eventually born. Four rotations and four reflections of a square form the group of symmetry of the square. More complex symmetries can be obtained by combining elementary symmetries (Du Sautoy 2008).

Thermodynamics allows us to emphasize a counterintuitive characteristic of symmetry. Let's try a little mental experiment: Pick up a white sheet, divide it into two parts in the vertical sense, and draw two black squares in symmetric positions with respect to the vertical axis. Then draw another two, always symmetrical. You can keep going like this until all the whole piece of paper becomes black. What happens at this point? We have achieved perfect symmetry. And, yet, we cannot distinguish any form, no object, no order. Total symmetry produces absolute uniformity. To appreciate symmetry, the observer should be able to distinguish an entity from the others. Symmetry cannot be total. If it is, it cancels out the experience.

It is a surprising result. We have always been convinced that the more symmetry the more the order, but the relationship between symmetry and perception of order is more nuanced. The psychologist and art historian Ernst Gombrich (1979) states that only the breaking of total symmetry gives rise to the perception of patterns. And the mathematicians Golubitsky and Stewart (1992) point out that we begin to appreciate symmetry in physical forms only when total symmetry breaks up into partial symmetries, as it is possible to observe in the beautiful picture captured through high resolution photography of a drop of milk hitting a liquid surface (Fig. 4.10).

Physics also teaches us that if energy in a system is homogeneously distributed, the system is incapable of performing work. Work is executed and energy is liberated when this uniformity is broken. A steam engine can work only if steam is separated into a hot container and channelled into a colder one. Water falls down from a higher position with higher potential energy. The electric current flows because there is an asymmetry in the electron distribution between the positive pole and the negative pole of a battery.

Boltzmann called entropy the measure of total uniformity in energy distribution (Atkins 1984). Gas particles in a container collide randomly with each other and tend to be distributed uniformly in this closed space. Under these conditions, it is very unlikely to find all the particles in one corner, although this configuration is possible in theory. It's like tossing a coin up twenty times: a sequence of twenty heads is unlikely to be achieved.

Psychological symmetry looks for diversity: there is a right side and a left side of the body (two things), the starfish has five distinct arms (five things), the square has four sides (four things). We then work on these distinctions to look for unity to find a relationship between A and B, whereby A = B is set when symmetry is detected. In other words, to see the square we need to be able to see its sides and understand how they are related to teach other.

Our brain is, in fact, hardwired to recognize symmetry. The analysis of neuronal activity stimulated by the presence of symmetric objects shows that the ability to identify symmetry is processed by what neuroscientists call the 'what pathway', an information flow that starts from the occipital brain, where the activity of the 'visual brain' mostly takes place and moves towards the temporal lobes. This circuit deals

FIGURE 4.10 Symmetry generated by a drop of milk hitting a liquid surface.
It is possible to appreciate the symmetry of milk wave because it breaks the symmetry of the liquid surface. Symmetry is only evident if it is partial.

with the processing of the spatial relationships among discrete objects, such as, for example, the proportions of the various elements in a face, but it is insensitive to the relationships between the perceived object and the surrounding environment, to which another brain circuit is dedicated (Kandel 2016).

The fact that evolution has endowed our brain with specialized neuro-circuitry able to detect and process symmetry clearly spells out the important role that symmetry has in evolution.

The importance of symmetry for living organisms is self-evident. All animals capable of movement, whether they crawl, fly, swim or walk, are provided with bilateral symmetry. Symmetry can be also circular, as for jellyfish, octopi, starfish, and other organisms that move in a fluid that is denser than the atmosphere. Organisms having bilateral symmetry tend, however, to move faster (Golubitsky and Stewart 1992).

The biologist Robert Trivers and his colleagues at Rutgers University measured the knees, ankles and feet of 73 Jamaican athletes and compared them with the same measures of 116 non-athletes of comparable age, sex and weight. The comparison revealed that the sprinters' knees and ankles were significantly more symmetrical than those in the control group (Trivers et al. 2014).

Symmetry is also dominant in the vegetal world: Trees and flowers have circular symmetry; leaves have bilateral symmetry. Marcus du Sautoy (2008: 23) points out that, for a living organism, symmetry is not an easy conquest: 'A plant must work hard and divert important natural resources to achieve the balance and splendor of the orchid and sunflower'. Both animals and humans tend to opt for symmetrical shapes in their choices (a symmetrical flower, a symmetrical fruit, or a symmetric mating partner).

Alberto Roselló-Díez, a developmental biologist at the Australian Regenerative Medicine Institute of Monash University, conducted a study on how a mouse foetus maintains symmetry as it develops. By forcing one of the foetus's limbs to grow slower than the other, the team has observed how the cells communicate to correct the asymmetry. Conversely, lack of symmetry can be the effect of distress: the eggs produced by hens raised in batteries are less symmetrical than those that live cage free (Roselló-Díez et al. 2018).

In ecological niches, where the different species compete and cooperate to ensure the survival of the species in a delicate dynamic balance, symmetry is typically a message of genetic superiority. Bees can recognize symmetry in flowers (Giurfa et al. 1996). Symmetric flowers are more likely to be found by insects, and thus symmetry gives a reproductive advantage. Something similar happens for the choice of a partner for sexual mating where highly symmetric bodies and faces are perceived as more attractive.

Conclusions

Symmetry is a principle that we use to give order to reality; on the other hand, a symmetric world is homogenous and boring. It is an organizing principle that preserves diversity and unity at the same time, by helping us to recognize individual parts and how they can be effectively connected to each other. Symmetry in art is a source of enjoyment because it is a compositional principle that plays with identity and diversity. A symmetric world is not static and inert: The tensions created through symmetry can be broken anytime by a minimal perturbation that can put everything in discussion.

Symmetry, like the other heuristics analyzed in this book, is a very general operator that structures our experience of the world. We find it at every level, from the organization of visual elements, such as lines and shapes in an image, to the social level, as expressed in the concepts of fairness and justice. We find it applied to scientific research to explain the birth of the universe, and as a key organizing principle in biological evolution. Finally, we can rediscover its power through mathematical theories, in the design of new products and in the management of group dynamics and other social processes.

It is worth stressing a principle that extends to all the other heuristics presented in this book. When a heuristic is applied with too much intensity, it produces negative results. Effective complexity is always obtained by a problematic balance of two opposing forces: the search for variety and the pursuit of unity. The search for variety requires breakages; the pursuit of unity requires the preservation of islands of order. The pursuit of order requires breakages; the search for variety requires the preservation of islands of order. Symmetry produces its benefits only if enforced up to a certain point. If this point is exceeded, symmetry gives rise to opposite results. When social symmetry is exasperated, it gives rise to uniformity, suppression of diversity, and impediments to social renewal and innovation, as has happened in totalitarian societies with disastrous consequences. Hyper-stable social organizations subsume a network of tensions that is just waiting for the right moment to surface and disrupt the existing equilibrium. Sometimes, all it takes is a small perturbation.

PUTTING IDEAS INTO PRACTICE

Key takeaways for this chapter

LESSON LEARNED	DESIGN IMPLICATIONS
Symmetry as fairness and equidistance: Symmetry favors information efficiency. Symmetry helps to stabilize meaning by freezing information in predictable and regular configurations.	• Your design is too messy? Identify symmetrical counterparts for functions and parts in your design that you had not initially considered. • Multiple points of view: There could be more than one symmetry. Identify alternative axes or focal elements.
Symmetry as emerging equilibrium resulting from competing forces: Symmetry can be an emerging order determined by opposite forces that achieve a state of equilibrium.	• The beauty mark effect: Experiment with a little asymmetry to create visual tension. • The harmony of the opposites: Play with contrast and use symmetric balance to help contrasting elements coexist.
Situational symmetry: Symmetry needs to be defined with respect to a background frame in a specific context. This frame could be socially situated or even arbitrary. Therefore, we need knowledge of this context to identify and create the type of right type of symmetry.	• Eye for an eye: Fairness and balance depend on what users expect to be fair and balanced. • Understand the 'natural' order of things in your design context: What's up, what's down? What is fair, what is wrong? What's on the foreground, what's on the background?

Creativity lab

The full description of each exercise is available on the book companion website: http://www.bloomsburyonlineresources.com/elegant-design

4.1 Case study: when faulty design creates catastrophes – the case of the nuclear accident at Three Mile Island

This case study shows how bad design of control rooms and dashboards led to the first accident in the history of nuclear energy at the plant of Three Mile Island.

4.2 Anatomy of a masterpiece: the use of symmetry in Renaissance paintings

In this exercise, you will analyze ways in which symmetry is constructed or violated in some Renaissance masterpieces.

4.3 The art of noticing: market 'asymmetry' – the art of visual merchandising and its impact on shoppers' experience

Observe how department stores use symmetry (or lack thereof) to organize their shelf space for the twofold objective of improving the shopping experience as well as their economic performances.

4.4 Design exercise: how to improve interface design through symmetry

Learn how to use symmetry and asymmetry to improve the design of everyday devices. This time we will look at the hated/beloved remote control.

5 Group

ABSTRACT

In this chapter, we will explore a seemingly obvious strategy to simplify a design: grouping. In addition to the obvious objective of allocating the elements of our design into clear categories, the ultimate goal of this strategy is to group elements through different criteria (space, time, and network relationships) to create powerful narratives that help users to connect the dots and quickly understand how they can browse information in our design. Through several examples from art and product/service design, the chapter illustrates that grouping can be used to create persuasive storytelling or to build mind tunnels that make us blind to novelty.

KEYWORDS

classification

clusters

storytelling

gestalt laws

memory

Seek? More than that: create. [My mind] is face to face with something which does not yet exist, to which it alone can give reality and substance, which it alone can bring into the light of day.

Marcel Proust (*Swann's Way*, 1913)

A stroll down memory lane

In 1468, Cardinal Bessarione donated to the Senate of the Republic of Venice a collection of 482 Greek and 264 Latin manuscripts. This group ended up forming the nucleus of St. Mark's Library (Biblioteca Marciana). Bessarione was one of the most influential intellectuals of his time and committed his entire life to the dream of reuniting the Catholic and the Orthodox Churches and liberating Constantinople, modern-day Istanbul, from Ottoman subjugation[21]. That dream never became reality.

The value of Bessarione's gift was exceptional for its political and cultural significance, but also in terms of sheer economic amount. Before Johannes Gutenberg invented print, books were so expensive that even affluent and avid book collectors could not amass in a lifetime the number of volumes that we can find today on a student's bookshelf[22]. Today we can rely on many devices to store information: our smartphones and laptops; the Internet; and the more affordable and simpler media, such as books, calendars, and notebooks. We tend to forget that this abundance is quite a recent achievement in humanity's history.

To cope with the shortage of external memory prosthetics, ancient savants developed quite sophisticated memorization techniques that they applied in various professional tasks and domains. The ability to memorize a large quantity of information became synonymous with prodigious intelligence.

One of the most renowned memorization techniques is the Method of Loci (in Latin, the word locus means 'place'), cited in several ancient Roman texts, including Cicero's *On Rhetoric*. The method consists of mentally visualizing a familiar building – your house, for instance – and associating specific locations within this place to chunks of information you want to remember. The second step is to visualize a walk in this building, moving through all the areas in the order in which you wish to remember these chunks. Using this technique, and with a little bit of practice, you can memorize a long sequence of events or an elaborate speech.

This chapter's focus is on our third strategy in the search for unity: grouping. Clustering events or objects into homogeneous categories is a straightforward approach through which people handle abundant information. This chapter's objective is to show that grouping is not just classifying – it's about creating mental 'places' that we arrange in a specific order to build action-oriented narratives. As in the memory walk, categories are topical chunks of information connected in a network that lead to one another. We need an artificial narrative, a memory stroll, to make sense of this information and transform a list into a temporal sequence that ends up being 'stickier' in our memory. We see remnants of this topological approach in English and many other languages (e.g. when we use expressions such as 'In the first place . . . In the second place'). The word 'topic' comes from the ancient Greek term 'topos', which means, again, 'place'.

The power of categorization lies in its dynamic, structuring property and in its ability to influence our actions. We will show that this power can be a curse and a blessing. It can lead us to identify creative connections, such as the one through which Starbucks' revolutionized the coffee business, or it can make us blind to the discovery of alternative points of view, as it happened to companies like Kodak and Polaroid when they refused to redesign their businesses around digital photography.

The power of grouping in art: seeking as creating

In Greek mythology, the Muses (i.e. the Arts) were the children of Mnemosyne, the goddess of memory, and Zeus. Thus, for the ancient Greeks, artistic creation was the combination of divine inspiration and memory.

A great example of this connection is a passage Marcel Proust's *Swann's Way* (1913: 48). In this text, the author describes the feelings evoked by the simple act of savouring a madeleine on a Sunday morning in a little French town. After the first bite, the artist writes:

> No sooner had the warm liquid mixed with the crumbs touched my palate than a shudder ran through me, and I stopped, intent upon the extraordinary thing that was happening to me. An exquisite pleasure had invaded my senses, something isolated, detached, with no suggestion of its origin.

Then, after another couple of mouthfuls, enlightenment occurs when he discovers that 'the truth I am seeking lies not in the cup but in myself'. He puts down the cup and examines his mind (Proust 1913: 48):

> It alone can discover the truth. But how: What an abyss of uncertainty, whenever the mind feels overtaken by itself; when it, the seeker, is at the same time the dark region through which it must go seeking and where all its equipment will avail it nothing. Seek? More than that: create. It is face to face with something which does not yet exist, to which it alone can give reality and substance, which it alone can bring into the light of day.

Memories are a crucial ingredient in artistic creation. Artists can find inspiration in apparently insignificant memory fragments that surface to their consciousness from the past. A good example is Alfonso Iaccarino's account of how he creates his plate from memories triggered by a single ingredient's flavours (chapter 2). It's that complex mix of memories and their associated feelings that allow Iaccarino to uncover the subtle qualities of an otherwise humble and ordinary vegetable.

What sets this creative thinking apart from more mundane information processing is artists' ability to re-group stimuli by mapping them against existing memories to create unlikely, surprising and aesthetically pleasant compositions. Through such reorganization, the taste of a tea-soaked cake is not just a mundane food memory for Proust. Instead, he finds out that 'this new sensation' was a 'precious essence that was not in me, it *was* me' (1913: 48).

This realization has tremendous implications for designers. First, introspection can provide a formidable source of good ideas. Second, our memory must be continuously nurtured by experience and curiosity to provide our creativity with suitable inputs. Third, any good idea requires emotional validation.

Grouping helps designers to identify fundamental units of meaning, clumps of sense, around which they can re-invent by re-organizing. The proper arrangements of these units into a cohesive and compelling message will then appear to observers as emerging naturally from the interaction among the various parts.

A masterful example of the arrangement of groups and shapes and how these parts connect seamlessly into a story is Leonardo da Vinci's *Last Supper* (Fig. 5.1). The visit to the Convent of Santa Maria delle Grazie in Milan is one of the most thrilling art appreciation experiences. Unlike other museums, visitors are not overwhelmed

FIGURE 5.1 *Last Supper* (Leonardo da Vinci, 1494).
Leonardo's *Last Supper* stands out among the countless paintings depicting this crucial scene in Christian religion because of its cinematic character. Da Vinci uses grouping to build visual episodes tied to each other in a grand narrative of friendship, salvation and betrayal.

by too many masterpieces and noisy crowds. The painting stands alone on one of the walls of an empty large, white room, which once was the Refectory where the convent friars had their meals. Only a limited number of visitors are admitted each day. The painting survived the construction of a door that partially destroyed the lower part of the fresco, Napoleon's soldiers using the Refectory as a barn, and even one bomb in World War II.

Surrounded by the silence in the big empty room, we can almost hear the apostles' voices reacting to Jesus' shocking revelation that someone among them will betray him that very night. What makes da Vinci's last supper stand out among many other attempts to depict the same

scene is its cinematic nature. The scene seems alive and thus very different from more conventional, hieratic representations of this crucial moment in Jesus's life and Christian faith. A comparison between Leonardo's version and the painting of the same scene by Ugolino da Siena (Fig. 5.2) shows the power of Leonardo's grouping.

The central point of the scene and the painting's main vanishing point is Christ, who has just uttered the terrible announcement. Jesus's figure is in a triangle with one vertex centred on his head and the other two on his hands, which point to the bread and the wine (Fig. 5.3). His serene expression strongly contrasts with the commotion that his words spark among his followers.

FIGURE 5.2 *Last Supper* (Ugolino da Siena, 1325–30 ca.).
In this version of the supper, the artist does not use grouping but organizes the various characters and their parts in the scene in a sequence, as if they were elements in a list. A list is much more difficult to memorize and understand because it lacks a narrative structure.

The other figures are arranged in four groups of three, symmetrically positioned to Christ's right and left. On Jesus's right, Peter grabs a knife to attack the traitor. Judas retracts his hand from the plate he shares with Jesus because the saviour has just said, 'The one who has dipped his hand into the bowl with me will betray me.' Judas's other hand grips the bag with the money he has received to betray Christ. Judas' dark and tense face contrasts with John's innocent expression, the youngest and Jesus' favourite disciple, who bends his head after he receives the terrible news.

To Jesus' right, James is horrified; Philip points to his chest and asks; 'Surely not I, Lord?' while Thomas points his finger toward the sky, perhaps asking whether what is happening is God's will, but this is also an iconographic concession to allude to Thomas' lack of faith when, after his resurrection, Jesus will invite the sceptical apostle to insert his finger in his chest wounds. Matthew, Simon and Thaddeus are having an intense exchange emphasized by expressive hands gesturing to the extreme right of the painting.

FIGURE 5.3 *Last Supper* (Leonardo da Vinci, 1494) image analysis.
This picture shows the groups of characters as organized by Leonardo following the biblical tale in John's Gospel 13:21. Four groups of three, two on each side of Jesus, whose face corresponds to the vanishing point of geometric perspective of the painting. Groups are graphically connected to each other by pointing arms and by Jesus' hands.

By articulating the scene in a series of four connected episodes, Leonardo was able to tell a powerful story, painting a conversation among thirteen men around the most solemn and theologically pregnant moment of the whole New Testament.

Aggregating characters into separate scenes is another way the grouping strategy can be used to convey a story. This technique has been used across various human cultures and at different times in history in a way that is similar to modern cartoons. In this approach, stories are told in a linear fashion through sequences of scenes that tell mythological tales or lives and accomplishments of kings and conquerors. These survive today in the Indian tradition of cloth-based scroll painting (Fig. 5.4).

What is your product? the danger of cognitive inertia and the wonders of creative categorization

Until the beginning of this century, giants such as Kodak and Polaroid dominated the photography industry[23]. A couple of decades later, neither company has been able to survive the digital photography revolution. On the other hand, other companies who were market leaders in the film photography era, like Canon, Olympus, Pentax, and Nikon, adapted quickly. What happened?

The question of why good companies fail has been answered in many ways (Christensen 2013). Contrary to what many people think, the answer seldom lies in the company's inability to

FIGURE 5.4 Patachitra, the ancient art of Bengal, display on a cloth.
Almost sixty families of Naya Village, in the Midnapore District of West Bengal, India, are associated with the art Patachitra, an ancient folk art of Bengal, appreciated by art lovers all over the world for its style of drawings, shapes, patterns, textures and colours. The art is based on mythological tales and stories from Indian history displayed as sequences of scenes and events.

adopt new technology. Kodak, for instance, was a pioneer in digital photography, and the first to develop digital cameras. Polaroid invested up to 40 percent of its R & D budget in digital imaging at the end of the 1980s.

Their mistake wasn't the lack of understanding of digital photography as a technology but their stubbornness in persisting with an outdated view of what photography was about and with a business model heavily grounded on film commercialization.

An often-overlooked explanation behind leading companies' failure to catch up with market disruption are the cognitive and emotional attachments preventing them from critically reassessing their assumptions about a foundational question: What is your product? (Tripsas and Gavetti 2000). The answer has deep repercussions on the way a company is designed and managed (and on why it won't change).

What was the crucial assumption at Polaroid and Kodak? Despite all the investments that they had diverted towards digital imaging, management firmly believed that customers valued a physical print. Under such an assumption, a picture is a print, *not an image*. This nuance had tremendous consequences on how these companies dealt with the digital revolution.

First and foremost, if a picture is a print, the razor and blade business model made perfect sense. In such a business model, a company subsidizes the razor to sell the blades: high margins and customer retention rate from selling the blades compensate for the losses on the razors. This was the case for Kodak and Polaroid (if we replace the razor with a cheap camera, like the iconic Kodak Instamatic in Fig. 5.5, and the blades with film and printing materials and services). Switching to digital photography would have meant getting rid of film, something that was hard to accept for companies who derived most of their profits from film manufacturing[24].

What the digital revolution changed was the assumption about what a picture is. Today, a picture is *supposed to be* an image that can be creatively edited, shared, and integrated with other media. None of these processes requires printing. Camera manufacturers other than Kodak and Polaroid did not have a hard time adapting because this new assumption did not question their business model and product architecture: All they had to do was replace chemical photo-sensible material (the film) with electronically photo-sensible material (the chip). Canon, Nikon, and the like benefited from this transition because the value, in terms of image quality, shifted from the print to the taking of the image.

More recently, however, these companies are losing significant market shares to smartphone makers. Phone cameras are now enormously powerful and able to take pictures of stunning quality for most uses (Fig. 5.6). Camera-making companies' inability to catch up with this new trend can once again be explained as a categorization failure. Photography is not just about taking good quality pictures; it is increasingly the sharing of emotions and status and the expression of self through the production and publication of creative and original image. Value then shifts from the hardware (e.g. lenses, mechanics, chip) to software and AI able to correct quality in real time and provide functionalities for easy sharing and creative editing on the go.

These examples show how the attachment to an outdated product categorization led some market leaders to miss this shift in the value proposition. The next story, instead, shows a case of how creative product recategorization led to a market breakthrough.

It was, in fact, intuition and unbiased observation that led to creating a global chain of almost 29,000 stores employing 240,000 employees with 20 billion dollars turnover. In an interview released to the NPR radio podcast *How I Built This* (Raz 2017)[25], Starbucks founder Howard Schultz narrates how one day in 1981, he walked into a small coffee shop in Seattle and decided to change his life. He left his job and New York, where he was working for Xerox, and dedicated himself to the coffee business. The Seattle Starbucks coffee place, unlike today, neither brewed nor served coffee, but only sold coffee beans. Despite the early founders' reluctance to move to what they thought was 'a restaurant business', Schultz managed to convince them to start serving coffee. Long lines began to form around the corner of the little Seattle coffee house. It was an overnight success, the start of a fantastic company that revolutionized coffee drinking in America and then globally.

What was the secret behind this success? Schultz says the idea came to him as an epiphany, just two years later in Milan, Italy. In his own words (Schultz in Raz 2017):

FIGURE 5.5 Kodak Instamatic 1965 model, Getty Images.
The Kodak Instamatic was one of the most successful cameras ever built. This "one-button" camera was extremely cheap and easy to operate for users without shooting skills. It made photography accessible to everyone and allowed Kodak to build a very profitable business model centred on the sale of films and photo development and printing services.

FIGURE 5.6 Apple iPhone 12 Pro and Samsung S20, Getty Images.
Smartphones are now offered with powerful cameras and creative software that are transforming the nature of photography from an act of capturing one image to the process of creating socially salient updates to showcase individual creativity, emotions and status.

That's when I was walking the streets of Milan and every 20–30 yards you are intercepted literally with an Italian coffee bar. And I walked in all of these places and kept seeing the theater, the romance, and the nectar of the gods, which is espresso . . . All the elegance, the style, but what really struck me was the sense of community. And I started going into these stores almost the same time every day and start seeing the same people, so realizing this was a third place between home and work, but the beverage was the draw! And so I realized, while I was in Italy, that Starbucks was in the coffee business but perhaps the wrong part of the business.

This was the eureka moment that triggered the company's conversion from a coffee beans store to a global powerhouse. Schultz could have noticed that the Italian word for coffee, 'caffè', also means 'coffee bar' and that 'prendre un caffè' (to have coffee) is about a beverage as much as it is about a social moment in which the coffee refreshment is an excuse for social networking. The European cafe tradition dates back to the end of the eighteenth century, when the drink became popular in Europe, and cafes in cities like Paris and Wien became places where intellectuals and creative people gathered to discuss and share ideas. In Milan, *Il Caffè* was one of the first Italian modern newspapers founded by Illuminist thinkers and philosophers.

By re-categorizing the coffee shop as a 'third place' and having coffee as a social practice, Schultz designed a customer experience model that was consequential with the initial idea: creating a community space centred around one of the most familiar products ever (Fig. 5.7).

FIGURE 5.7 Argentina, Buenos Aires, Starbucks Coffee's interior with customers.
Starbucks revolutionized the coffee business by creatively re-thinking coffee as an experience to be had in a third place, a social space halfway between home and office.

The science of grouping

One reason humans simplify complexity by grouping is the limitations of our working memory. In a well-known paper titled 'The Magical Number Seven, Plus or Minus Two: Some Limits on Our Capacity for Processing Information', George Miller (1956) showed that, on average, individuals could memorize up to seven (plus or minus two) different stimuli at the same time in a variety of tasks, including the ability to recognize musical tones, taste solutions with different salt concentrations, and identify and memorize visual stimuli. Miller referred to this limitation as 'channel capacity', borrowing ideas from the then-emerging information theory[26] (Shannon 1948). If our attention can handle only seven different items at the time, how can we process and manage more complex information? A solution is through hierarchy: Once we recognize familiar connections among different units, we can zip them into a more meaningful and compact representation.

Gestalt psychologists (Wertheimer and Riezler 1944; Koffka 2013) identified a set of heuristics that we apply to perform this aggregation, known as Gestalt[27] laws of grouping (Table 5.1). Here are a few examples.

The principle of similarity states that individuals tend to group objects that look similar to one another. This also implies that objects perceived as different stand out as noticeable anomalies: the relatively isolated figure of Jesus in Leonardo's last supper is an excellent example of how dissimilarity was used in the composition to give special status to the most important character of the scene. The second most important character is Judas. Here Leonardo masterfully plays with the similarity heuristics by portraying the traitor retracting from his group, turning his body and face away from Christ.

The closure principle states that we tend to complete figures in which we notice that something is missing by filling the gaps. Figure 1.6 is a good example: most people fill the gap and identify a square, although there is no square. Another Gestalt principle is continuation: Our eyes move from one item to another to identify connections among separate objects, as happens again in Leonardo's *Last Supper* in which the several subgroups of people connect into a sequence of micro-events.

Cognitive scientists have identified in 'chunking' one of the mechanisms our brain uses to group information (Neath et al. 2003). A 'chunk' is a collection of elementary units that are stored in memory and recalled together. The typical size of the chunk is – you guessed it – seven, plus or minus two. An everyday application of chunking is the structure of telephone numbers in the US: two groups of three digits, followed

TABLE 5.1: The Gestalt laws of grouping

LAW	OBJECTS, CONCEPTS AND IDEAS TEND TO BE GROUPED TOGETHER WHEN THEY . . .
Proximity	are close to one another.
Similarity	are considered similar based on certain criteria.
Closure	connecting them helps to fill the gaps and create a new form.
Continuation	guide our eyes to find connection among them.
Common fate	seem to have to or want to move in the same direction or evolve in the same way.
Connectedness	are explicitly connected.

by one group of four: *xxx-xxx-xxxx*. While it is hard to retain ten digits, it is easy to remember three groups of numbers. You should apply this simple heuristic anytime you communicate – for instance, in a PowerPoint presentation, make sure you display no more than five to seven chunks of information.

As we showed in the case of Kodak and Polaroid, while categorization helps us to learn and remember, it can be at the same time an obstacle for the acquisition of new information. Learned categories typically function well, and anytime that they do, we tend to reinforce them thanks to the positive feedback we receive. However, this can turn quickly into a competency trap in two ways. First, existing categories may impede us in making sense of novel information: Because we are unable to connect the new piece of information to pre-existing knowledge, we ignore it. Second, we squeeze novel information inappropriately into existing categories. For instance, Polaroid managers considered digital images to be just another input for the printing process instead of reflecting on how digital pictures were redefining customer value. If images are memories, the very first thing humans do with memories is share them, and printing was a suboptimal way to accomplish this objective.

Interference theory provides some evidence and scientific explanation for the dark power of categorization (Gordon et al. 2001). Have you ever had a hard time remembering a movie title because another, similar title, one that you knew was not correct, insistently surfaced to your memory, crowding out the correct guess?

One explanation is that information processing involves competition among existing and newly acquired information. Since previously acquired information might be more readily available for whatever reason, it has the upper end in this competition (remember also that success gets rewarded at the emotional level, so 'good

old knowledge' also comes with an emotional attachment). This phenomenon is called *proactive interference*. It explains why individuals are more likely to be conservative and blind to innovation, especially when they are competent and successful.

Sometimes the opposite case occurs. We let go of old information because newly acquired information interferes retroactively with it. In a classic experiment, researchers found that subjects were less likely to remember a sequence of words after being provided with a new list (Tulving and Arbuckle 1966). A mundane example of retroactive interference happens when we forget the grocery shopping list at home; when we are at the supermarket, the act remembering some items on that list will increase the probability of forgetting the others we are supposed to buy.

Conclusions

Grouping is a powerful heuristic. It helps us to build categories as mental 'places' often associated with powerful visual images. Images can be associated with virtual mental locations where we store concepts and ideas we want to remember. Such locations' sequence makes sense only if we rearrange these images into an ordered structure.

We have shown that categorization is much more powerful when we associate categories to some course of action. The idea that a picture is a print had enduring consequences on how film manufacturers conceived and executed their business, to the point that it made them unable to embrace digital photography. The idea that coffee is a social moment and a coffee shop a community space is at the base of Starbucks' success and the invention and design of their 'third place'.

Creative thinking is more about looking for a new place to reposition an old idea than about sheer invention. As Proust reckoned, creating is seeking.

PUTTING IDEAS INTO PRACTICE

Key takeaways for this chapter

LESSON LEARNED	DESIGN IMPLICATIONS
Grouping as logical categorization: Grouping items into clusters is a straightforward way to organize information. When an item is included in a group, the group identity prevails over the specific differences. The same action can be associated with all the items belonging to that group. This logic increases efficiency in information processing, but grouping can trump diversity and create cognitive inertia that can prevent us from seeing and understanding differences.	• *Become familiar with conventions*: There is no harm in accepting types and labels if they are based on valid and accepted criteria of information organization. • Beware of stereotypes and the commonplace: Always question taken-for-granted grouping criteria.
Grouping as storytelling: Grouping helps us organize information in time as well as in space by clustering events into episodes and by connecting episodes over a timeline. In design, a narrative could be constructed around sequences of actions that make sense for a user when interacting with a new design, such as do X, then do Y and Z.	• *Tell people stories they want to hear*. Build user-stories that users can understand and that reflect their spontaneous behaviour. • *Tell a story – period*! Build a story when it's hard to find one: A crowded display or a long list are hard to understand precisely because they are hard to remember and make sense of.
Grouping as networking: Objects and concepts can go together not just based on time and space but also in terms of other relationships (see Table 5.1 for Gestalt laws). The identification of such relationships can be particularly useful when obvious ways to organize information are not applicable or not helpful.	• *Connect the dots*: Some apparently unrelated behaviours may actually reveal a user's need. • *Mind the gap*: Use a Gestalt-inspired checklist to analyze your design and search for connections based on perceptual relationships. • *Disconnect*: Sometimes spurious or unwanted connections are created by chance and can lead to errors and confusion.

Creativity lab

The full description of each exercise is available on the book companion website:
http://www.bloomsburyonlineresources.com/elegant-design

5.1 Case study: the (re)invention of the bicycle

Learn how the design of innovative product can happen through the 'discovery' of untapped users' needs by analyzing alternative bicycle designs.

5.2 Anatomy of a masterpiece: painting complexity

Learn a few ways in which great painters use grouping to organize complex scenes.

5.3 *The art of noticing:*
using photography for storytelling

Practice the grouping strategy in the organization of visual stimuli in a narrative fashion through a photography exercise.

5.4 *Design exercise:*
the Gestalt laws of grouping

Redesign a remote control to minimize information overload through the application of the Gestalt principles.

6 Split

ABSTRACT

In this chapter, we will explore the last of our search-for-unity strategies: splitting. Splitting content across different levels helps users to process abundant information. Another fundamental function of good splitting is to provide users with easy ways to move back and forth across these layers, so that they do not get lost in the complexity of a design. We can accomplish this result by, for example, clearly identifying foreground and background and by connecting details to the whole.

KEYWORDS

design hierarchy

layering

navigation

recursiveness

hypertext

levels

Mr. Palomar's mind has wandered, he has stopped pulling up weeds. He no longer thinks of the lawn: he thinks of the universe. He is trying to apply to the universe everything he has thought about the lawn.

Italo Calvino (*Palomar*, 1986)

Mirrors, infinite lawns, and the invention of the hypertext

If you have ever read *If on a Winter's Night a Traveler* by Italo Calvino (1981), you know that this novel is about a reader trying to read a book. It's a headache-inducing literary experiment whose visual analogy could be Diego Velasquez's portrait of himself while depicting Philip IV's daughter, the Infanta Margaret Theresa, along with other characters of her court entourage (Fig. 6.1).

Another example is Escher's *Reptiles* (1943) lithograph, in which some lizards exit from a two-dimensional drawing and 'come to life' as three-dimensional animals crawling in a circle around some objects surrounding the drawing. They go back into the image at the end of their short walk in the 'real' world[28].

Very much like the lizards, the reader, who is the main character in Calvino's work, enters and exits the novel he is reading. The chapters of the story are organized according to this structure. The first part is about the reader and his reflections or feelings about what he is reading; the second part is about the story he is reading. With this invention, Calvino anticipated the advent of the hypertext: links to navigate a corpus of documents connected in an information network. In plain English, this is the way we access information on the Internet.

Similarly, the observer of Velasquez's painting moves back and forth from the main scene to the act of painting it.

Calvino, Escher, and Velasquez's works are enigmatic, and multiple interpretations of what the artists were trying to communicate are available. We are not interested in whether these artistic experiments' primary purpose was the concealing of a secret message or hidden truth. Instead, we want to focus our attention on how the artists explored the relationship between a work of art and its observers and how the aesthetic experience requires us to move between two 'realities': the fictional level of the artistic representation and the real world of the observer. Their work invites us to reflect on what we experience when we move back and forth between these two realities.

In addition, their message is even more universal. Understanding our everyday experience requires we engage in this immersion/emersion dynamic, perhaps across multiple iterations. First, we need to deep dive into the complexity of the object or experience we are analyzing; then, we have to re-emerge at a higher, more general level in which we make sense of what we observed.

Does it sound familiar? Isn't our everyday life very much like this? Isn't our mind continuously wandering between the details and the general, the concrete and the abstract, the physical experience of something and its abstraction? The digital reality of the infosphere and the physical world?[29]

In this chapter, the point we will make is that one fundamental way to deal with complexity is to find effective mechanisms to navigate across these levels. We refer to the strategy as 'splitting'. If we can organize our experience by splitting information across levels, then it is critical to identify effective ways this organization occurs and can be supported in our designs. We will argue that a key indicator that this organization is useful is the ease with which users can move back and forth across the levels.

FIGURE 6.1 *Las Meninas*, Diego Velasquez (1656).
Velasquez portrayed Philip IV's daughter, the Infanta Margaret Theresa and her court, while in the act of painting the scene itself, inserting his self-portrait in it. The mirror and the many other paintings in the background reinforce this idea of circular references between reality and fiction, art and life.

The devil is in the detail

Hieronymus Bosch is a fascinating painter. Despite the fact he lived when the modern world was emerging in Europe during the Renaissance and the age of geographic discoveries in the fifteenth century, Bosch remained a quintessential Middle Age artist. His paintings are hyperdetailed, fantastic representations of religious subjects, populated by human and bizarre beings whose meaning and genesis are often very hard to decipher[30]. Most of his works represent sin, vice and perversion. Bosch used visual metaphors inspired by proverbs, legends and other myths deeply rooted in the 'pop' culture of the time, based on the rhythms and rituals of rural life in the fifteenth century in the Netherlands. This subculture coexisted along with the official science and religion doctrines.

In the *Temptations of St. Anthony*, a 52 by 90 inches tryptic depicting various episodes of the saint's life in a single painting, it is possible to observe dozens of characters (Fig. 6.2 for the whole tryptic; details in Figs. 6.3 and 6.4). Let's linger a little on one of these figures, a little devil that appears in the bottom right corner of the tryptic left panel (Fig. 6.4). This mysterious creature has a deformed human body, two giant dog-like, black ears, and a bird's head; it wears wooden ice skates not visible in the picture, has a funnel as a hat and bears a little dead tree branch from which a small red ball is hanging by a tiny rope. The devil is a messenger delivering an accusation notice with the Latin word 'protio', an abbreviation for *protestatio*, meaning 'court notice'. The message is an allusion to the sins the saint committed in his youth and his upcoming trial. The other elements of the figure are all references to human sin. The skates suggests that sinning is as untrustworthy as skating on ice. The funnel refers to intemperance in drinking,

FIGURE 6.2 *Temptations of St. Anthony*, Hieronymus Bosch (1501 ca.).
In this painting, Bosch tells the story of the redemption of St. Anthony by interlacing episodes from the life of the saints with metaphors, legends and bizarre characters. He uses the rural Dutch landscape of his time as background.

FIGURE 6.3 Detail from the central panel of *Temptations of St. Anthony*, Hieronymus Bosch (1501 ca.).
This single scene, which occupies a small part in the central panel, offers an example of the abundance of details Bosch used in his paintings. While these details appear enigmatic to us, they were easily interpreted by observers that were familiar with the religious worlds of a Dutch farmer in the sixteenth century.

FIGURE 6.4 Detail from the bottom of the left panel of *Temptations of St. Anthony*, Hieronymus Bosch (1501 ca.).
Bosch's paintings are filled with bizarre and scary characters. What does the little devil in the bottom corner represent? Much information is compressed in that little detail.

the red ball and coat to the flesh's pleasures, the naked tree branch to the deadly nature of human immorality that is easily bent by carnal temptation.

We have used a third of a page to describe a few square inches of the painting and just one of the many puzzling characters, objects and scenes appearing in it.

Was this proliferation just an attempt by the artist to show the power of his imagination and his extraordinary artistic skills? Were these visions just the creation of a tormented soul and an abnormally visionary mind? While we can admire his mastery, Bosch was not someone who would brag about his art. Despite his horrific artistic visions, his biography tells us he was a trustworthy, modest and well-respected individual; head of a prosperous household; and a high-level member of religious fraternities that were influential in the life of those communities. Bosch was not a wicked artist. He would portray a religious tale so that farmers and other uneducated people could understand it: through visuals associated

with references, sayings, proverbs, stories and metaphors that were part of the popular culture and literature familiar to the lower-class churchgoers. Contrary to the Renaissance paintings made to satisfy the sophisticated tastes of rich lords, merchants and intellectuals, Bosch's art was speaking to the humblest and the poorest using the stories they knew and wanted to hear.

What does all of this have to do with splitting information and resolving complexity?

Using rich and terrifying imagery, Bosch was particularly effective in narrating stories in which the observers would move from single episodes to the more general meaning. The *Temptations of St. Anthony* is a tale of redemption of a human being who managed to ascend to sanctity after experiencing perdition. Anthony entered God's grace only after a chain of trials, tests, fights and mistakes that put him on the right path. To represent this narrative, Bosch needs plenty of details that can stimulate and entertain observers. The numberless details are not supposed to be distractions or digressions but contribute to the story's consistency. A little monster can be a reference to a line in the Bible (the devil's messenger) connected to a broader scene (the saint crossing the bridge as a symbol of the walk of shame he has to undertake), which contributes to the more general storyline of the painting (human redemption through repentance).

What makes Bosch's art so mesmerizing is his wild imagination and the ease with which an average Joe living at that time and place would navigate this complexity by getting absorbed in a particular detail without losing sight of the work's broader meaning. This easy reading is not accessible to us because we lack those farmers' cultural references.

Let's visit a few more examples of how artists have used splitting. Vermeer plays with the dualism between the whole and the detail in his painting titled *Little Street* (Fig. 6.5). The structure of the image is the façade of the house, with its geometric regularity. However, some open doors and windows break the monotony and let the observer peek inside the building and observe scenes happening behind the façade. Our eye can move between the two levels: from the exterior to the interior, from the general to the particular. Vermeer's visual solution, an open door, is a simple but effective device to address our spontaneous need to dig into the obvious (the façade of a building) to find the meaningful (the life taking place behind it).

Fede Galizia[31], a Baroque Italian female painter and a pioneer of the genre known as still life, attempts to capture the essence of

FIGURE 6.5 *Little Street*, Johannes Vermeer (1657). In this painting, Vermeer provides a straightforward application of splitting by using the building façade as the first layer and the interior scenes as the second level, while the roof on the background creates a third level that confers tridimensionality to the whole scene.

her subjects, different types of fresh fruit, by exploring in detail their colour, texture and the way their surfaces reflect the light (Fig. 6.6). However, what makes Galizia's painting different from a botanist's drawing is how she worked to integrate those shapes into a whole composition. With some imagination, we can picture the artist experimenting with multiple alternative visual arrangements of the items appearing in the painting until settling on the final layout.

In his book, Rembrandt's eyes, the art critic and BBC commentator Simon Schama describes at length a seemingly minor detail in one of Rembrandt's self-portrait (Schama and van Rijn 1999): a crack on the wall that appears in the

FIGURE 6.6 Fede Galizia's *Still Life with Fruit* (1607). In this still life, splitting works as the eyes move between the amazing realism of the details of each element and the overall composition.

FIGURE 6.7 *Artist in His Studio* (Rembrandt, 1628). In this unusual self-portrait, Rembrandt provides many layers of information to illustrate the material and symbolic condition of a poor artist in the Netherlands of the seventeenth century.

lower right corner of the *Artist in His Studio* (Figs. 6.7 and 6.8). The painting is one of the most unconventional self-portraits ever made. The artist is represented in the background, barely recognizable, in full figure rather than the more traditional close-up format, in a distant corner of his studio. The forefront is almost entirely occupied by his easel. The studio is a bare room, whose material conditions clearly spell out the poverty of the artist during his early career (later on, Rembrandt accumulated wealth and had an affluent life, only to lose everything during his older years and die in poverty). Let's explore a short excerpt from this beautiful description (Schama and van Rijn 1999: 16):

> In the corner of his room, Rembrandt's eye ran over the fishtail triangle of a decomposing wall, coming apart in discrete layers, each with its own pleasingly distinct texture: the risen, curling skin of the limewash; the broken crust of the chalky plaster, and the dusty brick beneath; the minute crevices gathering dark ridges of grunge. All these materials, in their different states of deterioration, he translated

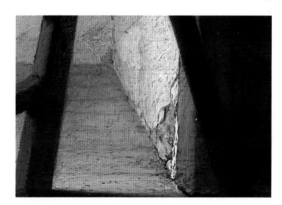

FIGURE 6.8 Detail from *Artist in His Studio* (Rembrandt, 1628). The amazing level of detail of this crack in a wall cannot be just ornamental. We speculate that this and similar details have a critical role in providing consistency and strength to the message the artist is conveying.

> faithfully into the paint and did so with such intense scrutiny and devotion that the patch of crumbling fabric begins to take on a necrotic quality like damaged flesh. Above the door, another venous crack is making swift progress through the plaster.

According to Schama, the crack is a telling example of Rembrandt's fascination with ruin and decay, of his poetry of imperfection. We offer the crack as an admirable instance of the application of the splitting strategy. Try to cover the crack and observe the painting: You will notice that the image loses some of its power without this detail. This crack and the multiple mould stains and fissures shown on the walls are powerful details because they convey a considerable amount of meaning. These particular signs occupy less than 5 percent of the painting surface but tell us a lot about the young artist's life. They narrate his poverty, his aspiration to emerge from anonymity. His art is offering an emancipation opportunity, but, at the same time, is a barrier to everyday life (that's why the easel is so prominent, and he is in a far corner). They indicate the living conditions of poor people in seventeenth-century Netherlands, its humidity and inclement weather. The fact that we do not notice, on the first inspection, the richness of this information is a sign that the splitting is working very well. Our mind can wander seamlessly between the detail and the higher-level narrative to the point that we are not aware of the lower level, even if we perceive it.

Splitting has tremendous implications for designers. If we are mindful of details' role and power, we can design products that speak effortlessly to users. Rembrandt's crack example also offers a way through this problem: Can you imagine how much time and energy the artist spent being absorbed in the contemplation of that crack on the wall before he started to paint? How much he had to ponder about what to include in and what to exclude from his representation? To understand how each detail would contribute or detract from his message?

The first step in constructing an effective split is to get lost in contemplating a dull object and observing it as if it were the most novel of the things (think back to Flaubert's advice in

chapter 2). This research is often triggered by a gut feeling that we miss something important, just in front of our eyes, that we cannot decipher and articulate. That something is talking to us; it is struggling to emerge to the surface of our conscience. The world is trying to give us directions and pointers.

It takes patience, time and a remarkable ability to listen before we set out to say something. The second step is to determine how we can connect the rich information embedded into critical details with the broader message we intend to convey. Again, it is about splitting information across two or more levels and allowing users to move flawlessly across them.

The ergonomics of simplicity: the NEST thermostat

The story goes that Tony Fadell[32], a former Apple executive and founder of NEST, a leading company in home automation, was working on the project of building an energy-efficient home near Lake Tahoe. His insight was that the whole energy system hinges on a minor device: the ugly thermostat that we find on the wall in most homes, hotel rooms, and offices. Like many good designers, Fadell is obsessed with bad design, of which, unfortunately, there are plenty of examples around us. In an interview (Simonite 2013) he released to the MIT magazine *Technology Review* he stated: '[Thermostats] were 500 bucks a pop, and they were horrible and doing nothing and brain-dead. And I was like, "Wait a second, I'll design my own."'

If you have ever tried to use a programmable thermostat, you know what Fadell is talking about: They are not only aesthetically unpleasant but are hard to use and install (Fig. 6.10). Their interface is complicated and counterintuitive. One needs to read the user manual, which is typically even more confusing than the device. Frustration mounts, and most users end up not programming their heating system and wasting their money and precious environmental resources because of inefficient control of the temperature in their homes and offices.

By his training as a designer, Fadell knew that a promising place to look for most of the design pain points is the user interface; in the case of an energy system, this place is the thermostat. Once you know this 'rule', identifying the thermostat as the attack point to the design challenge becomes more apparent. Fadell's following design question was perhaps the result of his long experience at Apple and his involvement with the design of the iPod: 'How do I design this energy-efficient home when the primary interface to my world is the thing in my pocket?'

Fadell and his design partner, Matt Rogers, another Apple expat, started with the simple observation that 99.9 percent of the time, the only thing we do when we use a thermostat is turning it up or down. So, what is the simplest form that can facilitate this interaction? A knob or a dial.

However, while a knob is a device with which users are very familiar, its simplicity also hinders the possibility of performing more sophisticated operations. A plain knob would not do the job. It would be dull and, even worse, boring. As other famous designers such as Donald Norman and John Maeda have observed, users need some complexity, through the right mix of novelty and familiarity. The thermostat industry's answer to this challenge was to clutter the humble thermostat interface with an excess of buttons, displays, control panels hidden under sliding doors, or displaced on equally confusing remotes. Bad design is often due to a well-known design rule's misapplication: The interface's complexity must reflect the functionalities a device has to support. While this can be true for

FIGURE 6.9 Airbus A350-1000 cockpit.
The cockpit of an airplane such as the Airbus A350-1000 – an example provided by Donald Norman (2016) of how an interface's complexity must reflect the functionalities a device has to support and the ability of the intended users to absorb and process a certain level of complexity. To a jet pilot the cockpit looks much simpler than it does to most of us.

genuinely complex systems – for example, think of the dashboard of an airplane (Fig. 6.9) – this principle is often overapplied in the design of much more mundane tools that end up being loaded with unnecessary complexity, such as many thermostats (Fig. 6.10).

The opposing mistake would be to suppress complexity entirely to make the user experience very smooth and unproblematic; unfortunately, complexity is a state of the world that we cannot compress arbitrarily or pretend to ignore.

The NEST solution was to simplify the interface to the highest possible degree and to hide complexity in layers of the system that were not immediately accessible to users, but that could be made easily available whenever the users wanted. This is an application of the split strategy design: Split information at different levels and support the users as they navigate them.

Fadell and Rogers applied this strategy at every stage of the user's experience: They adopted Apple style, minimalist packaging. They patented a

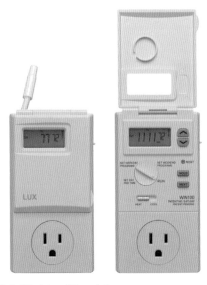

FIGURE 6.10 A traditional thermostat.
An example of a thermostat, showing how most of these devices tend to be unnecessarily complex and unattractive. In this design, while the use of the door solves the aesthetic problem, it just sweeps complexity under the carpet without providing effective guidance on how to program the device in an intuitive way. Hiding complexity without helping users to learn to use it is a serious design mistake.

particular type of screws, screwdriver, and cabling for easy installation and connection to the HVAC system. They relocated to a smartphone app all the most sophisticated control functionalities so those could be managed remotely (Fig. 6.11). They added some emotional touches to the design of the knob: a sleek, elegant shape and luxury black colour; an anxiety-killing time-bar showing the time needed by the HVAC to achieve the desired temperature; and even a little green leaf to make the use of the thermostat emotionally salient by indicating efficient consumption through a badge for virtuous, environmentally conscious users.

The NEST thermostat contains an essential lesson about splitting: Splitting is not about

defining a top-down hierarchy but about providing a dynamic organization of information at different levels of depth and mechanisms that support smooth navigation across the levels. The invention of the iPod's control wheel, which NEST adopted for its thermostat, is an appropriate example of such a mechanism: The wheel allows users to move horizontally within one level, with a button to dive down into the lower levels. The wheel-plus-button system supports fluid navigation by seconding a very natural movement of our finger. It's an admirable synthesis of cognitive and physical ergonomics.

On the other hand, the failure of Google Glass, at least as a consumer product, can be offered as an example of bad application of the splitting strategy. As in many digital products, the design of the Google Glass was inspired by the incorrect assumption that users are better off when they are provided with more information. While we generally appreciate having information, the provision of too much real-time data clashes with the limited ability of our brain to process all this information at once. Users are willing to take only so much complexity.

The Glass wearable digital device was equipped with a web-connected micro-camera that would superimpose an information dashboard over what the user was looking at in a certain moment. For instance, a cyclist (like the one wearing the glasses in Fig. 6.12) could see real-time data about his bike ride, such as speed or weather forecasts. This is an example of augmented reality.

Google Glass was a huge market flop. We argue that one reason behind the failure was a design flaw due to the misapplication of the splitting strategy. By providing users with layers of information that were all contemporarily available, the glasses caused information overload and made navigation across layers virtually impossible.[33]

(a)

(b)

(c)

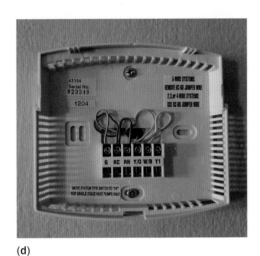

(d)

FIGURE 6.11 NEST thermostat design innovations.
(a) NEST thermostat; (b) NEST screen; (c) NEST app; (d) NEST installation picture posted by a user celebrating easy self-installation. These pictures show how NEST designers integrated various technologies and designs into the thermostat by displacing complexity and by providing, at the same time, ways to navigate it through the user's experience.

FIGURE 6.12 Google glasses.
Pairs of glasses outfitted with Google Glass are displayed for online sale. Sales on the consumer markets were disappointing because customers found little value in the abundant information that the Glass system would provide them with. We argue this unwanted complexity was due to the bad layering of information in the attempt to create the experience of augmented reality.

The science of splitting

The splitting strategy is ubiquitous in nature. Pattern recognition, an ability that the human brain exhibits to a remarkable degree, as described in chapter 1, is about the automatic identification of details and their connection to higher-level concepts. For instance, when we recognize a familiar face, our brain detects some telling features of that face that we might not even be aware of at the conscious level. Try to describe in words the eye orbit or the shape of the nose of a familiar face, and you will likely find out that your description is rather inaccurate. However, you will notice that something is different if your friend shows up after he has had a touch of plastic surgery to the nose. Conversely, when we segregate the detail from the background it belongs to, it becomes uninformative. Imagine you are shown the close-up image of another friend's nose, detached from her face. You may not recognize it as her nose, even though each nose is unique. This holistic nature of pattern recognition and understanding is the result of hierarchical and parallel mechanisms through which our brain processes information. The integration of input coming from parallel processing is a process called binding (Kandel 2016).

Intense focus on an object facilitates the binding process in two steps. Low-level information helps our brains quickly recognize essential features like size, colour and shape of an item in the pre-attentive phase. In the attentive phase, higher-level visual centres in the brain identify specific features and infer that, since several features occupy close or related visual space positions, those features must be bound together.

This is how our brain detects Rembrandt's crack in the wall (Figs. 6.7 and 6.8) and gives it a meaning in a context. The automatic and unconscious nature of the binding process is also responsible for recognizing details and connecting them to higher-level meaning. Thus, we detect the crack on the wall, but we don't really 'see' it until we engage in a deliberate analysis of the painting.

In a recent book, historian Peter Cowie (2018) offers countless details and anecdotes on the making of *The Godfather*, the 1972 Francis Ford Coppola cult movie that changed mob movies forever. Marlon Brando's stunning performance as the Godfather resulted from his painstaking preparation and maniacal attention to detail. For instance, he would spend hours every day in make-up sessions. Brando's make-up included the insertion of 'steel-bar dentures that sat below and in front of his lower teeth, with blobs of resin (known as "plumpers") at either end to give him that imperious jawline' (Pine 2012) (Fig. 6.13).

Some facial traits, such as a more prominent jawline, are associated with masculinity and can be predictive of a man's testosterone generation capability[34]. Excess testosterone is associated with aggressive and other types of macho-style behaviours that viewers would expect to find in the rough, competitive, tribal arena of organized crime.

The unconscious recognition of lower-level details is behind gut feeling decisions (see chapter 1). During the first Gulf War, Royal Navy Lt. Cmdr. Michael Riley was checking his radar screen when he identified a flying object approaching an allied US aircraft carrier[35]. However, the radar's signal could be interpreted either as a coalition A-6 aircraft or as an enemy missile.

Riley was torn between giving the order to strike down the object and avoiding the risk of killing US pilots with friendly fire. On gut feeling, Riley gave the order to shoot it down.

It turned out he was right, although the lieutenant could not articulate a reason for why he acted that way. Riley only reported that the

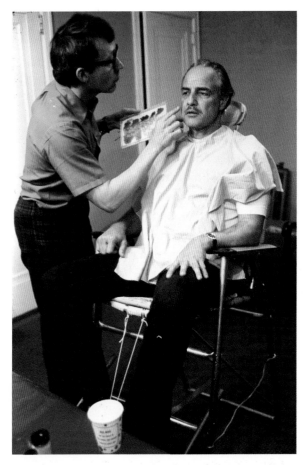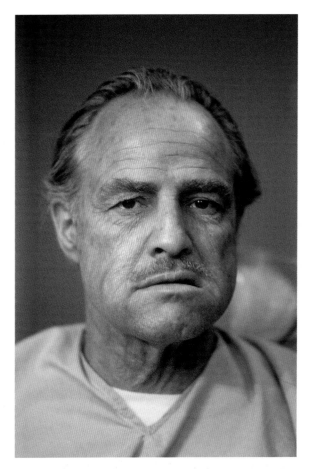

FIGURE 6.13 Marlon Brando with make-up artist Dick Smith.
Marlon Brando with make-up artist Dick Smith on *The Godfather* movie set (left) and after the dental treatment aimed at creating a more prominent jawline (right). The magistral interpretation of the Godfather by Marlon Brando was partly due to exceptional make-up that created physical traits typically associated with masculine leadership stereotypes.

blip didn't *feel* like an A-6. An investigation showed that his 'gut' decision was consequent to a subliminal recognition that the missile entered the screen at a slightly different interval from the planes. While Riley's conscious attention could not discriminate among the two blips, his brain had already classified that property of the stimulus in a deeper information layer that his mind was able to process in the background, very much like we process Rembrandt's crack in the wall in the context of the *Artist in His Studio* (Fig. 6.7).

The organization of information into a self-organizing hierarchy is a property of complex networks, of which the human brain is a superb instance. Albert Barabasi and his collaborators have widely studied the importance of preferential attachment mechanism to explain the emergence of complex, structured networks (Barabasi 2003). Preferential attachment means that members of a network tend to gravitate toward and connect to the most connected members. This definition is self-referential because it captures the recursive nature of preferential attachments. Consider the Internet: We know that the most referenced websites will show up at the top of the Google search page, in addition to paid advertisements for websites. Because over 90 percent of Internet users do not scroll down over the top links appearing in the search results page, the top websites will increasingly receive disproportionate attention. It's the 'rich get richer' phenomenon, according to which those who are already in a vantage position will further their advantage because they have a small head start.

Preferential attachment is an example of the 'split' strategy because it creates a self-emerging hierarchy, and it provides for smooth mechanisms to navigate across the layers of this hierarchy. It also shows how, once formed, this hierarchy can become a stable way to organize information. This stability can also hinder change and be very undemocratic. Since the splitting gives prominence to a dominant choice architecture, the prevailing nodes will suppress diversity and limit competitors' possibilities to emerge.

Conclusions

As with any other strategy belonging to the search-for-unity group, splitting can simplify the system's design by helping users allocate attention and effort where and when it is needed. These strategies increase the design's effective complexity when the design is too rich, chaotic and overwhelming. Of course, the price to pay is the potential loss or hiding of details that matter and the consequent suppression of diversity. The risk is that the design can become too simple for the complexity of the world it is supposed to handle.

When that is the case, we need to resort to a different set of strategies. These heuristics will help us question and sometimes destroy pre-constituted order in search of new meaning and creative possibilities. We will refer to this new group as search-for-variety strategies, and explore them in the next four chapters.

PUTTING IDEAS INTO PRACTICE

Key takeaways for this chapter

LESSON LEARNED	DESIGN IMPLICATIONS
Splitting as vertical depth (hierarchy): An obvious way to organize abundant information is to allocate it into layers of a hierarchy, as in a computer menu.	• *Identify a hierarchy among the functions*: Observe what users do with your product, identify functions, and map functions in a hierarchy (e.g. a tree). • *Make the hierarchy visible*: Create visual devices that make this hierarchy visible, accessible and easy to operate. • *Make the hierarchy easy to navigate*: Make sure users have easy ways to move across levels and that they won't get lost.
Splitting as horizontal depth: Clearly identify background and foreground. The human eye can move smoothly between the foreground and background of an image if they complement each other. The foreground provides accessibility and immediacy, the background provides context.	• *Make your foreground prominent*: What are the critical tasks, and which are the essential functions and controls? Are they clearly prominent and visible? • *Do not hide your background*: Something that is in the background still needs to be accessible and visible.
The Gestalt of splitting: According to Gestalt psychology, perception works holistically. Our brain looks for the big picture and makes information relevant in a context. While partially unaware of this information richness, we navigate it and look for consistency between the big picture and the details, and we can spot inconsistency.	• *Be whole*: What is the honest key message your design is communicating? You don't know? You'd better find it! • *Connect the whole and the small*: Are the details of your design helping users to converge towards the message? Is there anything that is inconsistent or distracting?

Creativity lab

The full description of each exercise is available on the book companion website: http://www.bloomsburyonlineresources.com/elegant-design

6.1 Case study: the desktop and the map

Observe how splitting works in either a bottom-up or top-down fashion through the analysis of popular computer interfaces: the desktop and the search engine.

6.2 Anatomy of a masterpiece: splitting in Titian

Learn a few ways in which great masters use splitting to organize complex scenes, as Titian did with his Venus.

6.3 *The art of noticing: using photography to create a narrative*

Analyze a TV commercial to understand how splitting of information at different levels can improve the effectiveness of the communication.

6.4 *Design exercise: splitting websites*

Learn how to apply the splitting strategy to the redesign of a website.

7   Use the Power of the Centre

ABSTRACT

Our brain tends to organize visual stimuli by fixating on focal elements and their connections. In this chapter, we will learn how to harness this natural information processing strategy through a strategy that helps improve our design by reorganizing it around visual centres. Visual centres create lines of force in an image and can be introduced to rebalance a composition through a more effective redistribution of visual weight across an interface. They can also help us to re-structure our design in different ways by rewiring the connections among them to create more expressive configurations.

KEYWORDS

visual center

visual weight

gestalt

narrative centers

eye-tracking

focal elements

lines of force

An object placed centrally between the two halves of a composition necessarily has a double function. It divides and it connects.

Rudolph Arnheim (*The Power of the Center*, 1983: 90)

May the force be with you

In his bestselling book, *The Cathedral of the Sea*, Ildefonso Falcones provides a fictional but informative account of a fundamental moment in the construction of one of the most important churches in Barcelona, the cathedral of Saint Mary of the Sea. At the beginning of the thirteenth century, Barcelona was the thriving capital of a maritime empire that stretched from Catalunya to Sardinia, Sicily, and West Africa, contending for trade supremacy in the Mediterranean with other naval superpowers of the time, such as the maritime republic of Genoa, Pisa, and Venice. As happens in cities when they go through moments of startling economic expansion, in the fourteenth century intense construction activity was going on in the town, and the Cathedral of Santa Maria del Mar was one of the most prominent examples of this renaissance.

The moment narrated by Falcones is about positioning the apse's keystone, a massive stone weighing more than six tons. Dozens of workers, using only pulleys, scaffolding and the strength of their muscles, heave the keystone high in the air until it reaches the exact point where it is supposed to be, under the careful supervision of the chief architect, Berenguer de Montagut. The moment is tense. One can feel the excruciating pain of the physical effort of raising the stone and the stress of preventing that one single little mistake that could cause massive damage to the expensive scaffolding and, even worse, threaten the lives of those working underneath it (Falcones 2009: 99):

> When the keystone finally reached the topmost platform, a few smiles appeared on tightly drawn lips, but they all knew that the most

crucial moment had arrived. Berenguer de Montagut had calculated the exact position where the keystone had to be placed so that the vaults of the arches would fit perfectly around it. For days he had used ropes and stakes to calculate the precise spot in between the ten columns. He had dropped plumb lines from the scaffolding and tied ropes from the stakes on the ground up to the top. He had spent hour after hour scribbling on parchment, then scratching out the figures and writing over them. If the keystone was not placed exactly right, it would not support the stress from the arches, and the whole apse could come crashing down.

The critical aspect is that the construction of these amazing temples started from a virtual point: the centre of the vault, where all the forces keeping up the dome would converge[36]. Only after the keystone was posed in its right place would the workers raise the arched ribs converging toward that centre. If the keystone were shifted even a little off the centre, the whole dome could collapse at some point after its construction due to the imbalance created by dysfunctional structural tensions. It is important to reflect on the fact that the centre of the vault is, at the same time, the point in which the lines of force converge and from which they emanate.

Whether we realize it or not, we often design structures, systems and products around one or a few dominant and structuring centres. This chapter will show how the search for these centres drives perception and understanding and how we can build around this principle a design strategy that, following psychologist Rudolf Arnheim, we will refer to as the power of the centre (Arnheim 1983).

The power of the centre in art: equilibrium as dynamic tension

The Guggenheim Museum, a well-known iconic New York City attraction, is one of the most impressive buildings designed by Frank Lloyd Wright. While you can go there to admire Vassily Kandinsky's works in the permanent collection or to attend the latest temporary exhibition by some well-known or emerging artist, the building deserves a visit just to enjoy its innovative design.

You do not need to know or do much to appreciate it. Just enter the central atrium, a large rotunda from which you can observe the whole structure, a giant white and circular open space. Then, walk to the elevator, get off at the last floor, and stroll along the ramp that leads you back to the rotunda through the gallery, following a gentle slope along a breathtaking spiral (Fig. 7.1 and 7.2).

The smooth walk is functional to the act of viewing the paintings. The light slope downward makes walking and standing less wearisome.

FIGURE 7.1 The New York City Guggenheim Museum.
The Guggenheim Museum, by Frank Lloyd Wright, is one of the first examples of adoption of unconventional solutions for museum design. Its white and round mass, in stark contrast with the surrounding buildings, hosts a huge open exhibition space in which works of art are displayed along a descending spiral.

FIGURE 7.2 Guggenheim Museum's interior.
The museum's interior is built through the connection of two architectural centres: the big atrium and the semitransparent dome, connected by a spiral that is at the same time the exhibition space and a stairway.

You are liberated from the stress of climbing stairs, taking elevators, looking for the room of the painting you are interested in, fighting the crowd that gets in your way, and the other gimmicks you have to deal with in more ordinary museum buildings.

The Guggenheim building is a fantastic example of human-centred design[37]. Frank Lloyd Wright's[38] focus was on the museumgoers' experience, which he visualized as a flawless flow from the ticket desk to the artworks and back. The structure has a functional centre in the ample atrium, which is the start and the end of the visit, and the space where the downward spiral lands. The atrium is also central in the visitor experience from both the functional and the emotional point of view. From the rotunda, you can spot the other visual centre of the building, a skylight oculus ninety-six feet above you. Two lines of force connect the upper and the lower centres: a downward one drawn from gravity that leads from the top of the spiral to the rotunda, and an ascending one that leads our gaze through the huge white open space towards the luminous ceiling. Compressed and exalted at the same time by these two centres, the spiral seems to act as a spring that prevents the building from falling apart.

The tension between these two powerful centres creates the dynamism that is well described by the architectural historian and critic Paul

Goldberg, as cited on the Guggenheim website (Goldberg 2018):

> In many buildings, you observe them best by staying in one place and taking it all in. But the only real way to experience the rotunda is to move along the spiral. . . . Because it's the experience of . . . feeling the space change, feeling yourself go round and round at this remarkable pace that Wright sets for you . . . seeing a piece of art that you have just seen close-up again across the rotunda from a distance. All those things are essential to the experience of the Guggenheim. It's a building that you cannot experience by sitting in one place. . . . It was Wright's idea that the building is about movement through space as much as it is about space itself.

Visual artists use the idea of creating balance among competing visuals extensively. According to Arnheim, compelling images achieve dynamic equilibrium through the tension created among different visual centres. Van Gogh offers an application of this principle in his *Starry Night* (Fig. 7.3).

FIGURE 7.3 *Starry Night* (Vincent Van Gogh, 1889).
This is one of the most popular paintings by Van Gogh, representing a nocturnal rural landscape under a rotating firmament whose energy and motion contrast strongly with the tranquillity of the terrestrial scene.

The most critical visual centre is the vortex located in the middle of the sky. Another minor visual centre, the moon in the top right corner, competes for our attention. Still, the conflict is resolved by the diagonal horizon that drags these rotating masses toward the picture's left side. The combination of the diagonal and the vortexes sets the whole landscape in motion and creates the illusion that the sky and, with it, the entire landscape rotate around the central vortex. By creating this system of tensions and the motion that it conveys to the whole scene, Van Gogh communicated the drama, the intense emotion, and the anguish that he felt when he observed an otherwise peaceful and quiet starry night over a sleeping village (try to eliminate the imbalance between these two centres by mentally flattening the diagonal connection between them and you will see how the energy of the rotating sky is immediately lost).

Another example is a painting by Claude Monet, the *Station of Saint Lazare* (Fig. 7.5).

FIGURE 7.4 *Starry Night's* **visual analysis.**
The painting is structured around two visual centres: the central vortex and the moon on the left. The diagonal horizon emphasizes the direction and speed of rotation and creates a relationship between the two centres, which appear to move together.

FIGURE 7.5 *Gare Saint-Lazare*: Arrival of a Train (Claude Monet, 1877).
The locomotive on the right counterbalances the visual mass of the train on the left and creates a dynamic effect, inducing the illusion that the two trains are moving in opposite directions. The painting shows that visual centres work if they are connected through some form of perceptual, spatial or logical relationship.

Let's follow Arnheim (1983) in his description of how Monet plays with the main visual centres to achieve a powerful composition. The painting is built around two conspicuous elements. The first is the roof of the station that peaks on the central vertical of the canvas. The second is the black locomotive on the right, surrounded by the smoke that occupies the whole upper part of the painting. The decentralized position of the locomotive and the perspective give us the sense that the machine is advancing. The framing effect created by the station roof and by the other train car on the right side balances the locomotive's massive visual weight. It is interesting to compare this painting with another version of the same work in which Monet did not include the big black locomotive (Fig. 7.6). The absence of an object with considerable visual weight on the right side of the image makes the whole composition unbalanced, flat and, overall, less effective.

FIGURE 7.6 *Gare Saint-Lazare* (Claude Monet, 1877).
In this version, the absence of a clear visual centre in the right side of the painting makes the overall composition very unbalanced and compositionally flat.

The power of obsession

A jet of hot water at 88°–93°C (190°–200°F) passes under a pressure of nine or more atmospheres through a seven-gram (.25 oz) cake-like layer of ground and tamped coffee. Done right, the result is a concentrate of not more than 30 ml (one oz) of pure sensorial pleasure.

Stamp (2012)

According to the Italian coffee maker company Illy, this is the recipe for the perfect espresso. With time, espresso has become a trendy and stylish

way to make and consume coffee. However, the espresso machine was invented at the end of the nineteenth century in Italy for more prosaic reasons: to drastically reduce the time needed to make a coffee from five or six minutes to less than one minute to increase coffee shops' productivity[39].

However, it was not an Italian company that made espresso truly global. It took the Swiss multinational Nestle's marketing genius to create around espresso an entirely new business that revolutionized the coffee industry. It is the Nespresso System, a combo including a stylish espresso machine and specially designed coffee pods that make espresso preparation a flawless and enjoyable experience.

A carefully designed value proposition drives the Nespresso revolution. According to Christensen et al. (2009), a value proposition is a product or service that makes it more convenient, affordable, or effective for customers to do a job they were already trying to do. The way a company crafts and articulates its value proposition will have profound implications on the design of the other building blocks of its business model. In other words, the value proposition is the keystone around which the whole strategy and its execution are built.

We can see strategy as a structure, an architecture of choices linking principles and objectives to plans and actions. Leading companies' strategies often hinge around a few key assumptions and values, and they appear deceptively simple. The hard part is not the strategy implementation but the centrepiece's identification, as the keystone's precise location drives the construction of a gothic cathedral. To apply this metaphor to strategy, let's describe the Nespresso business model using a popular strategy visualization: the business model canvas (Osterwalder 2016).

The business model canvas is a one-page visual description of the way a company makes money. It includes nine building blocks related to upstream and downstream business processes, respectively, to the left and the right of the value proposition block. Left-side activities such as sourcing and operations will generate costs, while right-side activities will define the company revenue model.

Nespresso's business model is a combination of two models in one. The Nespresso system includes a coffee machine and pods, but Nestle's way of producing and profiting from these two components is very different.

The development of the machine required Nestle to invest in patents[40] and brand building

as crucial resources. Nestle decided to outsource the machines' production to third party manufacturers and focus its upstream activities on marketing. As for the downstream part of the model, the company decided to distribute the machine through retailers. Roughly speaking, the highest costs for this part of the business model were marketing costs, and the company made (little) money by reselling the machine with some mark-up. This business model is illustrated in Fig. 7.7a.

The profitable part of the model is making and selling pods (Fig. 7.7b). Nestle is not an appliance manufacturer, but a food company, so it made sense to focus on their core skills of mass-producing and distributing alimentary products on the global market.

Since espresso is marketed as an upscale, high quality product, it was imperative to source good quality coffee from selected producers. Nestle decided to be directly in charge of the production and distribution of the coffee pods. The channels to reach the final customers were a combination of online and brick-and-mortar dedicated outlets, including the Nespresso website, the exclusive Nespresso stores, and a dedicated call centre. The revenue model was the classic razor-and-blade system. Consumers are held captive through a proprietary platform (the machine) and engage in repeated and frequent purchases (the pods). In this way, Nestle transformed a commodity (coffee) into a high-end product. Of course, margins went considerably down when the Nespresso patents expired, and the market opened to competition. Nevertheless, Nestle was able to secure several years on the market without competitors.

The Nespresso case shows that effective design is the result of stubborn perseverance in implementing a few principles and associated courses of action. As visual artists, good designers use those principles as strategic centres to build consistent delivery for users' enjoyment.

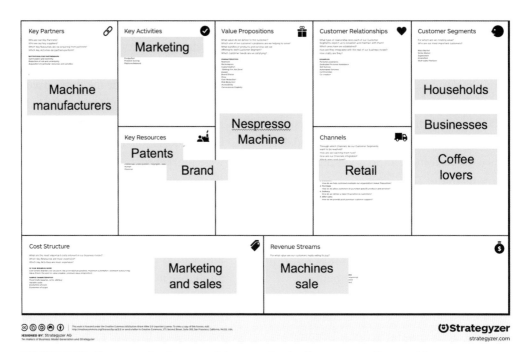

FIGURE 7.7A Nespresso business model canvas for the Nespresso coffee machine.

This model shows how Nestle acquires espresso machines from specialized manufacturers and then resells them through ordinary retail channels. While Nestle needs the coffee machines as a platform for the selling of coffee pods, the design, production and distribution of these appliances are not central in the Nespresso strategy.

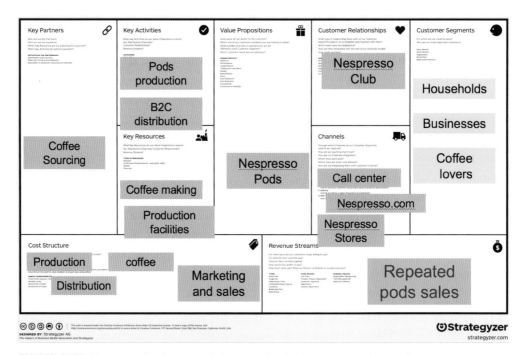

FIGURE 7.7B Nespresso business model canvas for the Nespresso coffee pods.

The business model canvas for the Nespresso coffee pods helps us understand how the production and distribution of the coffee pods are the strategic centres that allow Nestle to retain customers and achieve high margins through the sale of coffee. The Nespresso pods are, in fact, manufactured internally and distributed through proprietary channels, creating revenues through repeated pod sales.

FIGURE 7.8
The Nespresso system composed by the pods and the machine (Magimix M-100 model in this picture) are designed to provide a smooth and posh coffee experience. The pods and the machine are the centrepiece of a business strategy designed to transform coffee from a commodity to a fancy and elegant user experience.

In art and design, identifying good centres makes the whole system coherent with the message and the performance it intends to convey.

The design of the coffee machine and the pod reflected these strategic choices through contemporary, sleek design, based on higher quality plastic and steel details and the coffee pod presented as an upscale chocolate bonbon box (Fig. 7.8). The design of the machine-pod combination was also aimed at minimizing the fatigue and the inconvenience of making an espresso at home without the skills, the clean-up and the time.[41] The pod containing the right amount of coffee can be just slipped in the right spot with a click or through a handle bar; then all you have to do is push a button and the machine will operate at the right level of temperature and pressure that are needed for a good espresso.

Handling visual weight

Gestalt psychologists were among the first scholars to recognize the importance of structuring centres in perception. In *The Power of the Center*, Rudolph Arnheim (1983) provides plenty of examples on how the search of visual centres and their connections in an image drive our interpretation of complex visual stimuli. The analogy is with the centre of gravity of an object, which in physics is the position that determines, among other things, the object's static equilibrium. Even more critical in Arnheim's theory is the concept of a field of forces that emanate from a visual centre. The keystone in the vault of a church is the endpoint, where the lines of forces that keep the building up converge. This centre invites our eyes to identify a point from which energy radiates.

Understanding an image is the result of identifying these centres and how they are related or connected. To explain the effects of visual centres in perception, Arnheim often refers to the visual weight metaphor. The visual weight of an element in an image does not depend on objective properties such as its colour and shape, but on how our brain processes these features. For instance, our visual perception is generally asymmetric because the right hemisphere is dominant in an image's visual organization.

As a result, objects on the left side are considered more relevant. Since our bodies are subject to gravity, our eyes tend to give more weight to anything located in the bottom part of an image. By combining these two forces, anything in the left bottom part of an image tends to assume visual salience.

This is perhaps why Henry Cartier Bresson applied this rule in his famous portrait of Marilyn Monroe sitting at a café table[42]. The whole composition seems based on the artist's effort to show Marilyn as an ordinary woman with problems and dreams. But how to not be distracted by her extraordinary beauty, charisma, and the sexual energy that more ordinary portraits of the diva based on the pin-up canon would convey?

Cartier-Bresson positions the subject in a crowded, ordinary space, divided into two parts. The confusion and the many details of the crowd in the café floating in the upper part balance out the simplicity of the bottom part. Then he puts the main subject on a neutral background while she seems lost in her thoughts and is not paying attention to the photographer. A 'heavy' black object in the left bottom corner contrasts with the portrait's bright right side. The picture is taken from above to make the main subject appear smaller and give her some gravity with the added visual weight we associate to the lower parts of a picture. We can engage in a mental experiment in which all of these decisions are reversed, one by one, and then imagine the final result: We will find find that at each step the image loses something.

Data collected through eye-tracking technology provides empirical evidence that our eyes actively search, find and fixate on visual centres (Fig. 7.9). Subjects wear smart glasses connected to a computer able to track their gaze paths as the eyes explore an image. By processing the data recorded by the camera mounted on the glasses, the eye-tracking system detects a network

FIGURE 7.9 Eye tracking technology application to marketing.
A pair of smart glasses connected to eye-tracking software allows marketers to identify the visual spots customers focus their gaze and attention on.

(Fig. 7.10). The nodes are the visual centres on which the subject's gaze rests for a few seconds. The links trace the movements between the centres generated when the observer explore the image.

Replicating a previous experiment carried out by Yarbus in 1967, researchers tracked eye movements when subjects were asked to observe a painting titled *The Unexpected Visitor* by Ilya Repin (Greene et al. 2012; Tatler et al. 2010).

In the first experiment, subjects explored the image freely. The glasses recorded the spots in the picture upon which observers would rest their gaze for a short time as nodes in a network. The arches connecting these nodes were the traces left by the observer's eye movements between the spots. The result was a random network.

In the subsequent rounds, Yarbus asked his subjects to explore the painting to answer a specific question – for instance, to guess how old the characters are or to estimate the family's material circumstances. The eye-tracking experiment confirmed that different questions produced different networks, structured around

FIGURE 7.10 An eye tracking analysis of *The Unexpected Visitor* (Ilya Repin, 1884–88).
Maps of the eye fixations of a single subject asked by Yarbus to examine the painting freely (top) or assess the ages of people (bottom). The pictures show how an observer's gaze moves among different fixation points that act as visual centres, as detected by eye-tracking technology. The visual centres change depending on the question asked to the observer (authors' graphic reconstruction based on Yarbus' experiment).

specific visual centres. These empirical results show that our expectations drive subjective visual analysis and that fixation points change depending on the meaning we are searching for in the image. As with effective design, some centres are more salient than others, depending on the purpose we intend to achieve.

Yarbus' experiment shows that the way we look for connections among different visual centres plays a crucial role in interpreting an image. This cognitive activity finds some supporting evidence in neuroscience studies on the functioning of the visual system. Human vision is the result of several processes taking place simultaneously in different areas of the brain. The analysis of visual input is organized following hierarchical levels: the low-level processing occurs on the retina and consists of detecting the image. The intermediate level processing puts together elementary stimuli into higher-level categories, such as the separation between foreground and background. The high-level processing integrates information from several regions to make the image meaningful and the object of conscious attention.

The integration of input coming from parallel processing is a process called binding (Kandel 2016), which we mentioned in chapter 6, a combination of a pre-attentive selection of relevant low-level information and the binding of these into higher-level visual centres and conscious elements to which we assign more prominent visual salience.

While the ability to identify visual centres and their interconnections helps us detect and interpret images in a reliable fashion, the imposition of a rigid interpretative scheme over an ambiguous image can lead us astray.

In a famous experiment developed by psychologist Karl Duncker in 1945 (Duncker and Lees 1945), subjects were given a candle, a tray with thumbtacks, and matches, as displayed in Fig. 7.11 (top). The problem they were asked to solve was to attach the candle to the wall. In this condition, most subjects tried different solutions, none of which worked, including stitching the candle to the wall with the thumbtacks, melting some wax and using it to stick the candle to the wall surface or a combination of the two approaches. The second group of subjects was given the same task, but the tools were arranged differently, as illustrated in Fig. 7.11 (bottom). This time the thumbtacks were not in the tray. Most subjects in the second group found a viable solution by using the tray as a base, fixing it to the wall with the thumbtacks, and sticking the candle on the tray.

This test detects functional fixedness, a cognitive limitation that prevents us from seeing or using familiar objects in unusual ways[43]. When we see the tray containing the thumbtacks in the candle experiment, we tacitly assume the tray is just a container and not a support. The simple change of presenting the thumbtacks outside the tray helps us see this object as another tool.

We can interpret this result in terms of recognition of visual centres and possible ways to connect them. In this case, the connection is driven by the need to visualize a plan's execution to solve a practical problem. In the top part of Fig. 7.11, the tray is in the background, so it has no visual weight, and it is relegated to the periphery of our perceived world. As a blank or neutral background, it is just a poorly informative layer that is not connected to the rest. When the thumbtacks are taken out, instead, the tray becomes another tool that could be potentially recombined to the other elements to solve the problem.

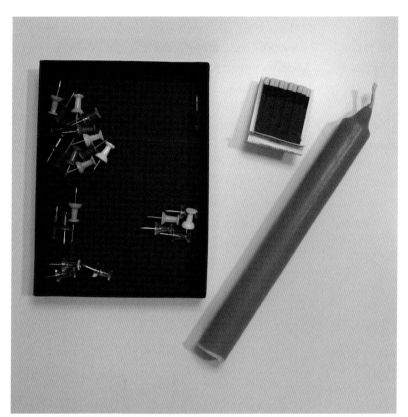

FIGURE 7.11 The candle experiments. This simple experiment shows how the individuation of additional or different visual centres can help us to solve difficult problems. When the thumbtacks are in the tray, participants do not consider the tray as a resource to solve the task because they only see the tray's obvious function as a container. Extracting the thumbtacks from the tray reveals that the tray can be used as a base to support the candle.

Conclusions

We speculate that functional fixedness can make designers blind to innovation. Initial assumptions that worked well in the past are acritically applied to novel situations, or, even worse, they prevent us from seeing novelty. The Kodak and Polaroid cases presented in chapter 5 are good examples of managerial functional fixedness. Knowing the power of the centre helps us now to understand better why this happens. Wrong assumptions can lead to catastrophe when associated with powerful centres shaping the behaviour and functionality of all the other essential components of the system.

Technological change sometimes works as an earthquake that shakes beliefs and organizational charts altogether, very much as an earthquake shakes the keystone in the dome of a cathedral; the whole edifice may collapse under its own weight.

On the positive side, though, the easy identification of appropriate and well-connected visual centres can make our design extremely intuitive and expressive. Users will be naturally drawn towards the centre and, from there, will be able to figure out how the functional logic of the design unfolds. Designers and users can exploit the aesthetic appeal of the power of the centre.

PUTTING IDEAS INTO PRACTICE

Key takeaways for this chapter

LESSON LEARNED	DESIGN IMPLICATIONS
Structuring centres: Visual centres are prominent elements in an image working as the origin or the endpoint of lines of force that define a scaffolding structure around which the image is organized, like energy radiating from or absorbed by a source. This imaginary force field helps the observer in the exploration and understanding.	• *Focus on the centre, the rest will follow*: Build your design around and from centres and the details will follow, driven by the forces emanating from the centres. • *Centres ain't nothing if users don't call them*: Test your design to check that the users can easily spot the centres or whether they identify other centres you had not initially designed. • *May the force guide you*: Find the lines of forces connecting the centres. Are they easy to identify? Do they connect centres in a way that make sense? Do they help focus or provoke distraction?
Balancing visual weight: Competing centres can work together if they balance each other out and help create a dynamic equilibrium. This equilibrium is the result of tensions originated by the lines of forces. One way to identify this tension is to assign an imaginary weight to each centre and make sure weight is fairly distributed so as not to cause rupture, distraction, confusion and contradiction.	• *Relationships matter*: How many centres do you have? How many centres do you need? Do they work well together or create conflict and confusion? One way to work this out, although not the only one, is to establish a hierarchy of centres. • *The importance of endpoints*: Visual centres are sources of energy, but where does this energy go? You need to identify other centres capable of absorbing it.
Narrative Closure: The centre is not just a source from which we depart when we explore an image but also the arrival point to which we return to conclude our exploration. We can leverage this property to help users to navigate our design as in an imaginary walk that translates into a narrative sequence in which the centres are stations and lead to one another in a consistent fashion.	• *Users' stories*: Reimagine the sequence of actions that users perform when using your design in typical situation as a little story. Ideally, every moment of the story should have a focus and a design element that supports it. • *Point of view is everything*: Reconfigure your centres – for instance, by altering the connections of the centres' hierarchy – and observe how your design changes and how users' behaviour change. • *Dangling conversation*: One way to look at a story is as a conversation in which the teller answers the listeners' questions and expectations. What happens next? Why does that happen? Use your centres to make sure the story you tell is aligned with the story they can follow and enjoy.

Creativity lab

The full description of each exercise is available on the book companion website:
http://www.bloomsburyonlineresources.com/elegant-design

7.1 Case study: the power of the centre in Wright's architecture

Learn how the identification of a centre inspires and directs both the development and the fruition of a design in Frank Lloyd Wright's iconic buildings.

7.2 Anatomy of a masterpiece: the power of centre in Klee's paintings

Observe a few ways in which great masters use the power of the centre to organize complex scenes, as in Paul Klee's masterpieces.

7.3 The art of noticing: the power of narrative centres in framing news

Observe how changes in the choice of the attention centres can substantially alter the narrative in a visual ad.

7.4 Design exercise: the power of the centre in inclusive design

Rethink and redesign a common everyday object by assuming a strong focus towards the needs of a special group of users, following the idea of inclusive design proposed by Don Norman.

8   Emphasize

ABSTRACT

Emphasizing is a design strategy that can help you to pursue novelty and variety by making your design more extreme, and, in this way, more exciting, intriguing and original. In this chapter we will show that this result can be achieved by adding deliberate distortion to your design to give prominence to a particularly important user need or message the design intends to convey. We will illustrate through examples how this result can be achieved by aligning design features with the intended emphasis.

KEYWORDS

distortion

halo effect

stereotype

caricature

positioning

first impression

law of instrument

Est modus in rebus sunt certi denique fines,
quos ultra citraque nequit consistere rectum
There is a mean in all things; and, moreover,
certain limits on either side of which right
cannot be found

Quintus Horatius Flaccus (*Satire*, BCE 35)

An umbrella on four wheels

On 27 July 1990, at four o'clock in the afternoon, the last 2CV6 left the Citroen plant in Mangualde, Portugal. More than 5 million exemplars of these little French cars had been sold for over forty years in Europe, Asia and Africa. The Deux Chevaux nickname (meaning 'two horses'), a pun based on the French pronunciation of the model name (2CV), alluded to the small (horse)power of its engine. The 2CV would not be marketable today, given its incompatibility with the current regulations, technical standards, and customers' tastes. Still, it made total sense in 1934 to design a very small car (TPV, Toute Petite Voiture) for the broad public[44]. Until then, cars had been quite expensive and exotic objects that only affluent consumers could afford. The times were ripe, however, for mass motorization. The Ford T-model in the US, the Volkswagen Beetle in Germany, or the FIAT Topolino in Italy were all developed in those years to democratize cars by catering to a working-class customer base. The 2CV stands out in this crowd for the ingenuity of some design solutions, all oriented to one crucial design objective: build the cheapest functional car in the world.

According to Citroen's management's intention, the new car had to serve those who had to travel by car because of their work and for whom ordinary vehicles were too expensive – namely, a rural clientele, including country vets, doctors, midwives, priests and small farmers (Reynolds 2005).

Anecdotally, the initial project brief was to design a car that was cheap to buy and maintain, able to carry two people, 100 pounds of potatoes, a casket of wine, and two baskets of eggs for 35 miles with half a gallon of gas, while traveling mostly on unpaved roads, without breaking the eggs!

The obsession with cost minimization pushed Citroen engineers to develop a minimalist design based on innovations that helped make this car very affordable and revolutionized the design of some components to benefit the whole automotive industry.

For start, the designers had to find ways to minimize the number of components and use of raw materials to reduce the vehicle weight and make it consume less gas. A superlight car, however, is hard to stabilize and control. Thus, to improve roadholding, Michelin equipped the vehicle with radial tires. Among other advantages, radial tires supported better traction and control for lighter vehicles and soon became an industry standard.

When aluminum's cost skyrocketed after World War II, Citroen had to switch to steel for the body and chassis. Thus, the 2CV was equipped with four gears instead of three to pull the extra weight. Citroen designers opted for an air-cooled motor to eliminate the extra components of water-cooled vehicles, such as oil coolers, coolants, radiators, water pumps, and thermostats.

A canvas in place of the roof to reduce weight and allow drivers to transport oversize load earned the little Citroen the nickname of an 'umbrella on four wheels'. There was no shortage of other low cost, creative solutions. Some early prototypes featured only one headlight. Direction blinkers were not available in the early models, and half-way tilting side windows allowed drivers to push their arms out to signal the intention to turn to the left, very much like cyclists do. The windscreen wipers were powered by a cable connected to the transmission. Therefore, the wipers' speed was dependent on car speed, which would be functional until the car idled at a stop, in which case the driver could operate them by hand with a crank.

FIGURE 8.1A Citroen 2CV.
The French car manufacturer Citroen launched this model after World War II to provide an affordable vehicle to farmers. In the late 1960s, the car became an icon for the youth revolution of 1968 and a symbol of France and French culture.

The car interior was no-frills, too: seats with tubular steel frames with rubber band springing, barely enough space to accommodate four passengers, fixed rear windows, and no air conditioning system. Interestingly, however, the lack of comfort was compensated by the of a superb suspension system, inspired by a similar design used in racing cars in the 1930s and able to keep the car glued to the road, despite its light weight.

Today the 'tin snail', another of the nickname of this car, is a vintage, iconic car considered a symbol of France no less than the Eiffel Tower and the butter croissant.

Citroen attempted to apply the same low-cost design approach to more contemporary models, such as the C4 Cactus (Fig. 8.1b). The design was inspired by frugality (and that is an understatement) as well as geared to convenience and reduction of the cost of ownership for people who mostly use their cars in big cities. It is admirable, however, how Citroen designers, once again, did not compromise on style and aesthetically valorized some technical solutions that were conceived to reduce cost. An example is the use of bumpy, rubber surfaces on two sides of the car and on the bumper that prevent door dings and scrapes. Frugal design appeals to environmentally conscious consumers, who appreciate the fact that the C4 Cactus weighs 15 percent less than a similar car because of reduction in components and use of lighter materials.

We offer the 2CV and the C4 as outstanding examples of the design strategy we call emphasizing. Emphasizing is uncompromisingly stressing one or few design principles. In the case of the little Citroen, the stress was on frugality, affordability and highly focused functionality. The result was the introduction of a deliberate distortion in the design that magnified one trait and put everything else in its shadow, bending many other features to serve the intended emphasis. We will show how the use of this strategy allows us to choose design trade-offs and provides designers with ways to differentiate their product from competitors.

FIGURE 8.1B Citroen Cactus.
Citroen applied the same design approach, inspired by frugality, in another successful model, the C4 Cactus, released in 2014.

Emphasizing in art

Deliberate deformation is frequent in visual art. Primitive art offers early examples, such as the Neolithic Venus of Willendorf, representing a feminine body with exaggerated sexual attributes.

The deformation of the body, hands and face is frequent in Expressionist works, reflecting the soul's internal torment through the contraction, bending and twisting of the body (Fig. 8.2). In Schiele's self-portrait, hands are gnarled and unnaturally long. The contour of the body and face is interrupted by frequent sharp edges. Front wrinkles are almost engraved on the canvas, and the pose is tense and constricted, ready to blow out its energy. In many works, it feels as if Schiele wants to capture his subjects at the exact time they are about to snap.

FIGURE 8.2 *Self-portrait*
(**Egon Schiele, 1911**).
The deformation of the body, hands and face is frequent in Expressionist works, reflecting the soul's internal torment.

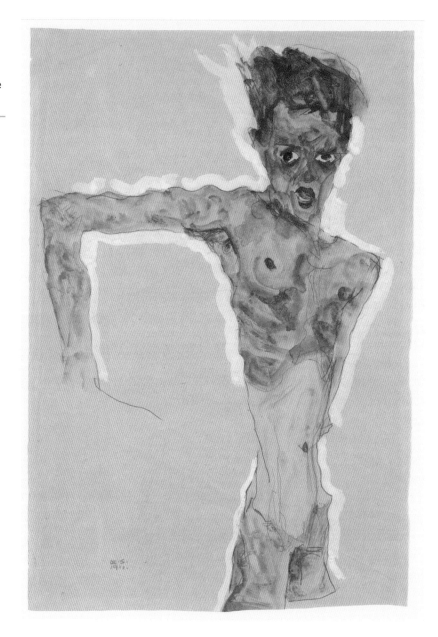

The Vision of Saint John by the seventeenth-century Spanish painter El Greco is a proto-Expressionist painting (Fig. 8.3). The bodies are abnormally stretched and appear like ghostly figures. The deformation communicates the body's resurrection and liberation on the day of the final judgment. El Greco depicts the tension towards salvation through the deliberate violation of anatomic proportions, resulting in unusually long necks, small heads, long arms and the contrast between the bodies stretching and the serene expression of the Saint's face[45].

FIGURE 8.3 *The Vision of St. John* (El Greco, 1608–14 ca.).
Elongated figures and lack of respect for the proportion of the human body are frequent in El Greco's works and confer spirituality to his characters.

Very long necks are a signature for Amedeo Modigliani, a French Italian painter who lived and created his most important works during the years between the two world wars (Fig. 8.4). While Modigliani is hard to classify in any of the *-isms* that were popular during his time, such as Cubism, Dadaism or Surrealism, he felt the influence of those movements and Picasso's studies on African masks[46]. As a scholar of the Italian Renaissance, he was undoubtedly familiar with the classic beauty canons for drawing the human figure. Nevertheless, his female portraits were deliberately deformed, usually through a disproportionately stretched neck. A long neck

is generally considered a female beauty marker in different cultures worldwide (Fig. 8.5). By emphasizing this feature, Modigliani managed to capture female beauty.

Note how Modigliani had to modify other features of his subjects' face to apply emphasis consistently – for instance, by stretching their noses and face ovals and reducing the size of their eyes and lips. As illustrated in the opening story for this chapter, this is a likely consequence of emphasizing. All the other elements in the composition need to adapt to serve the function or feature that the artist wants to highlight.

Good examples of emphasis can be found in the art of caricature. Caricatures typically emphasize a few prominent details of a subject by blowing them out of proportion to magnify what makes that face unique. In political satire, caricatures can either offer facetious portraits of famous public figures or attempt to ridicule political adversaries.

Caricature can also capture personality traits, or even cultural, ethnic or racist stereotypes, by boosting only those traits representing the intended typecast. In *The Bench*, William Hogarth

FIGURE 8.4 *Portrait of Jeanne Hebuterne* (Amedeo Modigliani, 1928).
Very long necks and noses, along with small eyes – signatures of Modigliani's work – exalt the femininity the young ladies he painted.

FIGURE 8.5 Kayan Lady in Pan Pae village, Myanmar.
The use of neck rings to exaggerate the length of women's necks can be found in different cultures, from Myanmar to South Africa.

shows some judges sitting in session in the attempt to ridicule the 'shallow discernment, natural disposition, or willful inattention, [that] is here perfectly described in their faces' (Trusler 1983: 119) (Fig. 8.6). Leonardo Da Vinci also indulged in caricature drawing to practice the art of drawing human attitudes, dispositions, vice, and virtues that could surface on a face. This ability is evident in his *Saint Jerome* (Fig. 8.7), showing the signs left by age, deprivation and the hardships of the eremite's life on the saint's body.

Caricatures allow us to elaborate on the power of emphasizing from the cognitive and perceptual points of view. Fig. 8.8 shows a picture extracted from a drawing manual (Weigall 1850). The model is supposed to help beginners become familiar with the shapes, proportions and expected features of a human face. Still, this picture is so standard that it cannot be considered a realistic portrait of a specific individual, not to mention that these canons are biased by implicit ethnic stereotypes. It reminds us of shop window mannequins that are purposefully designed not to resemble anyone so that buyers can picture themselves wearing what is on display.

FIGURE 8.7 *Saint Jerome* (Leonardo Da Vinci, 1480 ca.). Da Vinci often used caricatures to study human types and to capture the personalities of his characters through the exaggeration of peculiar face or body traits, as he does in his Saint Jerome, portrayed as an old, emaciated eremite.

FIGURE 8.6 *The Bench* (William Hogarth, 1758). In this caricature, Hogarth's irony targets the indolence, apathy and lack of humanity of the judges in the courts of eighteenth-century England.

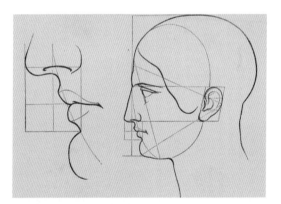

FIGURE 8.8 A simple model to learn how to draw the profile of a face (Charles Weigal, 1850). In drawing manuals, the human figure is often idealized into standard types to teach students face and body proportion. Any particular face can then be derived from this base by exaggerating the traits that make that face unique.

The reality is that every face is unique in its own right, and a well-done portrait is the one that captures features and expressions that are distinctive to the subject and that tells us what's exclusive about the portrayed person. In this sense, we could say that every good portrait is a caricature in which salient and prominent traits are layered on a standard face type.

Interestingly, early work in industrial design was based on a similar idea of designing for the 'average Joe'. In 1959, Henry Dreyfuss (1967) actually proposed standard human models for both genders that he named Joe and Josephine (Fig. 8.9). These models were based on the

supposedly standard measures of the average American and were to be used by designers for the creation of user-centered products. Of course, those idealizations were not representative of the actual diversity of the American society in those years, but only of the market they intended to serve.

Think different

A key concept in Marketing is Positioning. This concept was invented by the marketing gurus Al Ries and Jack Trout and defined in their book (2001) as a marketing strategy that aims to make a brand/product occupy a distinct position, relative to competing brands, in the mind of the customer.

In practice, positioning develops products or brands that stand out among the crowd of competitors. Positioning is primarily psychological, as spelled out in the original definition. The objective is to make a message memorable and able to tell something unique

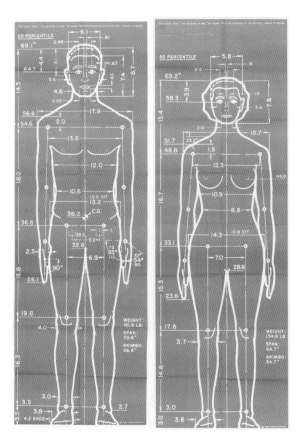

FIGURE 8.9
After extensive study, Henry Dreyfuss created Joe and Josephine, two models representing 'average Americans' in the 1960s that could be used as a standard to design products that were compatible with the average human body size and shape.

FIGURE 8.10
A billboard depicting John Lennon and Yoko Ono promotes Apple Computers on 1 August 1998 in Los Angeles, CA. Numerous famous and historical figures are featured in a series of Apple's 'Think Different' advertisements, including Picasso, Muhammad Ali, Ted Turner and the Dalai Lama. The campaign made a clear reference to the IBM Think computer family, alluding to the impersonal, corporate and conformist style of IBM products.

about a product by emphasizing its distinctive traits. Since the message must be memorable, it must be straightforward and compact, typically condensed in one short sentence.

With its 1990s 'Think Different' campaign, Apple used only two words (Fig. 8.10).

The campaign was all about communicating Apple technology's nonconformist character. These traits would implicitly transfer to customers who were flattered to be considered equally rebellious and original. It took L'Oréal four words to create a revolutionary tag line in the 1970s that is still used today: 'Because I'm worth it'[47]. It was a Copernican revolution in the beauty industry that had, up to that point, framed cosmetics as tools women were supposed to use to 'please him' instead of taking care of and feeling better for themselves.

Apple's campaign showed some of our age's most original geniuses as examples of anti-conformist innovators while never mentioning, let alone showing, computers in their ads[48]. L'Oréal would air spots underlying women's independence, portraying them alone without the dominating male presence seen in competitors' ads.

In a 2002 survey on brand perception in the automotive industry, market researchers found out that customers typically associated car brands to one dominant feature. Toyota was related to 'great value cars', Volvo to 'safety and family', Honda to 'visionary technology', Chrysler to 'old American car'. It was perhaps surveys like these that caused KIA and Hyundai to start vigorous marketing campaigns to shake off the unflattering label of making 'cheap', 'low value' cars, reputations these companies had gained in the 1990s after their aggressive entry in the US market.

These brands managed to become new market stars after several years of growth and sustained efforts in technological and communication innovation. Such intense and expensive communication campaigns were necessary; repositioning a brand with a bad reputation turned out to be very hard. The product's image tends to stick and change slowly only after consistent and prolonged product innovation efforts. However, the pay-off can be substantial: According to the authors of the same survey, 'The price consumers expect to pay for otherwise almost identical luxury vehicles can vary as much as $4,000, depending on the car's brand', which in a hypercompetitive industry like car manufacturing is a huge advantage.

Positioning messages are built using the 'emphasize' strategy in three steps:

1. select the trait or feature you want to magnify;
2. bend secondary traits or features to serve the key message;
3. obscure or put everything else on the background.

The same steps are applicable to the design or redesign of products as well. The iMac marked the rebirth of Apple at the end of the 1990s. The first iMac looked like a coloured, plastic, egg-shaped screen that, with the exception of a keyboard, came without any external parts, such as peripherals, cables, and wires. This was a major shift compared to the dominant design for personal computers in the 70s and 80s (Fig. 8.11 and Fig. 8.12).

Apple had pursued this strategy already in the mid-1980s with its Macintosh Classic line. The novelty this time was the 'i' in the machine's name, a reference to the Internet, an indication that the new generation of computers was born to be connected. The design was consistently liberated of external input devices; it assumed information would primarily come to our computers from the Internet. The floppy drive was gone, a pioneer design choice that raised several complaints in those days, even among Apple fans, but that proved to be victorious. Simultaneously, the new USB socket was added, together with embedded ethernet and modem ports to plug the computer to the network with a click. The CD ROM player had to stay because the Internet was not fast

FIGURE 8.11 Dominant design for personal computers.
The three computers that *Byte Magazine* referred to as the '1977 Trinity' of home computing. The TRS-80 Model I, the Apple II, and the Commodore PET 2001. The design of a personal computer as a typewriter with a screen had become dominant and ubiquitous in the 1970s.

FIGURE 8.12 Apple iMac.
The iMac marked the rebirth of Apple and revolutionized the design of personal computers, popularizing the idea that computers should be aesthetically pleasant objects. Through its i-line, Apple emphasized that the computer's value was in its ability to access data through the Internet, and, for this reason, Apple designers decided to get rid of the then-popular floppy disk drive.

enough to transfer multimedia content, but it was hidden in the computer's body. Apple got rid of the CD ROM when high-speed Internet supported audio and video streaming. The coloured plastic shell was added to help the laptop stand out from the greyness typical of the dominant design for personal computers and help iMac users stand out as those who 'think different'.

The iMac did not revolutionize computer architecture, and many of the internal components were similar to those used by competitors. However, they were not visible and, more importantly, they had no role in creating the brand image that Apple wanted to put in the heads of its customers. So, why bother even mentioning them?

In some cases, emphasizing is applied even in the absence of technical or functional reasons. The Jaguar E-type, a successful roadster produced between 1961 and 1975, is an iconic sportscar. Allegedly, Enzo Ferrari, the founder of the well-known luxury rival car manufacturer, defined the E-type as one of the most beautiful cars ever designed. The E-type stands out from the other expensive sport coupes for the abnormally elongated front (Fig. 8.13, top).

The E-type was the commercial evolution of the D-type (Fig. 8.13, bottom), a model designed for car racing competitions between 1954 and 1957. The D-type had an equally stretched design to accommodate the large engine and the support frame needed to propel the car to race-level speeds. The car's commercial version did not carry the powerful 265 horsepower racing engine. Nevertheless, Jaguar's engineers decided to keep the long front-end. What was initially a technical choice that determined the car's shape became a purely aesthetic feature that visually conveys the sense of speed. Experiments in psychology of

FIGURE 8.13 Jaguar E-type and D-type.
The iconic shape of the Jaguar E-type was due to the exaggerated length of its hood. The E-type inherited this feature from a previous model, the D-type, that Jaguar developed only for car racing competitions.

perception showed that we see fast-moving objects as more stretched than they are. Thus, the E-type elongated form emphasizes that visual feature by creating an expectation for speed[49].

The emphasis of a specific product feature can have an invitational role: that magnified element 'speaks' to the user. It wants to be used in a certain way. The Jaguar E-type shape says 'speed'; the lack of peripherals on the first iMac says 'connect', a balanced-arm lamp says 'move me where you need more light'. When applied to product design, emphasizing can go beyond ergonomic and functional considerations. By aligning users' expectations and mental models to prominent features addressing those expectations, emphasis achieves instructional and communicational value that makes products intuitive and useful.

Sometimes the emphasized feature is perceived as exaggerated. In such cases, the design can become inelegant. Think of unjustifiably high prices, flashy fashion, media overexposure, extravagant furniture irrespective of human ergonomics and common sense. The wrong emphasis only aims to be heard and seen at any cost without providing any pragmatic solution to our problem. It is what we usually refer to as 'vulgar'. Using our invitation theory, we can explain why bad emphasis is so repellent. It is dumb because it communicates the obvious; it is obnoxious because it does so in a very loud way; it is useless because the proposed design does not improve people's lives. Vulgarity happens when designers run out of good ideas, lose their ethical compass, and add to the cacophony of bad art and questionable marketing.

The science of emphasizing

Why do we tend to appreciate the availability of prominent forms or features in a product? Why do we find at other times that this prominence is exaggerated, annoying, and undesirable?

One explanation is the halo effect, a cognitive bias playing a critical role in judgment formation. For instance, this bias is at work when we extend our judgment from one particular aspect of a person (e.g. a trait or a skill in a specific domain) to other, unrelated personality traits and fields. The expression was coined by Edward Thorndike, a psychologist who proposed it in a study published in 1920 to describe the systematic biases through which officers rated their soldiers. The halo effect sounds something like this: Because Claire is a brilliant engineer, she will also be a great manager. Human resource specialists and recruiters, in particular, are regularly trained about the perils ensuing from this bias. The main issue with the halo effect is that this bias often works at the unconscious level (Nisbett and Wilson 1977), so while we may be able to recognize it after the fact, we can be utterly blind to its presence when forming our opinion about someone or something.

While the halo effect is generally considered a dysfunctional and biased cognitive heuristic, one can also read it as a way our mind copes with uncertainty. While we could counter the halo effect by postponing judgment and collecting more data, we do not have this luxury in many practical life situations. This is especially true if we look at this issue from an evolutionary perspective: When decisions have an impact on our survival, it is often better to decide quickly – even if not accurately – than to be accurate and dead! More broadly, making the right decisions based on limited information constitutes an evolutionary advantage for any species.

One way to achieve this cognitive efficiency is to identify features or characteristics that are particularly telling about a situation, person or objects of interest. More importantly, these features are associated with easy-to-enact calls for action. For instance, we only need to consider a few features to judge whether a fruit is ripe, such as colour and size, and then we eat it or not. True, we could run sophisticated chemical analyses in a lab, but they won't tell much more than we already know about whether we should eat that fruit or not.

This saliency effect is at work in other survival choices, such as mating. In nature, sexual attraction can be triggered by a few conspicuous features, such as more massive horns, huge crests, or stunningly coloured plumage. Sometimes these prominent features have clear functional advantages. Still, more often than not, they are the result of arbitrary aesthetic mate choice, such as the extraordinary plumage and elaborate courting rituals in many species of birds (Prum 2017)[50].

In some cases, these overemphasized traits are residuals from previous evolutionary developments. For instance, a massive beak or a crest was a weapon that has lost its initial function but has kept its role for mating selection purposes. Sometimes, arbitrary aesthetic features have adapted to practical purposes, as when the dinosaurs' plumage evolved into wings and flight.

Whether physical traits have a functional or purely aesthetic purpose, assessing that single feature may entirely bias the judgment about whether the individual will be a good mate.

Halo-effect thinking is also at work in other domains – for instance, in experts' judgment. Experts are better than ordinary people in making decisions in their field because of extensive exposure to good practice and superior mentoring (Ericsson and Pool 2016). Exposure to many instances of good models allows experts to sift out features from irrelevant details much more rapidly and effectively than the rest of us. Interestingly, sometimes the process starts with some hunch that something is wrong and needs more in-depth consideration. This reasoning strategy also explains why experts occasionally fail miserably when applying their expertise to another context where the same rules do not hold.

Emphasizing a few prominent traits helps frame new stimuli in familiar categories. For instance, if a kid learns to recognize early signs of bullying behaviour, she may adopt adequate countermeasures before the bullying behaviour escalates. We have an analogy of this in nature when animals exhibit ritual versus actual fighting. A tail down is a sign of submission while showing fangs communicate aggressiveness, but in the end, nobody gets bitten.

Apparently, this capability of early recognition and even anticipation of significant signs is hardwired in our brain. fMRI results show activation of specific brain regions such as the fusiform cortex, the posterior cingulate gyrus and the amygdala when individuals identify previously seen faces as either 'friends' or 'foes'. (Vrtička et al. 2009). This research corroborates the validity of an evolutionary perspective to explain why quick and dirty judgments can make us better off (on average) when dealing with potentially hostile situations. If the decision is correct, our brain will store the first impression in our long-term memory for future uses, and this explains why first impressions tend to be very hard to change. Cultural transmission from one generation to another will further reinforce this propagation.

Whether validated by evolution or by relevant expertise and rational assessment, emphasizing can help form a sound judgment and communicate effectively. We have already provided examples of brilliant advertising campaigns leveraging the power of emphasis. In classic rhetoric, emphasizing is an approach to persuasion, and several rhetorical figures of speech achieve this purpose. Synecdoche, also known as 'part for the whole', is a figure of speech

that deliberately uses the halo effect to emphasize a relevant element in the discourse context. For instance, if I refer to my family members as 'mouths to feed', I am focusing on providing for them and on a perception of this task as a burden.

Good and bad rhetoric can generate anything along the spectrum, ranging from brilliant advertisement to crooked propaganda. In posters and fliers used in World War II, the enemy was an ugly character with rapacious features, ready to plunder and rob our country. In racist propaganda and ethnically biased communications, the disparaged groups appear with exaggerated traits or habits associated with negative connotations[51]. These distorted images appear in culturally biased discourse as well, with or without explicit terms. In anti-immigration political parties' jargon, for example, immigrants are called 'irregulars' or 'illegals', suggesting immoral or criminal conduct.

Conclusions

The use of racist, cultural, gender-based, and other stereotypes shows the dark side of the emphasizing heuristic. While emphasis should be used to add information by making salient what matters, it can unfairly suppress or obscure diversity.

Another psychological theory, known as the instrument's law, can help us show why emphasis can be a curse and a blessing. The law is often summarized with the sentence 'for a kid with a hammer, the whole world is a nail' (Maslow 1966). By design, an instrument constrains action to a limited set of possibilities because it concentrates attention and energy on where it needs to be. For instance, a hammer channels our strength towards the point where this energy can provide the highest impact.

What is interesting with design artifacts is that by constraining our actions, they also constrain our thinking. A hammer can be very effective at fixing things; we can use a metaphorical hammer to 'nail down' other problems – even when another tool or action would provide a better solution.

Instruments can drive us into a competency trap. When we become very good at hammering, we receive positive feedback from each success. In the long run, this translates into positive reinforcement and bends our preference towards hammering even when other tools could be better suited for the task.

As we showed in the examples of good design by emphasis, good products 'talk to us' through their features. When these features are particularly evident, they scream at us and even give us orders. In actuality, a design cannot 'make' us do anything. Still, it can activate those hard-to-silence, inner voices that stem from our experience, preference and mental models.

PUTTING IDEAS INTO PRACTICE

Key takeaways for this chapter

LESSON LEARNED	DESIGN IMPLICATIONS
Emphasis as difference from the average: Emphasizing is about departing from the average by exaggerating a few traits to achieve better performance or differentiate design from competitors. The emphasis of a particular feature can affect other traits that end up being subservient to the emphasis. Adding emphasis implies adding distinction and novelty to exalt specific properties of the design; as such it is a strategy that helps to innovate the average, taken-for-granted solutions.	• *Who is the average Joe?* In order to differentiate you need to know what 'average' means in your case. You need to know your point of departure . . . before you depart. • *Beware the consequences:* Consistency is everything when you look for emphasis; make sure you understand the implications of going more extreme.
Loudness: Emphasizing can lead to unwanted loudness. Loud designs emphasize for the sake of provocation – to gain visibility no matter what. Sometimes, this could be a legitimate pursuit in research and avant garde work or to follow some hot and fashionable trends, but most of the time, loud means noisy, obnoxious and wasteful.	• *What's all the fuss about?* Sometimes we must scream, and that's fine if we have a reason. Do you have one? • *Form follows function*: This is particularly true when emphasizing. Again, you need have a solid reason to justify exaggeration.
Emphasis as metaphorical thinking: Metaphors map one concept over another, but they are not respectful of the original proportions. When we say that this man is a lion, we probably refer to the fact he is ferocious or courageous, not that he has a tail and mane. Metaphors magnify some commonalities and obscure the rest. In doing so, they can free our imagination.	• *Think visually*: Metaphors tend to come easily to mind if embedded into real or symbolic imagery. It is not by chance that the words *image* and *imagination* have the same root. • *Translate*: When you use a metaphor, you are entering a different linguistic world in which your design needs to reflect a different vocabulary. If a man is a lion, you need feline verbiage to describe the man. • *Take it to the limit*: Do not be shy with your metaphors, take them to the extreme. It might turn out to be a silly game, but what if it leads you to an eureka moment?

Creativity lab

The full description of each exercise is available on the book companion website: http://www.bloomsburyonlineresources.com/elegant-design

8.1 The case study: emphasis for beginners

Learn how emphasizing is commonly applied in the design of products for the youngest users – kids – and what this can teach the rest of us.

8.2 Anatomy of a masterpiece: the art of caricature

Learn a few ways in which great masters use emphasis to create ironic and, at the same time, extremely powerful, although unrealistic, portraits.

8.3 The art of noticing: benchmarking for elegance

Collect and compare products that are quite prone to exaggeration: welcome to the world of women's shoes!

8.4 Design exercise: design through metaphors

Practice the art of metaphor and learn that there might be countless ways to articulate what your design does or, even better, could do.

9 Remix

ABSTRACT

In this chapter, we will explore a key design strategy to search for variety: remixing. Remixing consists in recombining existing ideas and information in novel ways determined by an overarching and deliberately biased narrative. This narrative must precede our design; it must tell a story in which we believe and that can give a direction to casual reshuffling while supporting a serendipitous search process.

KEYWORDS

adjacent possible

evolution

mutation

recombination

brainstorming

metamorphosis

change

Walkman

dreams

The young lieutenant of a small Hungarian detachment in the Alps sent a reconnaissance unit out onto the icy wasteland. It began to snow immediately, snowed for two days and the unit did not return. The lieutenant suffered: he had dispatched his own people to death.

But the third day the unit came back. Where had they been? How had they made their way? Yes, they said, we considered ourselves lost and waited for the end. And then one of us found a map in his pocket. That calmed us down. We pitched camp, lasted out the snowstorm and then with the map we discovered our bearings. And here we are.

The lieutenant borrowed this remarkable map and had a good look at it. It was not a map of the Alps but of the Pyrenees.

Miroslav Holub (1977: 169), cited in Weick (1995)

Mission impossible

The history of geographic discoveries through which western European countries expanded their trade network and built colonial empires across the globe between the fifteenth century and the first half of the eighteenth is a fascinating account of advancements in trade practices, navigation technology and geography, as well as a story of faith, ambition and shocking brutality.

In the fifteenth century, some of these future colonial powers, such as Portugal, were relatively marginal. Portugal's population amounted to slightly more than one million people, the same as a big Chinese city during the same period, such as Beijing or Nanjing. European technology was significantly below par compared to Arab and Chinese sailors' know-how.

One of the most accurate 'global' maps available to Europeans was the one Fra Mauro[52] drew in 1450 for the King of Portugal (Fig. 9.1). The map exhibits a coarse and sometimes blatantly wrong representation of lands that were not under the Europeans' direct access or control at that time – basically almost everything outside the Mediterranean basin and its proximities.

Nevertheless, the prospects of the financial gains deriving from the control of the spice trade between Europe, India and Far East Asia were so attractive that the European emerging superpowers would stop to nothing to secure a monopoly over these routes, despite the enormous technical difficulties they had to face[53]. How did they do it? It turns out they had a significant advantage: They knew so little about the world that their ignorance ended up being one of their most important assets.

Designers and innovators work often under similar level of uncertainty, but lack of information does not prevent them from trying. What do we do and how do we behave when we have less information than we should? One way to cope with this problem is to stop thinking and start tinkering, by remixing resources and knowledge we already have. Surprisingly, this knowledge does not need to be that accurate. For instance, while Fra Mauro did not really know the shape of the African continent, his map was one of the first showing that Africa could be circumnavigated. It was this detail that sparked the interest of the King of Portugal Joao I and pushed Portuguese navigators to explore the west African coast, looking for a southeast turnaround. It was thanks to these attempts and to the knowledge they accumulated by trial and error about the Atlantic winds that the Portuguese literally stumbled into Brazil.

The other fundamental ingredient we need in order to act despite substantial uncertainty is motivational drive, sometimes coming to us in the form of a good story. In the Portuguese case, this drive was certainly financial, but the ideological engine used to justify even the most horrible crimes, including slavery, was a narrative built on religious fanaticism. Colonizers felt, or wanted others to believe, that they were on a mission on behalf of God. The official narrative was souls' salvation. And salvation was the story they used to legitimize horrible crimes, such as slavery[54].

The Portuguese also remixed astrological information to claim that Prince Henry was 'the chosen one' to make Portugal great. The rivers Senegal and Congo were believed to join the Nile at some points, so they thought the mythical Christian Kingdom in East Africa, ruled by a Priest John, could be reached by ascending their course. That's why Portuguese explorers ventured inside the continent and explored some important rivers.

It was this remix of old and new knowledge, driven by a salvation story, that ended up being the recipe for the exploration and domination of the Indian Ocean and the construction of a Portuguese colonial empire.

FIGURE 9.1 World map – the north is on the bottom (Fra Mauro, 1450 ca.).

Fra Mauro's map was one of the best planispheres created before the age of geographic discovery changed forever the way Europeans knew the world. The map is oriented with the south at the top and it captures only small parts of Asia and Africa because the southern part of the African continent and the Far East were virtually unknown to the Europeans at that time.

Innovation scholars often refer to this remixing of information and events in terms of evolutionary mechanisms that promote random selection of the fittest solution. We embrace these accounts, but we add that those casual collisions and evolutionary 'fitness' are not enough to explain human creativity.

This chapter will show that remixing always happens in the presence of a strong shared narrative and in the absence of complete information. Through the usual combination of examples from art and design, we will show that the remix strategy requires four components:

1. parts to recombine (e.g. ideas or physical components);

2. "liquid" work environment favouring smooth but partially constrained movement of parts as opposed to purely random movement;

3. surplus (e.g. wealth, time and/or energy to support movement and recombination);

4. narrative polarization, orienting change towards one direction as pointed out by shared storytelling about what is fair and desirable, even against established rules.

Metamorphosis or the nature of change

The creation of aesthetically viable forms is intrinsically a remix operation. We experience this often in our everyday life, when, for instance, we try to match clothes or choose furniture for our house. We learn that colour and pattern matching have their own rules. Sometimes, we dare a more unusual combination and are surprised by its effect. Artists typically set out to recombine materials, shapes, and techniques through endless experimentation to identify novel aesthetic configurations that turn out to be extremely useful in conveying their intent or message.

Cubist artists adopted an analytic, bottom-up approach to recombination by dismembering reality into the perception of minimal geometric shapes, such as cubes and pyramids. Then, they took the liberty of reassembling them in unusual ways to violate the rules of perspective. Deliberate rule violation is necessary for recombination because remixing is always an attempt to obtain degrees of freedom. Remixing is biased by intention and does not just happen by chance (although it can benefit from it).

Cubists applied this method to represent traditional subjects, such as still life, portraits and landscape painting, because they intended to show that, by relaxing conventions, we can find other surprising and revealing points of view to observe the reality.

Robert Delaunay applied this idea to the representation of the Eiffel Tower (Fig. 9.2). Today, this monument is the symbol of Paris. It is impossible even to imagine the city skyline without this impressive landmark. Yet the tower's construction by the French engineer Gustave Eiffel to celebrate the 100th anniversary of the French revolution and the Paris Global Trade Fair was controversial. More conservative critics considered the monument an ugly concentration of steel in sharp contrast with the Ville Lumiere's elegance, a monument to human arrogance, a modernist slap in the face of centuries of beautiful neoclassic architecture[55]. Delaunay captured these feelings in his work: He understood that the monster tower was the combination of steel modules created through industrial production and no longer through experienced artisans' art and craft. He probably felt that this dehumanized, analytical construction technique was behind the aesthetic shock induced by modernist architecture.

So, we imagine that Delaunay conceptually disassembled the Eiffel Tower and rearranged the parts by stitching them together without being constrained by engineering necessity (Figs. 9.3 and 9.4). The result is a tumultuous arrangement of elements with inconsistent

FIGURE 9.2 The Eiffel Tower.
The Eiffel Tower, designed and built by Gustave Eiffel between 1887 and 1889 as the gateway to the World Trade Fair, is one of the most well-known monuments in the world. However, it was harshly criticized at the time of its construction by artists and intellectuals who considered the tower an offense to 'the untouched beauty of Paris' (Loyrette 1985).

directions and proportions that, coupled with the vibrant red colour of the structure, give this inert concentration of metal a pulsating vitality. The vigour of progress was a recurrent theme in Cubist and Futurist works, aimed at revealing the power of technology and questioning the traditional forms and canons in art and everyday life.

FIGURE 9.3 The Eiffel Tower remix.
In this picture, we took the liberty of disassembling the Eiffel Tower into several pieces; we stitched them back together in a sort of remix that looks like Delaunay's red tower in Fig. 9.4.

FIGURE 9.4 *The Red Tower* (Robert Delaunay, 1911–12).
Delaunay portrays the Eiffel Tower following the Cubist idea of multiple points of views. The crooked tower is in fact obtained by looking at the object from different angles and then remixing together contrasting perspectives in a single picture.

In fiction and poetry, a common method for remixing is metaphor. A metaphor is a linguistic device through which an unfamiliar concept is referred to in terms of another that is assumed to better convey or exalt one or more features of the original, typically in a visual way. An expression such as 'A blanket of snow had fallen over the countryside' means to allude to the silence and peace of the winter landscape, to the idea that nature is resting while waiting for a new awakening after winter is over, and that this blanket is at the same time protecting living beings from the harshness of winter. By remixing two words that are not frequently associated, 'blanket' and 'snow', this metaphor evokes a powerful visual to describe the quietness of winter landscape.

Ovid's poem *Metamorphoses* is a tale about the wonder, the necessity, and the pain of change. It is a collection of short mythological stories in which the main character eventually mutates into another form under the sortilege of some offended or benign god. Every story is typically a metaphor of a fundamental human feeling, such as love, jealousy, anger, compassion, or hubris.

In the tale of Daphne and Apollo, the young girl is transformed into a laurel tree by her father Peneus, a fluvial divinity, to protect her from Apollo's lust. Here is a brief passage in which Ovid describes the transformation while it is occurring:

In Figs. 9.5 and 9.6 we can admire two different and equally beautiful representations of the scene in which Daphne mutates into a tree. The transformation happens through a series of rhetorical 'moves' by way of contrast between opposites: what was tender becomes hard (the chest into the wood), what was flowing becomes rigid (the hair into leaves), what was fast and agile becomes still (the feet into roots). Working on opposites is a common way to attempt remix, one that can be experimented in design as well (see the Walkman example in the next section, where large becomes small and privacy becomes public). One trait, though, remains the same in both the girl and the plant: the glow. The transformation in Ovid is, in fact, the process of unveiling this essential trait, this invariant property that makes Daphne 'Daphne': her glowing. Not Gods, nor life, nor time can destroy this little fragment of eternity in every human being.

Ovid's metamorphosis offers a clear example that, far from being a random exploration of endless possibilities, remixing is about searching for essence. It is a discovery process driven by intention and contingencies that ultimately helps us identify what matters and the real meaning of what we are trying to accomplish.

Vix prece finita torpor gravis occupat artus,

Mollia cinguntur tenui praecordia libro,

In frondem crines, in ramos bracchia crescunt,

Pes modo tam velox pigris radicibus haeret,

Ora cacumen habet: remanet nitor unus in illa.

She has just finished her prayer when a heavy numbness crosses her body,

The tender chest is undone into subtle fibers,

Hair grows into leaves, arms into branches,

Her feet, once so fast, are nailed to the ground by lazy roots,

Her face disappears in the top of a tree: only her glowing remains.

FIGURE 9.5 *Daphne and Apollo* (attributed to Pietro del Pollaiolo, 1470–80).
In this painting, Pollaiolo indulges in realistic details of the main scene and of the landscape in the background. The mix of the ongoing drama with the serenity of nature portrays the transformation as an act through which Daphne liberates herself from the pains of loving and living.

FIGURE 9.6 *Daphne and Apollo* (Gian Lorenzo Bernini, 1622–25).
In this sculpture, the fight between Apollo and Daphne becomes a dance through which Daphne graciously escapes her assailant while her 'Hair grows into leaves, arms into branches'.

Connecting the dots: a chairman walks into a lab . . .

In 1978, a team of Sony's engineers developed a recorder with stereophonic capabilities, called the Pressman (Ranganath and Ketteringham 1993). The name was targeting an audience of professional users: journalists. However, the project failed because Sony engineers could not fit both stereo and recording technologies in a small portable device, even though the company was the market leader in the miniaturization of electronic components. The technology was not just there yet. The result was a small stereo player, just a prototype shelved by Sony developers in the unhappy category of failed developments, almost forgotten in a dusty closet. Only one year later, though, Kozo Oshone, the Sony general manager of the tape recorder division, was in charge of manufacturing millions of these players under the name of one of the most successful and iconic Sony products: the Walkman (Fig. 9.7). How did that happen?

The Walkman became an instant success thanks to the Pressman's pairing with a gadget that another team had independently developed. It was a pair of lightweight, affordable and adjustable headphones capable of shooting high-quality stereo sound directly into the users' ears (Fig. 9.8). Nobody connected the dots until one day, Sony Honorary Chairman and co-founder, Masaru Ibuka, paid a visit to the lab where the Pressman was developed and saw that some of

the designers listened to music played by this prodigious little machine. What if Sony combined these two little gadgets in a portable music player?

This connection may seem trivial in a world in which portable digital music is ubiquitous. However, in the late seventies, portable music was a market that was completely unheard of and in striking contrast to the premium home music systems that went under the name of hi-fi (high fidelity) systems.

The Sony Walkman turned out to be a planetary success, yet its development and launch were breakthroughs achieved under extreme uncertainty. Sony invented a market that did not exist around the very concept of portable entertainment.

FIGURE 9.7 Sony Walkman.
The Walkman was originated by remixing two failed projects: a stereo recorder that did not record and a pair of lightweight headphones for which Sony had not found a use. The combination created a new category of devices for portable and customized entertainment.

The company had to face its marketers' scepticism that portable music was not a legit market category and its engineers' obstinance that the Pressman was a technical failure. The endorsement of Akio Morita, Sony CEO at the time of the events, was critical to overcoming these internal resistances. Sony's corporate culture did the rest by leveraging values such as innovation, teamwork, discipline, a little dose of company paternalism, enlightened top managers and the Japanese collectivist view of management based on workers' involvement and consideration of your company as your *Ouchi* (home).

Ibuka's intuition could appear as the result of random collisions happening through a series of fortuitous events in the right place and at the right time. However, we argue that the Walkman is an excellent example in which evolutionary randomness mixes with human vision and deliberate action in a story in which serendipity plays a big role. But, as they say, good things happened to the prepared mind and the prepared company.

Contemporary apps for music streaming are the latest evolution of the Walkman idea of portable music. Spotify, the leading platform for online audio entertainment, brought Sony's idea of 'public privacy' to the next level, with the campaign 'Music for Every Mood', which publicized the app's ability to create playlists able to sync with everyday moments, such as 'Songs to Sing in the Shower', workout playlists such as 'Body and Soul', or party collections as specific as 'Yacht Rock'.

FIGURE 9.8 A pedestrian in Central Park, New York City, in 1980 'wearing' a Walkman (Photo by Jill Freedman). The Walkman was an instant market success that allowed its users to be immersed in social spaces while surrounded by a personalized soundtrack.

The company applies the remix design strategy at multiple levels. At the product level, the app interface is in a continuous state of flux thanks to a wave of functions that are constantly updated or just tested (Fig. 9.9).

This continuous remixing of new functions and controls is the result of how Spotify developers work. Spotify adopted an innovative organizational model inspired by Agile development methods (Kniberg and Ivarsson 2012). Developers work as members of little project units called *squads*, focusing on the design of a specific interface component, but they are also part of domain units called *tribes* and functional units called *guilds*. Unlike more

traditional matrix-based structures, coordination is achieved via informal coordination, ample level of discretion and autonomy, and a playful, open and homey design of the workspaces, all to favour the remixing of ideas and synergies between different projects.

We offer a reading of the Walkman's and Spotify's successes based on the ingredients for successful remixing that we anticipated at the beginning of this chapter:

1. *Parts to recombine.* It's about remixing different technologies: the stereo player with the portable headphones for Sony; the hundreds of digital components and systems that are on and behind Spotify's interface.

FIGURE 9.9 Spotify desktop and mobile interface.
Spotify's interface design is in a continuous state of flux thanks to the innovations in functionalities and usability improvements created by the continuous remixing of and experimentation with hundreds of technological systems developed and deployed independently by different squads of developers.

2. *'Liquid' environment* to favour the smooth but partially constrained movement of parts, as opposed to purely random movements: at Sony this was possible thanks to its unique organizational culture favouring initiative and discovery; at Spotify's, it is the Agile methodology and the informal coordination and workspace.

3. *Surplus*: In both companies, Surplus is available at different levels, including huge R & D expenditures channelled towards the development of many prototypes (potentially many failures but also a few breakthroughs), top management commitment and leadership, human connections, and relationships that helped to communicate laterally and overcome rigid authority. It's about creating slack, a short-term inefficiency, that could produce massive payoffs in innovation capability – something at which both companies excel thanks to their relentless focus on innovation.

4. *Narrative polarization and rule violation*: Sony's vision that portable music was viable, that customers would love it, that there was a need in society to fulfil an individual reaction to mass consumption, which translated to self-affirmation, and creation of a private sphere in which consumption becomes self-expression[56]: these were the key engines behind the Walkman success[57]. Spotify's campaign 'Music for Every Mood' equally enforces this narrative by making music not just entertainment but an indispensable companion, helping us to nurture our moods as we experience life.

The lesson learned is that the polarizing narrative does not need to be accurate to help meaningful recombination of fragmented information and ideas. And when it's about breakthrough products, there is no alternative: We cannot analyze a market that does not exist,

much like unknown lands cannot be surveyed in advance. A story, even an inaccurate, approximate account, provides at least a sense of direction and meaning to advance into unchartered territory.

The same model can be used to analyze a dominant practice in the management of creativity: brainstorming sessions. Brainstorming is a methodology to help teams generate as many good ideas as possible. The basic assumption is that a collective of minds can be collectively intelligent by leveraging internal diversity through the recombination aggregation of the information and perspectives held by different group members. The assumption is that the random collisions of diverse ideas can generate insights by sparking group creativity through active regeneration and fertilization of individual contributions.

If you have ever participated in a brainstorming session, you know that this approach generates mixed results. All brainstorming methods typically favour idea generation versus idea assessment by postponing feasibility considerations as much as possible to prevent early criticism that can inhibit expression and produce premature convergence on suboptimal solutions.

While this emphasis on exploration is desirable, it does not guarantee the success of a brainstorming session. Using the four components in our remixing model, we can offer some tips on how to make brainstorming more likely to succeed:

1. *Parts to recombine*: The team must have enough diverse and complementary information to be recombined.

2. *'Liquid' environment*: Facilitation and team composition can help to reduce or eliminate stiff team dynamics favoured by autocratic leaders, high power distances, bureaucratic mindsets, lack of trust, political rivalries, and lack of psychological safety (Edmondson 1999).

3. *Surplus*: Team members must have enough 'inefficient' slack in terms of resources and time to generate new ideas.

4. *Narrative polarization*: This is possibly the most crucial factor. Participants should collaborate and negotiate a convincing narrative. A portable stereo player and lightweight headphone make a Walkman only if we buy the 'portable music' narrative.

Miss even one of these ingredients and the success of any exercise of team creativity is compromised.

Dream a little dream of me: the science of remixing

The idea of generating new solutions through the recombination of existing concepts is directly inspired by natural evolution. In the book, *Where Do Good Ideas Come From*, Stevens Johnson (2011) offers a review of diverse mechanisms favouring innovation through remix, drawing mainly from evolutionary biology and complexity science. The concept of the *adjacent possible* proposed by Stuart Kaufmann (2003) assumes that evolutionary change happens when a possible mutation is close enough to be 'affordable' for an organism. Consequently, to increase the number of available options, organisms need to have enough of these low hanging fruits, either internally or in the ecosystem they inhabit, to efficiently engage in serendipitous discovery. Following this theory, systems exhibiting a high level of variety, such as cities or coral reefs, are more likely to generate creative solutions.

We find that a fundamental limitation of evolutionary explanations of creativity is that they do not explain *how* individuals remix ideas to generate novelty. We argue that individual motivation and volition have a profound role in directing creative remixing through purposeful recombination communicated via biased narratives.

Theories related to why we dream can help to understand creativity at the individual level (van der Linden 2011). While there are dream types and recurrent dreams, every single dreaming experience is different, and it's highly unlikely that two individuals can have the same dream. One reason is that our dreams always reflect unique aspects of our personality, experience and specific wants and needs.

While somewhat controversial, the theory according to which nightmares are functional is fascinating (Healy 2019). It turns out that the majority of dreams we remember are what we would consider, in retrospect, terrible dreams. For instance, bad dreams can refer to uncomfortable situations in which we are unable to react appropriately, conditions generating anxiety or the feeling of loss. Nightmares leave us with a very vivid emotional reaction that helps us remember them better when we wake up. According to this theory, dreaming fulfils a mental simulator's function that allows us to experiment with problematic, if not dreadful, situations without taking real chances. In this way, our brain helps us to prepare to prevent or overcome such crises.

The mental simulator theory contrasts with previous neurobiological theories, for which dreams are just the results of random remixing of neuronal circuits pulling together uncorrelated thoughts and images that we connect in a story to make sense of them. The oldest approach to the analysis and the role of dreams was proposed by Freud, who saw dreams as reflecting our psychological pathologies and the manifestation of inexpressible wants or desires from our subconscious.

Despite the controversies and the deep divide between different approaches, all dream theories assume that our brain engages in active recombination of experiential elements to construct new meaning, an idea that in art has been masterfully represented in Salvador Dali's work (Fig. 9.10). Whether this meaning is the anticipation about how to behave in painful situations, dynamic storytelling to support sense-making, or re-elaboration of truths we have a hard time articulating or sharing with others, dreaming is a cognitive mechanism that helps us reshuffle ideas.

The discovery of the benzene molecule structure offers an example of how dreams can generate insight (Browne 1988). The German chemist August Kekule came to the eureka moment in which he visualized the chemical compound's structure in a dream in which he saw the image of a snake biting his tail. It is unlikely that this dream had a recondite sexual meaning or that it was just a random image generated by the scientist's neurons while he was sleeping. It seems more reasonable to assume the dream was a consequence of the enormous amount of time the scientist spent working and thinking about

FIGURE 9.10 *The Persistence of Memory* (Salvador Dali, 1931).
A rider walks past a reproduction of a Salvador Dalì painting in the Atlantic Avenue subway station in New York City. Dalì captured the visionary character of dreams by recombining images into enigmatic figures. His remix is never random; it proceeds by assonance and suggestions, as if a secret message were embedded in the complex texture of this imaginary world.

benzene. Through that vision, Kekule found a novel framework to contemplate the specific problems he was trying to solve.

Let's apply our remixing theory to this case again. First, Kekule recombined bits of knowledge he already had (parts). Second, his mind was in a fluid state because our minds are free to wander in a dream. Third, scientists typically have enough slack in terms of time and funds for their research and can flexibly manage their work time. Finally, scientists tend to be obsessed with their research object and strongly motivated to accomplish (polarization).

Whatever their nature and function, dreams are even more interesting when it comes to their interpretation. In ancient cultures, dreams were considered prophetic or sometimes the medium through which the gods would speak to humans. A dream was not informative per se without recognizing its meaningful aspects through the association between concepts that are often metaphorical.

Metaphors are powerful linguistic devices through which we map one concept in terms of another. When we say of a person that he or she is a chicken, we transfer that animal's proverbial lack of courage to the individual we are defining as a coward. Lakoff and Johnson (2008) showed that metaphors are not linguistic ornamental devices but essential cognitive mechanisms to comprehend reality. Our understanding, and our language, are genuinely metaphorical.

Metaphors can support linguistic remixing to create novelty and variety. It is not surprising that metaphors are widely used in poetry because the most compelling metaphors are also aesthetically pleasing.

Conclusions

As we do in each heuristic chapter, we want to warn our readers about the dark side of remixing. While remixing can be used to search for more profound truth, this is not its primary function. Instead, its role is to search for novelty, and this means possibilities, not facts.

An example of the remixing strategy's perverse use is algorithms that create fake news for bots to diffuse on the Internet through social media. Online tools can create plausible stories based on a few inputs provided by a human user. The story is crafted by an algorithm that uses pattern recognition to simulate a general-purpose writing structure. Users can fill the blanks with names or words. The recombination can be very creative and may sound so realistic that many people find it believable. Truth-deprived novelty can travel very far on our electronic social highways, and the art of creating astounding lies generates revenue.

We should be careful in design to ensure that our stories are not only exciting but also honest and aimed at improving users' lives.

PUTTING IDEAS INTO PRACTICE

Key takeaways for this chapter

LESSON LEARNED	DESIGN IMPLICATIONS
Intentional remixing: Remixing is informed by the past, the present, and the future. The past provides us with previous knowledge, stories and values to be reinterpreted to address new challenges. The present offers resources that we can recombine and reuse. The future is described through a narrative that can guide our actions.	• *Surprise, surprise!* Stories are collections of events that lead a character from A to B. This is why a lot of stories are boring. What is your story? What is everybody's story? Is your design's story any different or any more exciting? Where is the surprising side? At the beginning (unusual look and feel), in the middle (in the way users discover your design) or at the end (reward) of your design? • *Back to the future*: Design can activate good or bad memories. What we memorize is a collection of events and objects that can be arranged in many different ways; our memories are actively reconstructed every time and driven by intention. Good memories can be analyzed to find inspiration; bad memories to identify pain points.
Emergent remixing: When we do not have the luxury of having a clear vision or powerful storytelling driving our choice, we can still experiment and remix what we have until we make sense of the chaos and a direction emerges from our action.	• *Just do it!* When you do not know what to do, just act. Action can come in many forms: Read, observe, talk, watch, visit, exercise. If your mind is open, anything can be a source of inspiration. If it is closed, then break out! • *Tinker, again*: Assembling, disassembling, stressing, re-organizing are all ways to play with your design and escape paralysis without being oppressed by the anxiety of finishing. Tinkering should be playful and free.
Situational remixing: Sometimes innovation is blocked by constraints that seem impossible to remove. It happens that some of these constraints are imposed on us by what we know already. Previous knowledge can be a blessing and a curse. Through situational remixing, we can question rules, tradition and even technological limitations and discover that some blocks are just mental.	• *Question the taken-for-granted*: List all things you would like to do but you can't and the reasons, then work on the list to find out which 'nos' are real impossibilities. • *Bricolage*: When the block is due to unavailability of certain expensive resources, look outside of your field to find out what others did to solve similar problems. You'll be surprised! • *Innovation garage*: Look around, ask around and use what you have to build a low fidelity prototype. It doesn't matter how weird it looks.

Creativity lab

The full description of each exercise is available on the book companion website: http://www.bloomsburyonlineresources.com/elegant-design

9.1 Case study: the Olivetti Programma 101 and the invention of the desktop computer

Learn how breakthrough products are created by remixing existing parts and ideas driven by a revolutionary narrative, as in the case of the invention of the first desktop computer.

9.2 Anatomy of a masterpiece: visual bricolage in Cubist paintings

Learn how Cubist artists applied the remix strategy to reinvent the representation of movement and perspective through visual bricolage

9.3 The art of noticing: faces everywhere!

Observe how our mental models re-organize our experience by looking for 'faces' in the most unlikely objects.

9.4 Design exercise: remixing through the power of collage

Learn how create images through the remixing power of collage.

10 Contrast and Balance

ABSTRACT

This chapter is about a strategy we call 'contrast and balance'. At the core of this strategy there is the creation of differences in potential in terms of energy or information, with the aim of moving the configuration of a system in a desired direction. When it comes to design, contrast and balance is about creating informational tensions by redistributing information and users' attention towards the creation of a pleasurable but dynamic equilibrium.

KEYWORDS

visual weight

foreground and background

tension equilibrium

loudness

black and white

anchoring

paradoxes

creativity

The perceived object [. . .], in the present case, a wooden jigsaw puzzle—is not a sum of elements to be distinguished from each other and analyzed discreetly, but a pattern, that is to say, a form, a structure: [. . .]. Knowledge of the pattern and of its laws, of the set and its structure, could not possibly be derived from discrete knowledge of the elements that compose it. [. . .] The pieces are readable, take on a sense, only when assembled; in isolation, a puzzle piece means nothing.

Georges Perec (*Life: A User's Manual*, 2009)

Chess and balance

On 2 December 1805, Napoleon Bonaparte accomplished one of the most impressive military successes of his career. The French army, outnumbered at 16,000 units and 139 artillery pieces by a coalition of Austrian, Prussian and Russian soldiers, and positioned on the unfavourable side of the battlefield, routed the enemy and laid out the basis for French military supremacy over Europe for the following decade.

According to military analysts, the Austerlitz victory was a masterpiece of military strategy and tactics in which Napoleon's genius achieved one of its peaks. The French victory was the result of Napoleon's ability to attract his enemies in a skilfully built trap by reducing the number of troops he had positioned on the right wing of the French Army. Napoleon then ordered them to create a fortified position on the hill of the Santon, close to the Pratzen plateau, where the largest and best part of the enemy army was concentrated, and finally hid part of his soldiers behind a thick fog at the base of the Pratzen (Fig. 10.1).

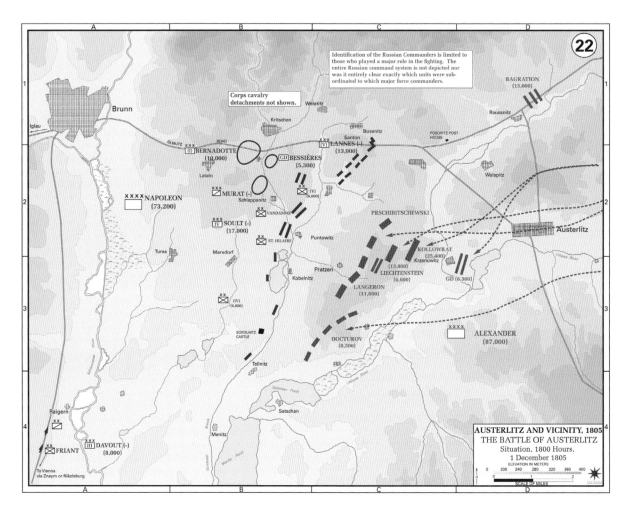

FIGURE 10.1 Initial troop deployment at Austerlitz on 2 December 1805.
Through the initial disposition of is troops, Napoleon offered a bait to the enemy by simulating a weakness in the right wing of his deployment and hiding other soldiers in the fog.

When the coalition troops focused their attack on the decoy prepared by the French, thus weakening the centre of their formation, the French squads, led by General Soult, came out of the fog and hit hard on the enemy on the Pratzen. They were helped by the troops positioned on the hill of the Santon. Surrounded by enemies, the Austrian-Russian army attempted a flight over the iced pond of the Satschan, a move that Napoleon had clearly anticipated, so much so that he ordered his artillery to crash the ice to drown the enemies. The battle resulted in one of the heaviest defeats for the coalition army, one that required the acceptance of a humiliating treaty and long time to recover from, materially and morally (Fig. 10.2).

Napoleon's success can be explained in terms of his ability to build a successful strategy through which he was able to anticipate the enemy's moves. The sequence of moves and countermoves can be modelled very much in the same way as a chess game. Winning a chess game is all about implementing a superior strategy to force the opponent to play on your terms. You can

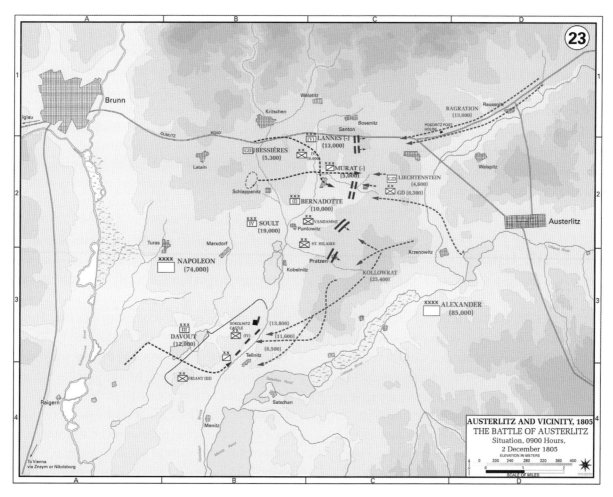

FIGURE 10.2 Battle evolution after Napoleon's attack.
The enemy coalition took the bait and was 'sucked' towards the centre for the French deployment while the hidden French troops organized a surprise attack and conquered the top of the hill.

dissimulate, decide to sacrifice some pieces in view of future gains, get the enemy to a hold, and take your chances. The successful player understands the system of tensions that is in place, the factors that determine the equilibrium and those that can be leveraged to break it[58]. To move from a stalled situation, the winner identifies the right sources of potential energy that could change things and liberates that energy in a controlled manner.

This is exactly what Napoleon did. He deliberately created a weakness in one side of his army, knowing that the enemy forces would be sucked into this artificial vacuum, and decided to sacrifice the troops that he had put in that difficult condition. The initial balance was broken through the creation of differences in potential energy that put things in motion, and the system of tensions was finally bent in favour of one of the two contenders.

When it comes to design, contrast and balance works in a similar fashion by creating tensions that will induce users to break the status quo to achieve a pleasurable and advantageous equilibrium. To see ways in which this result can be accomplished, as always, let's start with artists.

Present, tense

Artists use contrasting and balancing for two reasons: 1) to isolate salient elements; 2) to connect these elements in a web of tension. We can think of this web as a conversation in which elements talk to each other in a dialogic tension. As it happens in a conversation, one line calls for another, one speaker's turn makes an opening for the other speaker's turn. It is an invitation to action. Conversely, a bad conversation is one in which this dynamic is not at work. The conversation then evolves either towards the confusion generated by many speakers talking at the same time or comes to a halt because nobody knows what to say.

What happens when we are incapable of isolating meaning to add contrast to our experience? In a passage of Jean-Paul Sartre's novel *Nausea*, the protagonist Antoine Roquetin finds himself suddenly in a deep crisis in which he sees the world melting in front of his eyes (1965: 181):

All at once the veil is torn away, I have understood, I have seen . . . The roots of the chestnut tree sank into the ground just beneath my bench. I couldn't remember it was a root anymore. Words had vanished and with them the meaning of things, the ways things are to be used, the feeble points of reference which men have traced on their surface [. . .]. existence had suddenly unveiled itself [. . .]. the diversity of things, their individuality, were only an appearance, a surface. This surface had melted, leaving soft, monstrous lumps, in disorder—naked, with a frightful and obscene nakedness.

For Roquetin, the inability to isolate units of meaning from his experience translates into the anguish of being thrown into a meaningless world populated by 'monstrous lumps'. While a little bit extreme, this feeling is in fact not too different from the sense of disorientation that we might have felt in front of a visual representation that we are not able to make sense of, such as a piece of abstract art or a puzzling interface. How does our mind try to get rid of this feeling? By resorting to variety of ordering devices, including linguistic and visual tools, whose aim is to frame unstructured experience into a meaningful web of connections. There are at least two opposite ways in which such connections can be made meaningful: a) to express equilibrium and unity; b) to suggest imminent disintegration. Both these intents suggest the potential for action, to anticipate that something interesting has happened or is going to happen.

FIGURE 10.3 *The Star – Dancer on Stage* (Edgar Degas,1876–1877).
In this painting, Degas contrasts the levity and the energy of the dancer with empty space and an enigmatic back figure standing in the background.

Let's start with the first intent. In the painting in Fig. 10.3, Degas depicts a young dancer who floats lightly and harmoniously, presumably observed by a group of people, including other dancers and a gentleman in black. The dancer seems to hover weightlessly, and her posture is anticipating her body's rotation as in a pirouette. The painting communicates a sense of lightness, grace and harmonious movement. At the same time, it expresses a vigorous intensity and tangible presence. Let's use Arnheim's idea of visual centres to discover how the artist managed to communicate this feeling.

The dancer stands out with her white dress on a neutral green background, isolated from the rest of the composition. This figure takes almost one-third of the painting's surface. The rest is virtually empty, except for an upper triangle created by a diagonal line that separates the dancer from the observers (Fig. 10.4, left). The same diagonal also connects the two main visual centres of the painting, like the arms of a scale: the man dressed in black on the left and the dancer's face on the right (Fig. 10.4, right). The man in black weighs on the diagonal and pulls up

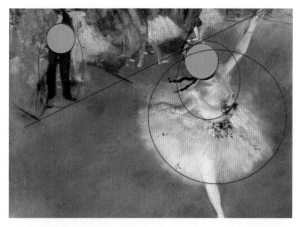

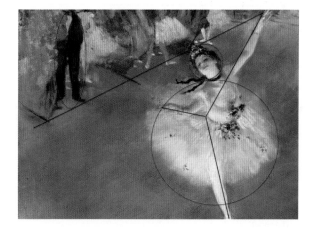

FIGURE 10.4 Contrast and balance in Degas' *The Star*.
This analysis shows the geometry of contrasting and balancing in Degas. The black figure in the back has a crucial role as a counterweight to the levity of the dancer; a diagonal horizon 'helps' the dancer rotate and advance in the empty space.

the dancer. The tutu's circularity and the axes of the arms and leg reinforce the sense of movement by suggesting a spiral[59].

As an immediate counterexample, try to cover the black figure, and you will experience a sudden loss of equilibrium and sense of movement.

Classic Greek sculptors were the first to create tension to suggest the potential for action and movement. One of the most well-known examples is the *Discobolus* of Myron, a fifth century BCE statue representing an athlete in the act of throwing a disc, of which only Roman copies survive nowadays (Fig. 10.5). Myron's intuition was that the best moment to capture the launch was when the athlete's potential energy was at its peak. Our mind is easily triggered into the illusion that the athlete is precisely at the point at which he will start the release procedure, and we know that the beauty and the launch's effectiveness are all self-contained in that instant. The spiral shape and the athlete's serenity compensate for the feeling of this impending explosion and create a sense of stability and control.

Let's compare Velasquez's portrait of Pope Innocent X with the same subject represented by Francis Bacon almost 300 years later (Fig. 10.6). This comparison helps us to illustrate the other intent of the contrast and balance strategy: disintegration.

In Velasquez, the portrait communicates a sense of stability induced by a pyramidal structure culminating on the red pointy hat. The hat drives our gaze towards the Pope's grave and serene expression that conflicts with the excitement created by the flashy cardinal red of the mantle, emerging from the dark background. The portrait is a game of contrasts whose objective is to make us experience the power of authority and subjugation.

Bacon instead has a different and more contemporary view of what power is. His portrait confines the Pope in a sort of fluorescent cage,

FIGURE 10.5 Roman copy of Myron's *Discobolus* (Myron, BCE 450–460).
In this classic pose, the discobolus is frozen at the moment at which he is about to throw the disc. The contrast between the athlete's focused but serene expression and the contracted muscles ready to explode gives vitality to the composition.

which we interpret as a metaphor of power. The cage bars represented through the yellow stripes separate the figure from us and communicate the distance and alienation that Bacon associates with power. The Pope is then exploding and vanishing away, along with his scream. The rays at the bottom release the force of this destructive explosion. Bacon represents power as a deadly

(a)

(b)

FIGURE 10.6 *Pope Innocent X* by Velazquez and Bacon.
(a) Pope Innocent X, by Diego Velázquez (1650); (b) Study after Velázquez's Portrait of Pope Innocent X, by Francis Bacon (1953). In Velázquez's representation, contrast of colours and shapes confer stability and unity to the portrait, while in Bacon's this equilibrium is deliberately broken to communicate the lies and destructive strength of political power.

force that consumes the man through the inhumanity of a raging and destructive power.

It is finally interesting to explore another use of contrast and balance positioned in the middle of the continuum between stability and disintegration. In some cases, artists create representations generating a sense of suspension between these two opposite outcomes.

An example is Hopper's painting, *Nighthawks* (Fig. 10.7). A few characters are in a night scene in a bar or diner. On one side, a man is portrayed from the back. On the other side, a couple, a young woman with a red dress and her partner, are absent-minded. The man's gaze seems lost

in the space while the woman is playing with something she has in her hand. The red dress contrasts with the navy of the two men's suits and the barman's white coat. The barman looks toward the couple, probably waiting for an order. The woman and the barman stand out while the two men seem to be camouflaged in the blue of the night and resemble each other. There is a dark and silent tension that immobilizes the figures in their activities.

Hopper dramatizes the situation in a few ways. First of all, he puts the observer in the position of an intruder spying from far away. The characters do not look at each other, nor do they

FIGURE 10.7 *Nighthawks* (Edward Hopper, 1942).
In this painting, Hopper resorts to different forms of contrast by juxtaposing light and darkness, complementary colours, and psychological or dialogical tension between the different characters in the scene.

watch us. They avoid emotional connection and are separated by a physical barrier (the bar) that divides the painting's space into distinct interior worlds. The upper part of the image is empty, and our gaze focuses either on the figure of the woman or the man, following the bar's profile to move from one to the other. The contrast between the street's darkness and the bright fluorescent lights of the interior accentuates the sense of drama and creates intimacy. We do not know how this situation will evolve: Will any character leave? Will the woman stop fidgeting and say something to her partner? Is there any hope for this couple?

Lost in transition

Contrast and balance is a widely used design strategy. A telling example of its application is in designing safety interfaces. Because of their complexity, many factors can threaten these systems' regular functioning to the point of generating economic disaster or putting human lives in danger (Reason 2016). For this reason, the design of an adequate interface is critical for the early identification of anomalies and potential risks as well as to ensure prompt intervention before an accident escalates to unmanageable levels.

The ubiquitous stop/emergency button (Fig. 10.8), whose standard design is a giant, clown nose–like red button on a yellow background, is a familiar example. Chromatic and geometric contrast give prominence to a device that anybody can operate. The red stop button of escalators and other systems with parts in motion is so attractive that you might have been tempted to push it just for fun. For this reason, the red button always comes with some threatening message reminding us of the punishment that will ensue for the unjustified use of the device (that's the balance side of the design). The bright colours' emotional valence and the inviting, toy-like shape trigger an immediate affective response, which is desirable when urgent action is required. Simultaneously, the written notice leverages our 'rational', slower brain that has the time to jump in and stop us from pushing the button when there is no emergency.

When monitoring a system's safety conditions, the operators should distinguish in the most reliable way when the system is working under normal conditions and when instead there is

FIGURE 10.8 The emergency red button.
Alert, danger and emergency signals create contrast through loud colours and shapes to attract immediate attention and prompt action.

an anomaly. Unfortunately, this was not the case at Three Mile Island, a location in rural Pennsylvania where the first serious accident in a nuclear plant happened. Unlike later cases, such as Chernobyl and Fukushima, this accident did not produce human losses. It provided many lessons that induced significant changes to nuclear energy production and regulation. Among the several causes that determined the accident (complex systems typically generate disasters only when a highly unlikely combination of threats and failures occurs), the investigation pointed out the control panel design (Malone et al. 1980). Some of the design choices included inaccurate indicators and alarms, so operators did not have a clear line of sight and easy access. During one of the critical phases of the accident, which started with a mechanical failure and was magnified by several human mistakes, an operator manually overrode the automatic emergency cooling system of the reactor because he mistakenly believed that there was already too much water present in the reactor. A hidden indicator light led to this mistake. Had this light been prominent and loud enough to attract the operator's attention towards the correct reading of the water level, the accident consequences would have been significantly less serious.

A properly contrasted interface needs to be balanced to prevent emergency considerations from heading the wrong way. In the Chernobyl accident, the 'red button' was too evident, and somebody pressed it at the wrong time. This action released the fuel bars in the coolant and created enormous pressure in the reactor due to a massive steam generation (for a more detailed examples of this and other issues in the design of the control dashboard at Three Mile Island, see case study 4.1, available on the book companion website).

A less dramatic application of contrast and balance is in the design choices of innovative products. In particular, we refer to breakthrough ideas that bring to market completely new objects for the first time, such as cars or computers. The introduction of something radically new requires balancing the novelty of the idea with some familiar elements that help users make sense and not be scared. For instance, early cars looked like carriages without horses. The first personal computers resembled a typewriter. The ubiquitous digital assistant we all have in our pockets was a phone (Fig. 10.9).

The same happened to radios. The early radios were bulky devices because their internal amplifier was built with a technology that did not support the level of miniaturization achieved in the 1950s after the transistor's invention. So, initially, the cumbersome radios ended up being enclosed into an even bulkier piece of furniture that would fit into a dining room of the 1930s and 1940s (Fig. 10.10, left). It was not until the 1950s that Dieter Rams questioned this design. Rams was an endorser of German functionalism, a minimalist design philosophy that traced its origin back to the Bauhaus movement (Rams 2014). As the leader of

the German producer Braun's design department, he reinvented appliance design based on the idea that technology was something that should be friendly and openly available to people instead of being concealed from their sight.

While designing a new radio and disc player, the SK4, Rams was still trying to enclose the device into a metal cabinet with wood finishes. The cabinet was supposed to be closed on the top by a metal or wood panel that was hurting the sound quality. Thus, Rams decided to use a new transparent plastic material known as Plexiglass for the first time in a consumer product (Fig. 10.10, right). The SK4 is today a design icon that strikes us for its modernity and stunning cleanliness. Along with other Rams' inventions, it had a long-lasting influence on consumer tech products[62].

Rams' bold choice to unveil the device's technological soul through the use of a transparent cover was balanced by a very restrained and otherwise simple design. It was based on a neat composition of white and grey controls, the use of elementary geometric shapes such as circles, squares, rectangles, and a 'list' of almost mesmerizing straight lines positioned on the speakers. Finally, the wooden finishes

FIGURE 10.9 Products in transition, from left to right: 1885 Benz velo; Olivetti Programma 101; IBM Simon smartphone. The design of radically new products sometimes inherits shapes and names from the ones they are going to replace, which helps to balance their extreme novelty and overcome the anxiety that such novelty can induce in users.

(a)

(b)

FIGURE 10.10 Radios' design.
(a) Kadette radio (International Radio Corp., 1933); (b) Braun SK4 disc player (Dieter Rams, 1956).
The SK4 questioned the traditional design of radios, which were typically embedded into a wooden cabinet and treated as a piece of furniture. It also represents one of the first uses of Plexiglass in home appliances.

created a discrete memory link to the heavy wooden cabinets that were the norm before Braun reinvented appliances' design.

The juxtaposition of old and new elements in the same design is a noticeable trait of the SK4. Studies on aesthetics judgment confirm that individuals prefer stimuli with both novel and familiar characteristics (Berlyne 1970). One way to achieve this result is to use contrast and balance and create an unresolved tension.

Contrasting and balancing is not only at work in the design of radically new products but can also service the intent of innovating traditional goods and services. In her book on aesthetic intelligence (defined as the 'new AI' – we love that!), Pauline Brown, former Chairman for the North American Division of the leading global fashion and luxury group LVMH (Moët Hennessy Louis Vuitton) offers an example of how Del Frisco steakhouse chain refreshened its image to make the dining experience of its clients 'big, bold, and sophisticated' but at the same time more trendy and contemporary without sacrificing the consistency of the brand.

Among the other innovations, the design of the restaurant interior (Fig. 10.11) contrasted and balanced elements that reinforced the appearance of a traditional steakhouse, such as warm colour palette, heavy utensils and boardroom atmosphere, with more modern design fixtures, such as high ceilings, iron and wood combined

FIGURE 10.11 Del Frisco's restaurant interior in Washington, DC.
The restaurant interior combines contemporary and sophisticated atmosphere with solidity, power and simplicity that are traditionally associated with American upscale steakhouses.

into modernist Bauhaus-like furniture, the transparency of glass screens and windows and unexpected bursts of colour.

The SK4 or the Del Frisco steak house offer examples of how designers can masterfully and deliberately introduce some ambiguity to satisfy opposite requirements. Commercial and political communication offer even more examples of the adoption of paradoxical statements by suggesting associations that can range from a biased view of the world to outright lies. Welcome to the fascinating art of the oxymoron, a figure of speech that deliberately merges words with opposite meanings into a paradoxical expression. Think of 'tax relief', an oxymoron that implies that taxes are a burden, or 'affordable healthcare', which subsumes the postulate that healthcare is something expensive but within reach, or the impossible fuel invented by Volkswagen known as 'clean diesel'.

If adequately applied, contrast and balance is a design strategy that can help us stretch out users' attention towards the full range of possibilities our design can offer. As with any other strategies proposed in this book, contrast and balance has its dark side. The overuse of contrast will make some elements wrongly preponderant and compromise the design's equilibrium. The dominance of balance will instead create too much compromise, and our design will fail to deliver what it promises.

The science of contrast

During one of his experiments, the psychologist Dan Ariely asked his subjects to estimate the price of a bottle of wine (Ariely and Jones 2008). Before offering their price guess, participants were also asked to write down the last two digits of their social security number. The data showed that the price estimates provided by the subjects correlated strongly with these random numbers. In other words, people who happened to have a lower two-digit number at the end of their social security number thought the wine was cheaper and vice versa. The simple exposure to a random and unrelated number significantly affected participants' judgment much more than any rational consideration[63].

Ariely explains this distortion occurs because we naturally tend to anchor our guesses on initial information that is offered or easily retrieved. While the anchoring effect is classified as cognitive bias and can lead us astray or make us prone to manipulation, it is also a heuristic that works well in many situations in which extrapolating a guess from a backlog of previously accumulated knowledge makes a lot of sense.

We can effectively predict the weather in the next hour or so based on the current conditions. We can anticipate the behaviour and choices of someone we know well, or know what to expect in a wide variety of social situations, just by observing a few clues.

Our brain likes to have a baseline and to make a judgment in contrast with it, and this attitude is deeply rooted in the biology of intelligent behaviour. In investigating the psychologic mechanisms that support art understanding and appreciation, Ernst Gombrich (1961) provides an excellent example from research on animals' behaviour. Let's get two pieces of paper of different shades of grey, and let's train chicks to expect food only on the darker one. At this point, if we replace the dark grey piece with a white sheet, the chicks will expect food on the light grey piece of paper – that is, on the relatively darker one. The chicks' brains, and our brains too, for that matter, learn and judge contrast based on relative gradients instead of absolute scales.

Gestalt psychologists have investigated the importance of gradients through the foreground/

background principle. According to this principle, human perception organizes information in layers characterized by different focus levels. What is more relevant and requires immediate or more attention is on the foreground and in focus; what is not is relegated to the background and blurred. This effect is common in paintings (think of aerial perspective in Renaissance painting), and it is taught in any Photography 101 class as a fundamental trick to isolate the subject from a noisy and uninformative background (Fig. 10.12).

In the third chapter of his book, *Creativity: The Psychology of Discovery*, Mihaly Csíkszentmihályi (2013) discusses whether creative people have distinctive psychological traits or personalities. His research findings show no trace of such a stable association. Instead, Csíkszentmihályi argues that creativity

is typical of complex characters: personalities that combine mutually exclusive traits to adapt to complex situations. From our perspective, these paradoxical combinations are a system of tensions that flexible minds can exploit to come up with original inventions and brilliant discoveries. We reinterpret Csíkszentmihályi's decalogue in terms of effective complexity (chapter 2). The ambivalence of the conflicting psychological traits associated with creativity helps handle the trade-off between searching for unity and searching for variety (Table 10.1). In other words, effective complex solutions are the creations of individuals endowed with an effectively complex personality.

According to the psychologist Mihaly Csíkszentmihályi, exceptionally creative people such as artists and scientists are able to balance and integrate opposite personality traits.

FIGURE 10.12 Contrast originated by blurred backgrounds.
On the left, an example of aerial perspective in Leonardo's *Virgin and Child with St. Anne* (1510–1513 ca.); on the right, Bob Dylan and Joan Baez portrayed with a blurred background by Rowland Scherman during a protest march in Washington, DC, in 1963. In both cases, blurring the background gives prominence and visual strength to the foreground.

TABLE 10.1: The conflicting traits of creative personalities as effective psychological complexity

SEARCH FOR UNITY (REDUCE ENTROPY)	SEARCH FOR VARIETY (INCREASE ENTROPY)	CREATIVE INDIVIDUALS ...
Rest	Physical activity	Alternate time of intense physical activity with rest and idleness.
Convergent thinking	Divergent thinking	Balance their effort between exploring new possibilities with the development of a deep knowledge of the domain of their interest.
Discipline	Playfulness	Stick to a strict working routine while having fun and even enjoying the hard work.
Realism	Imagination	Are able to unleash their imagination without losing contact with reality and feasibility.
Introversion	Extraversion	Enjoy introspection and loneliness as well as social life.
Humble	Proud	Are humble enough to acknowledge their limits but proud about what they know and learn.
Masculine	Feminine	Exhibit both traditionally masculine and feminine traits (e.g. preference for achievement versus relationship-oriented personality)
Tradition	Rebellion	Possess deep and sophisticated knowledge of a domain but are able to escape disciplinary boundaries and dogmas.
Objective	Passionate	Use data and facts to prove their theories but are driven by genuine passion and love for their work and objects of interest.
Enjoyment	Pain	Go through a time of enjoyment and satisfaction as well as through anxiety, disorientation, and pain.

Conclusions: keep on moving

'Omnia mutantur, nihil interit' [everything changes, nothing stays] states Ovid in the *Metamorphoses*. Nothing in Ovid's mythical world is stable. There is always the feeling that change can occur at any moment. In his poem, the passionate impulses of the gods, semi-gods, and men, subjugated to their passions' blind and violent strength, are the forces that keep the world going.

Through beautiful verses, Ovid reveals to us what our body already knows: every physical, social, conceptual or virtual entity is always and only a dynamic entity. Rest, fixed state, and idleness are illusions necessary for the mind to have references and fixed points. Reality is a concentrate of potential energy ready to unfold. When the world changes too fast, the solid ground of certainties prevents us from understanding and adapting to new conditions.

Mastering the ability to see reality as a web of tensions is critical to capturing the exciting richness of experience without being overwhelmed by its complexity.

When things change, we have to humbly accept the complexity of what we do not understand and occasionally experience the horror of the nonsense, as Roquetin does, sitting on a bench of a park observing the world as it goes liquid. To achieve superior design, we have to understand where the tensions are and how they generate pain for the users. Then, we must have the courage to break the toy when these tensions are not resolved, liquefy what we have already built, and get back to a fluid state in which everything can happen. It's a risky business, it can be painful and time-consuming, but the payoff can be enormous.

PUTTING IDEAS INTO PRACTICE

Key takeaways for this chapter

LESSON LEARNED	DESIGN IMPLICATIONS
Create information asymmetry: C&B is about re-distributing information to create tensions between opposite qualities that suggest some form of action. Lack of balance signals a noticeable difference, one we feel like we have to resolve. That resolution solicits a question, which may demand action aimed at resolving the tension. Think of this imbalance in terms of interface design: for instance, virtual buttons look like buttons because of the contrast created by a shade that surrounds them and invite us to push the button.	• *Escape flatland*: A hilly landscape is generally preferred to a flat one. So, think of your design as a landscape. How flat does it look? Where do you need to concentrate information and why? • *Contrast for action*: Inspect your design and look for anything that solicits questions and actions. If you can't find anything, consider adding contrast.
Balancing visual weight: C&B is about balancing visual weight to create a dynamic equilibrium. This aspect is akin to information asymmetry but is implemented more bluntly as a juxtaposition of forms and colour. C&B, in this case, is purely graphic and helps to identify salient differences. It can signal a property or quality very much like a red fruit in contrast with a green background signals the fruit is ripe or poisonous.	• *Checks and balance*: Think of your design as a graphic composition. Each part should have a counterpart that confers balance to the whole. This counteracting can be achieved in many ways (dark/light colour, full/empty space, complementary shapes, etc.). • *S.O.S. (Save our Signals)*: Graphic contrast should always be associated with some sort of aim or message that is intelligible to users. Make sure the message is there and that the users can read it.
Dual thinking: C&B plays with ambiguity because everything can be defined in terms of its opposite. Contrast adds dynamism and multiplicity through juxtaposition, while balance integrates the apparent contradiction into a new unity. A way to represent this dynamic is through oxymorons such as 'this piece of furniture is a modern classic'. Effective C&B does not play with words only but results from a design that manages trade-offs originally and more effectively.	• *Play the opposite game*: Try to define your design in terms of what it is not or what it does not do. Make a list and check if everything you have there is intended. Are there things that you would like your design to be or to do? Congratulations, you have a design trade-off you can play with. • *From 'either or' to 'and'*: Transform opposites into a two-dimensional space. For instance, transform the contradiction classic-modern into a diagram in which these dimensions are orthogonal and then place your design and its competitors in there (see the 'art of noticing' exercise in this chapter). See which one better conjugates the two opposites (a piece of furniture that is both modern and classic).

Creativity lab

The full description of each exercise is available on the book companion website: http://www.bloomsburyonlineresources.com/elegant-design

10.1 Case study: Alessi's houseware design

Learn how contrast and balance can be effectively applied to create psychological tensions through Alessi's design of its housewares for the "family follows function" project.

10.2 Anatomy of a masterpiece: contrast and balance in Japanese painting

Learn how to exploit the power of contrast and balance from how Zen painters represent the empty-full contrast.

10.3 The art of noticing: design by paradoxes

Use oxymorons to describe how products manage to contrast and balance opposite requirements.

10.4 Design exercise: the construction of a dynamic sculpture

Learn how to design equilibrium as Calder does in his dynamic structures.

11 Design as Aesthetic Intelligence

ABSTRACT

We are at the end of our journey, and we hope you enjoyed it. It is time to wrap up the key lessons and conclusions of this book. This chapter summarizes the theoretical background and the method we have proposed to achieve effective complexity by using the eight design heuristics described in this book. We outline how this book aligns with other contemporary approaches to design that are aimed at re-establishing design ethics and reducing the negative environmental and psychological impacts of design driven by consumerism and planned obsolescence.

KEYWORDS

Creativity

constraints

narrative

emotions

functionality

Nostro ingegno solo da sensato apprende
[our knowledge only comes from experience]

Dante (*Paradiso*, IV Chant, verse 41)

FIGURE 11.1 Tarot figures (unknown author, 1500 ca.)
This print part of the Cary collection at the Beinecke Library at Yale depicts several Tarot cards including mystical and enigmatic figures such as the Bagatto/Magician, the Empress, a female Bishop, the Emperor, the Star, and the Moon.

The clairvoyant designer

In 1973, the Italian writer Italo Calvino published *The Castle of the Crossed Destinies*, a short fantasy tale inspired by the magic and the mystery of tarot cards[64]. In the introduction, Calvino describes the method he used to create the stories contained in the book. He would arrange the tarot cards on a table to form a square (Fig. 11.1). Then he would read horizontal or vertical sequences until he spotted some intriguing connections that inspired an exciting plot.

Calvino (1973: 125) described his method as follows:

> First, I tried to compose narrative sequences inspired by the *Orlando Furioso* [an Italian epic poem] with the tarots. It turned out to be quite easy for me to reconstruct the intersection among these tales in a 'magic square'. Around that core, it sufficed for me to let other stories take shape by crossing each other, and in this way I ended up with a sort of crossword puzzle made up of figures instead of words, in which, moreover, each sequence could be read in both directions.

He wrote that the cards' meanings change depending on the order in which we read a sequence.

Thus, the Ace of Cups (Fig. 11.2) can be 'a source that flows between flowery mosses and whirls of wings' in the 'Story of the Ungrateful Punished' (1973: 9), a Fountain that 'seemed to originate, if you look closely, from a barrel on top of a grape press' and a 'Source of Life, the supreme point of the alchemist's research' in the 'Story of the Alchemist who Revenges the Soul' (1973: 15), or finally an elaborately made Altar-Chalice and a Cup whose Bacchic motifs guarantee libations of the purest wine in 'All the other stories' (1973: 47).

FIGURE 11.2 Ace of Cups.
A card from the Taroccchi by Bonifacio Bembo (fifteenth century).

In devising his stories, Calvino (1973: 124) is initially guided by the associations suggested by the images' details:

> I mainly applied myself to looking at tarot cards carefully, with the eye of someone who does not know what they are, and to draw suggestions and associations from them, to interpret them according to an imaginary iconology.

In *Six Memos for the Next Millennium*, a series of essays Calvino put together over ten years from his notes from a cycle of six talks he gave at Harvard University, Calvino reveals his own creative process in a more explicit way (1988: 88, our translation):

> In the creation of a story, the first thing that comes to my mind is an image that, for some reason, presents itself to me as extremely meaningful. As soon as the image has become clear enough in my mind, I begin to develop it into a story. Rather, it is the images themselves that form their implicit potential, the story that they carry within themselves. Each image generates others; a field of analogies, symmetries, and contrasts emerge. In the organization of this material, which is no longer only visual, my intention also intervenes at this point in ordering and giving meaning to the development of the story – or rather, what I do is to try to establish which meanings can be compatible and which are not with the general design that I would like to give to the story, always leaving a certain margin for possible alternatives.

We claim that this same method can be applied to design. Designing is about creating a foreseeable future, a desirable user narrative that unfolds via cause-effect relationships that are emotionally salient and ideally establish an unexpectedly pleasant surprise.

The oracle metaphor helps us to illustrate this definition better. The tarot reader puts together signs into a narrative tainted with emotional clues announcing the coming changes. Still, she or he passes this narrative to us with 'margins for possible alternatives' so that, by processing this intentional ambiguity, we can complete it and get a sense that we are in control of our life.

We summarize this design method in three steps:

1. *Everything starts with emotions*. It could be a body signal, a memory, or an aspiration triggering a sense of friction, annoyance, irritation, or, on the contrary, pleasure, cheerfulness, curiosity. Such emotional waves are fleeting and evanescent, but we should not ignore them since emotional clues contain the critical information we need to unwrap and process more in depth.

2. *Question the obvious*. In this phase, designers have to show their courage to shatter known and obvious forms, venture into unchartered territories, and explore fluid and unstable contexts. This courage should transform anxiety into curiosity, openness, and an attitude of playing with associations, differences, contrasts, irregularities, and redundancies. At this time, imagination and observation play with each other and act as our companions searching for sense. Designers have to put aside their egos and become passionate listeners.

3. *Re-order*. While fun, mind-wandering risks being fruitless if unnecessary prolonged, so designers must rely on a set of rules and constraints that help them to know when to stop. It is time to put order to the rich materials we have collected in phase 2.

Calvino's literary tarot game is a perfect summary of the design method we have tried to articulate in this book, and for which we want to provide a final wrap-up in this chapter.

What makes a good story? design is storytelling

What makes a good story? Indeed, its content, the narrative materials, and the sequence in which events occur and culminate. What about the imagery of a story? What role does it have? Is it ornament stitched on the plot to make it more appealing, or is it a substantial factor contributing to the story's unfolding?

Calvino's tarot experiment to build a story shows that this visual imagery does much more than decorate: it is the ingredient from which the plot germinates. Attractive or otherwise interesting visuals have an evocative power – they suggest, inform and drive our inspiration. More importantly, these visual stimuli help us build our mental imagery, an internal representation that provides the raw materials for sense-making and discovery. This multiplicity, in Calvino's word, 'is indispensable for any form of knowledge' (Calvino 2016).

However, such multiplicity must be 'taken out of the subjective' and made available to others through rational and intelligible intention. This approach is evident in Greek vase painting. The rich decoration and the abundance of elaborated figures representing gods, heroes and humans appear in linear narrative structures showing how the story unfolds in sequences, as told in the traditions and myths that every observer is supposed to know (Fig. 11.3).

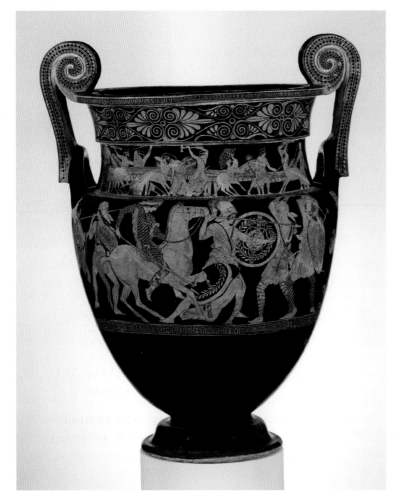

FIGURE 11.3 Terracotta volute-krater (Painter of the Woolly Satyrs BCE 450 ca.). This bowl for mixing wine and water is decorated with stories from Greek mythology that remind modern cartoons.

In this book's parlance, we need to get past the push towards multiplicity (search for variety) to a moment in which we sort out the abundance of stimuli and references into a coherent and consistent narrative (search for unity).

Calvino's experiment is an excellent example of how aesthetics can help us to navigate the complexity of a series of events. In this book, we argue that this artistic method can be applied to design as well[65]. A key argument we have advanced in this book is that there is a deep relationship between aesthetics and complexity. An aesthetically attractive design is not just there to appease our senses but also to facilitate sense-making by guiding our perception and increasing our ability to absorb new information. More specifically, elegant design helps us deal with complex tasks and situations by making our interaction with the world appear *simpler*.

The word *complexity* comes from the Latin *complexus*, meaning woven together. *Complexus* is also the perfect participle of the verb *complector*, to embrace. This perspective on complexity is an essential lesson of this book. A story cannot exist by itself. It can live if it is woven together with other forms because meaning can emerge only within a system. And this complexity needs to be *embraced* by the listener to become meaningful.

We have shown that the search for smart elegance is the search for an appropriate level of complexity that weaves various elements together and, at the same time, gives us the necessary scaffolding fabric in which this variety makes sense. We need such scaffolding because, as Donald Norman puts it (2016), complexity is a state of the world that cannot be avoided or suppressed. Complexity defines reality's underlying structure, a structure that we need to understand.

As users, we need *some* complexity because we long for such understanding, without which it would not be possible to assess performance and novelty. However, this complexity level needs to be commensurate with the amount that users can or want to absorb and handle. Such amount depends on many user-related factors, including personality (Pennycook et al. 2020), previous knowledge and background, motivation and will to commit time and resources to learn to use a new design proficiently. We can differ in terms of these and other factors, but the world's complexity stays there and stares at us in our face. The critical task for designers is to create *effectively complex* solutions to make a design as accessible as possible to most users.

Effective complexity is associated with the amount of perceived regularity in a design. The more accessible these regularities are, the simpler a design appears to our eyes. The designer's task is to find ways to identify and communicate these regularities most efficiently and effectively. Efficiency is the product of compressing information into easy-to-read regularities. Effectiveness is smooth and meaningful performance. Effectively complex designs maximize meaningfulness through a paucity of signs (i.e. with as little information as possible). Elegant design then aims towards the proper distribution of information over the product interface to facilitate understanding and interaction. This distribution tends to be optimal when the design peaks on effective complexity, and there is a balance between familiarity and novelty, ease of use, and arousal.

This smart simplicity is associated with aesthetic pleasure. Resolving complexity in surprisingly simple ways is responsible for the neurochemical rewards related to the feeling of pleasure. Part of this pleasure is aesthetic because we associate aesthetic validity with non-obvious configurations that are surprisingly easy to understand and operate.

This theory gives aesthetics an ecological validation: aesthetic pleasures can help us disentangle complexity and drive us towards more effective and efficient understanding and actions.

The combined effect of a non-trivial design that is effective and surprisingly easy gives joy to the users. Much design, unfortunately, errs on either side of the spectrum. Either we have a good design that works fine but does not excite us, or we have unnecessarily complicated solutions that speak aloud to our arousal centres but can be impractical and frustrating to use.

Designers should try to aim at the sweet spot among these opposite extremes, straight for joy and elegance.

Knowledge as experience of complexity

How does complexity resolution through aesthetic reasoning happen in our everyday experience? Everything starts with perception, and any perception triggers a feeling. The emotional response is the fastest reaction, followed by a slower assessment and understanding. Aesthetically valid stimuli balance these two reactions and integrate them into a rewarding experience in which the initial arousal is the starting point of the sense-making process.

This process is easy to experience through art, and this is why we have based this book on how our mind processes visual arts.

Great works of art attract us thanks to their strong emotional valence and provide us with novel and surprisingly effective perspectives in explaining and understanding life. For a few seconds, observe the painting of *Saint Anthony the Abbot in the Wilderness* (Fig. 11.4). The image triggers feelings of fear and loneliness. Our gaze is attracted by the naked and scary landscape, populated by lone animals and dead trees. The bright gold of the Saint's halo functions as a light to navigate the inhospitable land. The bright colours on the background offer relief for this anguish through a beautiful sunset and a church representing the gateway to a heavenly existence. Our knowledge of the religious narrative of saving our souls may help us make sense of these emotional readings and interpret our feelings within a broader message.

Why should design be any different? Good design triggers positive arousal and offers us novel and more effective ways to interact with the world.

FIGURE 11.4 *Saint Anthony the Abbot in the Wilderness* (Osservanza Master, 1435 ca.).
The use of simple colours and shapes in this image enable an immediate emotional response, combining anguish and hope. These contrasting emotions make sense thanks to the slower understanding and rational thinking based on the knowledge of the salvation narrative.

Designers should analyze users' experiences to consider these two levels of analysis and how they relate to each other. Any design should incorporate emotional and functional elements and ensure that these two levels are appropriately connected and do not stand in each other's way. An example of when these two levels are not well integrated is the aesthetic bias: the positive emotional response associated with a design's beauty makes us believe that it is also functionally excellent. When this expectation is violated, we feel disappointed. The opposite happens when a design is perceived as ugly and generates expectations of lousy performance. If such expectations are not verified, we experience a positive surprise. Yet the design's ugliness may keep people from even trying it out.

In both cases, we are in front of a design incapable of connecting emotional and functional features. Thus, in mediocre design, either the functional or the emotional prevails.

Our mind is often too busy to process this juxtaposition. Any time we make an aesthetic choice, we are using our aesthetic intelligence to choose something that will increase our fitness in the world in natural or cultural terms. We assess the objects that surround us in emotional and functional terms. Our mind moves back and forth across these two dimensions to understand how and whether emotional and functional features get along. For example, when we choose attire, we are driven by functional considerations (Is it appropriate for the event? Is it comfortable?) as well as emotional ones (Does it look good? Does it feel good?). It's easy to verify that our best outfits are the ones that score well on both dimensions.

As users, we can only choose among the possible alternatives on the market. As designers, we are the tailors that can combine both features. We can start on either side of the spectrum, perhaps by working on the functional side,

and then review to ascertain how we can make something very functional also exciting and attractive, without sacrificing functionality.

This search will activate our left brain and privilege subtraction of details and streamlining the design to minimize waste and increase reliability and accuracy. The search for emotionally salient design will push us to use our imagination to identify novel and alternative arrangements. Our mind will wander between these two poles and settle on a solution through a few iterations. Whatever is the logical closure justifying why we like something or why we made a particular decision, the final seal to that choice of design will always be emotional. We made that choice or decision because, yes, it seemed good, but more importantly, because it felt good. In conclusion, emotion marks the beginning and the end of any user experience.

This book proposes that this natural process through which the mind oscillates between the functional and the emotional, between subtracting details and searching for novel information, should be seconded and even imitated in the design process. For this reason, we have put together a method based on actionable design heuristics that can guide this exploration in a more disciplined way.

The elegant design method: question order, build order

In this book, we have provided eight design heuristics that designers can leverage to get as close as possible to the highest level of elegance (measured as effective complexity), and we have shown that these heuristics belong to two classes:

Search for unity heuristics fulfil the task of removing unnecessary information to achieve a higher degree of familiarity through the pursuit of known orders.

Search for variety heuristics help the designer to add meaningful information to increase the level of novelty through the pursuit of a new order.

The design process will consist of a series of iterations in which designers remove and add information until they reach the desired level of complexity.

The eight heuristics presented in this book and the iterative method to achieve effective complexity can help designers solve the most basic design trade-off between simplicity and performance. According to the approach we propose in this book, solving this trade-off requires exploring a continuum of design solutions that ideally lie between the absolute obviousness and chaos, determinism and randomness. Designers can err both ways, either by pursuing solutions that are too trivial and underperforming or by overwhelming users with too many functionalities and performance they do not need or cannot use. In the first extreme of the continuum, users will not have any freedom and flexibility. In the opposite extreme, instead, there is just too much choice and possibilities. All of this is relative to the complexity of the problem the design has to solve and the users' ability to explore, tolerate and even enjoy complexity.

The proposed heuristics can help each of us, whether our role is to be a user or a designer, to hone our aesthetic intelligence. The exercise of aesthetic intelligence requires an appropriate mindset based on two pillars.

First, designers should accept that complexity is out there, in the problem users are trying to solve, and that such intrinsic complexity cannot be avoided or neglected. The first step of any design attempt should be an honest assessment of the complexity we have to deal with, of course, evaluated from the users' perspective. Typically, grown-ups can process and have to deal with much more complexity than children, and experts can process and enjoy processing much more information than novices.

Second, the search for effectively complex design is a process that requires designers to experiment a lot and to have the courage to venture into unchartered solution spaces by questioning the existing order. While any design's objective is to bring order to the world, the pursuit of order is not always obtained by subtraction and reduction of the unknown to the known. Sometimes, we have to add entropy to our design deliberately; we need to break equilibria and rules to explore whether different orders are possible.

Conclusions: the pursuit of happiness through experience design

We wish to conclude our work with some final considerations on the ethical implications that our approach entails.

We want to leave our readers with how we see the role of design in society and express an opinion about some recent worrying trends, especially when it comes to the design of consumer products.

In one of its initial versions, the United States' declaration of independence included an article stating that all human beings have a right to private property. Benjamin Franklin was not happy with this article, probably because he found that too much emphasis on possession of wealth as a fundamental human right was uninspiring. His friend, the Italian philosopher and legal scholar, Gaetano Filangieri, suggested replacing the sentence with 'the pursuit of happiness' (D'Anna 2013). There is no need to comment on how this little change influenced the way people from other countries in the world have been looking at America and the American dream for centuries.

With the due proportions, nowadays, we are facing a similar challenge in the field of design. While initially, making technology more user-friendly through ergonomics and improved usability drove the discipline of industrial design, it soon evolved into another marketing tool, pushing users towards increasing levels of consumption.

It still seems that too many companies' main occupation is to use design innovations to persuade us to buy 'things we do not need, with money we do not have, for neighbors who do not care' (Papanek and Fuller 1972).

This trend has gone so far that some manufacturers openly consider planned obsolescence as a design criterion. Another nefarious design trend comes from the explicit attempts of creating products that generate addiction in their users. Digital technologies and the Internet have reinforced this trend further because digital businesses often monetize users' attention and time. Fogg (2009) introduced the concept of persuasive technologies, which some companies turned into a euphemism for designs that deliberately trick users into addiction. Sometimes, aesthetics is used unethically for this purpose, as the company Juul did by deliberately designing attractive and 'cool' vaping tools and sweet candy aromas to trick very young customers such as teenagers into smoking. And what about the festive and fancy presentations of junk food on packaging and commercials to attract children?[66]

In other cases, unethical consequences are not deliberate but still happen because designers have been inconsiderate about the negative impacts caused by their creations. A case in point is the Nespresso system that we presented as a great example of the power of the centre design strategy in chapter 7. The amount of non-recyclable garbage produced by coffee pod users emerged rather quickly as a huge problem. The company

tried to counteract this issue by implementing a recycling program for the collection of the coffee cases that, however, obtained mixed results because the task of setting aside and shipping (albeit for free) the exhausted pods fell ultimately on the users. Not to mention that other coffee companies that adopted the pod system were even less thoughtful than Nestle and the result is that today tons of unnecessary plastic goes into landfills because of the popularity of coffee pods.

We argue that these undesirable trends have in common a design paradigm that is driven by hedonic pleasure nurtured by excess or careless consumption. And this applies both to material and immaterial products (think of passive information consumption leading to information overload and misinformation, a sort of pollution of the mind).

This paradigm is unsustainable from the environmental point of view. Think of the amount of garbage, pollution and energy waste it produces (how much CO_2 was produced in making that espresso machine that we don't like anymore because we just got the new model?).

This paradigm is unsustainable from the business point of view, as well, since consumers are becoming more attentive and aware when it comes to aspects such as the environment, gender disparities, and respect for diversity. And when customers find that companies are neglectful or, even worse, manipulative or disloyal about these issues, the reputation and economic damage can be just immense.

Conversely, customers reward companies that embrace ethical design or reinvent their products to reduce their environmental impact or create value for society. For instance, the market is greatly rewarding Pepsi-Co's recent efforts to launch new products and reposition its brand to escape the category of junk food manufacturer. These efforts include the design of healthier lines of snack and soft drinks, investment in digital technology for the design of smart Gatorade bottles equipped with sensors that 'tell' athletes how much they have to hydrate themselves, or the project Life Wtr, a premium water brand that supports emerging artists by showcasing their work on the label, launched as special series (Fig. 11.5).[67]

We are also worried about psychological sustainability, the toll that excessive and passive consumption takes on our psychological well-being. Consumption-driven design generates anxiety, overwork, and, more recently, FOMO (an acronym meaning 'Fear of Missing Out'). This expression indicates the anxiety generated by the massive variety of desirable experiences that other people show off on their feeds that we feel we are missing.

Another adverse effect of this design paradigm is that it favours a very passive interaction. Habits, once formed, are passively activated, fast and acritical. When Netflix launches the next episode in a few seconds without leaving us the time to think if we want or should see it, it is playing with our addictive behaviour, love of passive entertainment and mindless choice. We are not claiming that it is wrong for people to look for some relaxation by enjoying binge-watching. Still, we are worried that this passive and acritical consumption is becoming mainstream and totalizing.

FIGURE 11.5 Life Wtr on display at DuJour's Jason Binn celebrating Winter Cover Star Diane Kruger at Vnyl on 25 January 2018 in New York City. (Photo by Sean Zanni/Getty Images for DuJour).
Through this premium water brand, selected young artists are given the opportunity to showcase their work on the bottle labels via special series.

The design approach we have presented in this book is based on a different paradigm, a paradigm we call experience-driven design. Experience-driven design is truly human-centred because it builds a positive experience to increase users' awareness and well-being through focus and joy. Focus promotes mindful, participated and aware fruition. Joy does not derive from the hedonic pleasure associated with buying and showing off new gadgets, but from the intrinsic motivation of enjoying a positive and meaningful interaction with the world facilitated by good design.

This meaningful interaction requires emotional salience, understanding, and, as mentioned many times in this book, some complexity. In our opinion, a good design facilitates our dialogue with the world through questions and answers that can drive a process of discovery and learning, and good aesthetics makes this learning effortless but not passive. For this reason, beautiful iconic design never gets old, and we call it classic. Old designs that are still highly sought by consumers embody the pleasure of using them in the very process of using them. The LC4 chair (Fig. 3.9) is still around because it makes the act of resting natural and rewarding. We never get tired of its beautiful shape. We feel joy from interacting with a form that seamlessly compresses ergonomic complexity into a surprisingly simple artifact. Classic design keeps talking to us because it consistently enables these meaningful and enjoyable experiences.

Experience-driven design optimizes both on the final performance and the process of interaction. It works at the functional and the emotional level by providing practical solutions, but it also engages the user in resolving the complexity of a task. It never stops producing positive reactions, the more it is reused. It makes users knowledgeable and stimulates their curiosity and willing to learn more.

Meaningful user engagement excludes the possibility of resorting to automatisms, habits, and does not frame users as the terminal point of a massive supply chain producing unsustainable waste. It helps users to navigate complexity but does not hide it away to create spoon-fed and gratuitous simplicity. Good design is honest about complexity; it does not lie.

A metaphor and an example come to mind: Musical instruments are designed not just to sound well but to play well. A jazz musician in a jam session, for instance, while having fun playing his or her instruments, also actively searches for an emerging order in the flow of musical information generated in a session. An excellent musical instrument gets better the more you play it, it never gets outdated, and musicians improve their skills the more they play. The instrument becomes a source of enjoyment and an enabler of that enjoyment. That is why good musicians love their instruments almost as if they had built them (and, in a sense, they do).

New approaches to design are, fortunately, emerging in opposition to consumption-driven design, such as positive design (Jimenez et al. 2015), design science research (Gregor and Hevner 2013) and the older but increasingly more popular design thinking (Brown and Katz 2019). More importantly, these approaches are applied beyond the traditional boundaries of the discipline, based on the idea that every human mind's product is a design object.

We hope this book will contribute to making design sustainable and mindful of authentic human and social needs beyond the satisfaction of hedonic urges and the short-term monetization of passive consumption that depletes both our planet and our psychological well-being.

BIBLIOGRAPHY

Alvarez, G. A., and Cavanagh, P. (2004). 'The capacity of visual short-term memory is set both by visual information load and by number of objects', *Psychological Science*, 15, no. 2: 106–111.

Ariely, D., and Jones, S. (2008). *Predictably irrational*. New York, NY: Harper.

Arnheim, R. (1965). Art and visual perception: A psychology of the creative eye. Berkeley: Univ. of California Press.

Arnheim, R. (1983). *The power of the center: A study of composition in the visual arts*. 2nd edition. Berkeley: Univ of California Press.

Atkins, P. W. (1984). *The second law*. New York: Scientific American Books: W. H. Freeman & Co.

Aviv, V. (2014). 'What does the brain tell us about abstract art?' *Frontiers in Human Neuroscience*, 8, doi: https://doi.org/10.3389/fnhum.2014.00085

Baldwin, C., and Linnea, A. (2010). *The circle way: A leader in every chair*. Oakland, CA: Berrett-Koehler Publishers.

Banathy, B. H. (1996). *Designing social systems in a changing world*. New York: Springer Science and Business Media.

Barthes, R., and Duisit, L. (1975). 'An introduction to the structural analysis of narrative', *New Literary History*, 6, no. 2: 237–272.

Barabási, A. L. (2003). Linked: How everything is connected to everything else and what it means for business, science and everyday life. New York: Plume Books.

Barabba, V. (2011). *Decision loom*. Axminster Devon, UK: Triarchy Press.

Bechmann, R., and Rivière, G. H. (1981). Les racines des cathédrales: l'architecture gothique, expression des conditions du milieu. Paris: Payot.

Berghman, M., and Hekkert, P. (2017). 'Towards a unified model of aesthetic pleasure in design'. *New Ideas in Psychology*, 47: 136–144.

Berlyne, D. E. (1970). 'Novelty, complexity, and hedonic value', *Perception & Psychophysics*, 8, no. 5: 279–286.

British Design Council (2016). *Eleven lessons. A study of the design process*. Available online: www.designcouncil.org.uk (accessed June 23, 2021).

Brown, P. (2019). Aesthetic intelligence: How to boost it and use it in business and beyond. New York: Harper Business.

Brown, T., and Katz, B. (2019). Change by design: How design thinking transforms organizations and inspires innovation. New York: Harper Business.

Browne, M. W. (1988). 'The benzene ring: Dream analysis', *The New York Times,* August 16.

Calvino, I. (1979). *The castle of crossed destinies*. Boston, Ma: Mariner Books (First Italian edition by Einaudi in 1973).

Calvino, I. (1981). *If on a winter's night a traveler*. New York: Houghton Mifflin Harcourt.

Calvino, I. (1986), *Palomar*. Boston, Ma: Mariner Books.

Calvino, I. (2016). *Six memos for the next millennium*. Boston, Ma: Mariner Books (First Italian edition by Garzanti in 1988).

Christensen, C. M. (2013). The innovator's dilemma: When new technologies cause great firms to fail. Harvard Business Review Press.

Christensen, C. M., Grossman, J. H., and Hwang, G. (2009). *The innovator's prescription*. Hoboken, NJ: McGraw Hill.

Cowie, P. (2018). The Godfather: The official motion picture archives. Carlton Books Limited.

Csíkszentmihályi, M. (2013). *Creativity: The psychology of discovery*. Harper Perennial.

D'Anna, S. (2013) 'L'italiano sogno americano', *Monsieur*, February.

Damasio, A. R. (1994). Descartes' error: Emotion, reason, and the human brain. New York: Putnam.

Damasio, A. R. (1999). The feeling of what happens: Body and emotion in the making of consciousness. Boston: Houghton Mifflin Harcourt.

Damasio, A., and Carvalho, G. B. (2013). 'The nature of feelings: evolutionary and neurobiological origins', *Nature Reviews Neuroscience*, 14, no. 2: 143–152.

de Saint-Exupéry, A. (2012). *Airman's odyssey*, New York: Houghton Mifflin Harcourt.

Devinsky, O., Farah, M. J., and Barr, W. B. (2008). 'Visual agnosia', *Handbook of Clinical Neurology*, 88: 417–427.

de Zurara, G. E. (1915). *Crónica da tomada de Ceuta por el rei D. João I*. Academia das sciências de Lisboa.

Dreyfuss, H. (1967). *Measure of man*. 2nd, revised and enlarged edition. Whitney Library of Design.

Duncker, K., and Lees, L. S. (1945). 'On problem-solving', *Psychological Monographs*, 58, no. 5: i.

Du Sautoy, M. (2008). Finding moonshine: A mathematician's journey through symmetry. London: Fourth Estate.

Dutton, D. (2009). The art instinct: Beauty, pleasure, & human evolution. London: Bloomsbury Press.

The Economist (2012). 'The last Kodak Moment', *The Economist Business Section*, 14 Jan, available online: https://www.economist.com/business/2012/01/14/the-last-kodak-moment (accessed 24 June 2021).

Edmondson, A. (1999). 'Psychological safety and learning behavior in work teams', *Administrative Science Quarterly*, *44*, no. 2: 350–383.

Enquist, M., and Arak, A. (1994). 'Symmetry, beauty and evolution', *Nature*, 372, no. 6502: 169–172.

Ericsson, A., and Pool, R. (2016). *Peak: Secrets from the new science of expertise*. New York: Houghton Mifflin Harcourt.

Fadell, T. (2016). 'How can we design for a better experience?' interviewed by Guy Raz. *TED Radio Hour*. NPR. Available online: https://www.npr.org/transcripts/478560438 (accessed 2 October 2020).

Falcones, I. (2009) *The cathedral of the sea*, New York: Penguin Books.

Feynman, R. P. (1963). *The Feynman lectures on physics*, ed. R. P. Feynman, R. B. Leighton, and M. Sands. Reading: Addison-Wesley.

Floridi, L. (2010). Information: A very short introduction. OUP Oxford.

Fogg, B. J. (2009). 'Creating persuasive technologies: an eight-step design process', In *Proceedings of the 4th International Conference on Persuasive Technology*: 1–6.

Freeman, M. (2007). The photographer's eye: Composition and design for better digital photos. Routledge.

Frugoni, C. (2019). Paradiso vista Inferno. Buon Governo e Tirannide nel Medioevo da Ambrogio Lorenzetti. Bologna: Il Mulino.

Galois, E. (1976). 'Ecrits et mémoires mathématiques', in R. Bourgne, Azra, J. P., Galois, E., and Dieudonné, J. (Eds.) *Écrits et mémoires mathématiques d'Évariste Galois: édition critique intégrale de ses manuscrits et publications*. Paris: Gauthier-Villars.

Gelernter, D. H. (1998). *The aesthetics of computing*. Phoenix: W&N.

Gell-Mann, M., and Lloyd, S. (1996). 'Information measures, effective complexity, and total information', *Complexity*, 2, no. 1: 44–52.

Gigerenzer, G. (2007). Gut feelings: The intelligence of the unconscious. London: Penguin.

Giurfa, M., Eichmann, B., and Menzel, R. (1996). 'Symmetry perception in an insect', *Nature, 382*, no. 6590: 458–461.

Gladwell, M. (1999). 'True colors', *The New Yorker*, 22.

Goldberg. P. (2018). 'Guggenheim on the inside', available online: https://www.guggenheim.org/arts-curriculum/topic/guggenheim-on-the-inside (accessed June 23, 2021).

Goldstein, D. G., and Gigerenzer, G. (2002). 'Models of ecological rationality: The recognition heuristic', *Psychological Review*, 109, no. 1.

Golubitsky, M., and Stewart, I. (1992). *Fearful symmetry*, New York: Dover Publ.

Gombrich, E. H. (1961). *Art and illusion*. New York (NY): Pantheon Books.

Gombrich, E. H. (1979). The sense of order: A study in the psychology of decorative art. Ithaca: Cornell University Press.

Gordon, P. C., Hendrick, R., and Johnson, M. (2001). 'Memory interference during language processing', *Journal of Experimental Psychology: Learning, Memory, and Cognition*, 27, no. 6: 1411–1423.

Greene, M. R., Liu, T., and Wolfe, J. M. (2012). 'Reconsidering Yarbus: A failure to predict observers' task from eye movement patterns', *Vision Research*, 62: 1–8.

Gregor, S., and Hevner, A. R. (2013). 'Positioning and presenting design science research for maximum impact', *MIS Quarterly*, 337–355.

Hansen, H., Ropo, A., and Sauer, E. (2007). 'Aesthetic leadership', *The Leadership Quarterly*, *18*, no. 6: 544–560.

Harari, Y. N. (2012). *From animals into gods: A brief history of humankind*. Scotts Valley, CA: CreateSpace.

Healy, B. (2019). 'Bad dreams are good – your night life prepares you for what's to come', *The Atlantic*, April.

Hirsh, E., Hedlund, S., and Schweizer, M. (2003). 'Reality is perception: the truth about car brands', *Strategy and Business*: 20–25.

Hodgson, D. (2011). 'The first appearance of symmetry in the human lineage: where perception meets art', *Symmetry*, 3, no. 1: 37–53.

Hoffman, D. (2019). The case against reality: Why evolution hid the truth from our eyes. New York: W. W. Norton & Company.

Hofstadter, D. R., and Sander, E. (2013). *Surfaces and essences: Analogy as the fuel and fire of thinking.* New York: Basic Books.

Holub, M. (2013, May/June). 'American scientist', *Research Triangle Park*, 101, no. 3: 169.

Iandoli, L. (2021a). 'Just like another person: How human-centered design led to the invention of the personal computer – the case of the Olivetti Programma 101', *Sage Business Cases*, doi: http://dx.doi.org/10.4135/9781529753578.

Iandoli, L. (2021b). 'Olivetti: The innovation factory', *Sage Business Cases*, doi: http://dx.doi.org/10.4135/9781529761887.

Iandoli, L., and G. Zollo (2007). *Organizational cognition and learning: Building systems for the learning organization.* Hershey, PA: IGI Global.

Inglehart, R. (2015). The silent revolution: Changing values and political styles among Western publics. Princeton University Press.

Jimenez, S., Pohlmeyer, A. E., and Desmet, P. M. A. (2015). *Positive design: Reference guide.* Delft University of Technology.

Johnson, S. (2011). Where do good ideas come from: The natural history of innovation. New York: Penguin.

Kahneman, D. (2011). *Thinking, fast and slow.* New York: Macmillan.

Kahneman, D., Slovic, S. P., Slovic, P., and Tversky, A., eds. (1982). *Judgment under uncertainty: Heuristics and biases.* Cambridge, MA: Cambridge University Press.

Kandel, E. (2016). Reductionism in art and brain science: Bridging the two cultures. New York: Columbia University Press.

Kauffman, S. (2003). The adjacent possible. *Edge*, 9 November, available online:https://www.edge.org/conversation/stuart_a_kauffman-the-adjacent-possible (accessed 24 June 2021).

Kawabata, H., and Zeki, S. (2004). 'Neural correlates of beauty', *Journal of Neurophysiology*, 91: 1699–1705.

Kelly, J. (2005). *The great mortality: An intimate history of the Black Death.* London: Fourth Estate.

Kijo, M. (1923). Haiku poetry in *Famous Haiku*, available at https://www.haiku-poetry.org/famous-haiku.html (accessed 2 July 2021).

Klein, H. (1952). *Symmetry.* Princeton: Princeton University Press.

Kniberg, H., and Ivarsson, A. (2012). 'Scaling Agile @ Spotify with Tribes, Squads, Chapters & Guilds', available online: https://blog.crisp.se/wp-content/uploads/2012/11/SpotifyScaling.pdf (accessed 24 June 2021).

Knight W. (2017). 'An algorithm summarizes lengthy text surprisingly well', *MIT Technology Review*. Available online: https://www.technologyreview.com/s/607828/an-algorithm-summarizes-lengthy-text-surprisingly-well/ (accessed 2 October 2020).

Koffka, K. (2013). *Principles of Gestalt psychology.* London: Routledge.

Kosner, A. (2013). 'Jony Ives' (no longer so) secret design weapon', *Forbes*, 30 November.

Lakoff, G., and Johnson, M. (2008). *Metaphors we live by.* Chicago: University of Chicago press.

Leder, H., Belke, B., Oeberst, A., and Augustin, D. (2004). 'A model of aesthetic appreciation and aesthetic judgments', *British Journal of Psychology*, 95, no. 4: 489–508.

Lehrer, J. (2010). *How we decide.* New York: Houghton Mifflin Harcourt.

Leroy, L. (1874). 'L'Exposition des Impressionnistes', Le Charivari, Paris. Translated by John Rewald in *The History of Impressionism*, MOMA, 1946: 256–261.

Lombard, P. (1150 ca.). Giulio Silano, trans. (2007). *The Sentences,* Books 1–4. Toronto: Pontifical Institute of Mediaeval Studies.

Loyrette, H. (1985). *Gustave Eiffel.* New York: Rizzoli.

Lupton, H. (2017). *Design is storytelling*, New York: Copper Hewitt Smithsonian Design Museum.

Maeda, J. (2006). *The laws of simplicity.* Cambridge, MA: MIT Press.

Malone, T. B., Kirkpatrick, M., Mallory, K., Eike, D., Johnson, J. H., and Walker, R. W. (1980). 'Human factors evaluation of control room design and operator performance at Three Mile Island-2', *NUREG/CR*, 1270, vol. 1.

Marković, S. (2012). 'Components of aesthetic experience: aesthetic fascination, aesthetic appraisal, and aesthetic emotion', *in-Perception*, 3, no. 1: 1–17.

Maslow, A. H. (1966) The psychology of science: A reconnaissance. Harper & Row.

McKinsey (2018). 'The business value of design', *McKinsey Quarterly*, October 25, available online: https://www.mckinsey.com/business-functions/mckinsey-design/our-insights/the-business-value-of-design# (accessed June 21, 2021).

Michellone, G., and Zollo, G. (2000). 'Competencies management in knowledge-based firms', *International Journal of Manufacturing Technology and Management*, *1*, no. 1: 20–41.

Milian, M. (2009). 'Why text messages are limited to 160 characters', *Los Angeles Times* blog, available online: https://latimesblogs.latimes.com/technology/2009/05/invented-text-messaging.html (accessed June 21, 2021).

Miller, G. (1956). 'The magical number seven, plus or minus two: some limits on our capacity for processing information', *Psychological Review*, *63*: 81–97.

MOMA (1952). 'Olivetti: Design in Industry', *The Museum of Modern Art Bulletin*, 20, no. 1.

Montesquieu, C. (1748). *De l'Esprit des Lois*, Geneve: Barillot & Fils.

Morieux, Y., and Tollman, P. (2014). *Six simple rules: How to manage complexity without getting complicated*. Boston: Harvard Business Review Press.

Mortimer, I. (2014). *Centuries of change: Which century saw the most change?* New York: Random House.

Neath, I., Bireta, T. J., and Surprenant, A. M. (2003). 'The time-based word length effect and stimulus set specificity', *Psychonomic Bulletin & Review*, *10*, no. 2; 430–434.

Nisbett, R.E., and Wilson, T. D. (1977). 'The halo effect: evidence for unconscious alteration of judgments', *Journal of Personality and Social Psychology*, 35, no. 4: 250–256.

Norman, D. A. (2004). *Emotional design: Why we love (or hate) everyday things*. New York: Basic Books.

Norman, D. A. (2016). *Living with complexity*. Cambridge, MA: MIT Press.

Osterwalder, A. (2016). Business model canvas of Nespresso, available online: https://www.youtube.com/watch?v=dhQh-tryXOg (accessed 24 June 2021).

Papanek, V., and Fuller, R. B. (1972). *Design for the real world*. London: Thames and Hudson.

Pennycook, G., Cheyne, J. A., Koehler, D. J., and Fugelsang, J. A. (2020). On the belief that beliefs should change according to evidence: Implications for conspiratorial, moral, paranormal, political, religious, and science beliefs. *Judgment and Decision Making*, *15*, no. 4: 476.

Perec, G. (2009). *Life: A user's manual*. 2nd edition. Verba Mundi.

Perotto, P. G. (2015). *Quando l'Italia invento' il Personal Computer*. Ivrea, Italy: Edizioni Comunita'.

Piaget, J. (1964). 'Part I: Cognitive Development in Children: Piaget Development and Learning', *Journal of Research in Science Teaching*, 2, no. 3: 176–186.

Piattelli Palmarini, M. (1996). *Inevitable illusions: How mistakes of reason rule our minds*. Hoboken, NJ: Wiley.

Picasso, M. (2001). *Picasso: My grandfather*. New York: Riverhead Hardcover.

Pine, H. (2012). 'How Brando gave the don his bite', *Shortlist*, February.

Pirsig, R. M. (2005). *Zen and the art of motorcycle maintenance: An inquiry into values*. New York: HarperPerennial.

Plimpton, G. (1958). 'Ernest Hemingway, the art of fiction no. 21', *Paris Review,* 18, no. 2: 60–89.

Proust, M. (2015). *Swann's way – in search of lost time, volume one*, first edition published in 1913, translated by C. K. Scott Moncrieff. Digireads.com Publishing.

Prum, R. O. (2017). *The evolution of beauty: How Darwin's forgotten theory of mate choice shapes the animal world—and us*. New York: Anchor Books.

Ramachandran, V. S. (2012). *The tell-tale brain: A neuroscientist's quest for what makes us human.* New York: W.W. Norton & Company.

Rams, D. (2014). *Less but better*. Berlin: Gestalten.

Ranganath Nayak, P., and Ketteringham, J. M. (1993). Breakthroughs! How the vision and drive in sixteen companies created commercial breakthroughs that swept the world. Pfeiffer & Co.

Raz, G. (2017). 'Starbucks: Howard Schultz', *How I built this podcast,* National Public Radio, available at 'https://www.stitcher.com/podcast/how-i-built-this/e/51626348 (accessed 24 June 2021).

Reason, J. (2016). *Managing the risks of organizational accidents revisited*. Boca Raton, FL: Taylor and Francis.

Reber, R., Schwarz, N., and Winkielman, P. (2004). 'Processing fluency and aesthetic pleasure: Is beauty in the perceiver's processing experience?' *Personality and Social Psychology Review*, 8, no. 4: 364–382.

Reynolds, J. (2005). *The Citroën 2CV*. Sparkford, UK: Haynes Publishing.

Rewald, S. (2004). 'Cubism', *MET Heilbrun Timeline of Art Essays*, available online: https://www.metmuseum.org/toah/hd/cube/hd_cube.htm (accessed June 23, 2021).

Ries, A., Trout, J. (2001). *Positioning*. Hoboken, NJ: McGraw Hill.

Roselló-Díez, A., Madisen, L., Bastide, S., Zeng, H., and Joyner, A. L. (2018). 'Cell-nonautonomous local and systemic responses to cell arrest enable long-bone catch-up growth in developing mice', *PLoS Biology*, *16*, no. 6: e2005086.

Sartre, J. P. (1965). *Nausea*. Milano, Italy: Mondadori.

Schama, S., and van Rijn, R. H. (1999). *Rembrandt's eyes*. New York: Alfred A. Knopf.

Schank, R. C. (1991). *Tell me a story: A new look at real and artificial intelligence*. New York: Simon & Schuster.

Schank, R. C. and Abelson, R. (1977). *Scripts, plans, goals, and understanding*. Hillsdale, NJ: Earlbaum Assoc.

Schein, E. H. (2002). 'The anxiety of learning', interview by Diane L. Coutu, *Harvard Business Review*, 80, no. 3: 100–6.

Schneider, M., and Somers, M. (2006). 'Organizations as complex adaptive systems: Implications of complexity theory for leadership research', *The Leadership Quarterly*, *17*, no. 4: 351–365.

Segall, K. (2013). *Insanely simple: The obsession that drives Apple's success*. New York: Penguin.

Semmann, D., Krambeck, H. J., and Milinski, M. (2003). 'Volunteering leads to rock–paper–scissors dynamics in a public goods game', *Nature*, *425*, no. 6956: 390–393.

Shannon, C. E. (1948). 'A mathematical theory of communication', *The Bell System Technical Journal*, 27, no. 3: 379–423.

Simonite, T. (2013). 'How Nest's control freaks reinvented the thermostat', *MIT Technology Review*, February 15, available at https://www.technologyreview.com/2013/02/15/114067/how-nests-control-freaks-reinvented-the-thermostat/ (accessed 24 June 2021).

Smith, K. K., and D. N. Berg (1987) *Paradoxes of group life: Understanding conflict, paralysis, and movement in group dynamics*. New York: Jossey-Bass.

Stamp, J. (2012). 'The long history of the espresso machine', *Smithsonian*, June 19, available online: https://www.smithsonianmag.com/arts-culture/the-long-history-of-the-espresso-machine-126012814/#EGjHqVRtfm0Wlbfj.99 (accessed June 23, 2021).

Stanska, Z. (2017). Stendhal Syndrome – The art fans sickness, DailyArt Magazine, April 3, available online: https://www.dailyartmagazine.com/stendhal-syndrome-art-fans-sickness/ (accessed June 23, 2021).

Statista Research Department (2021). 'Automotive electronics cost as a share of total car cost 1970–2030', *Statista*, February 5, available online: https://www.statista.com/statistics/277931/automotive-electronics-cost-as-a-share-of-total-car-cost-worldwide/ (accessed June 21, 2021).

Steegmuller, F. (1949) *Maupassant: A lion in the path*, London: Macmillan.

Strang, S., Gross, J., Schuhmann, T., Riedl, A., Weber, B., and Sack, A. T. (2015). 'Be nice if you have to - the neurobiological roots of strategic fairness', *Social Cognitive and Affective Neuroscience*, *10*, no. 6: 790–796.

Tatler, B. W., Wade, N. J., Kwan, H., Findlay, J. M., and Velichkovsky, B. M. (2010). 'Yarbus, eye movements, and vision', *i-Perception* 1, no. 1: 7–27. Available online: https://www.ncbi.nlm.nih.gov/pmc/articles/PMC3563050/ (accessed 17 June 2021).

Taylor, F. W. (1911). *The principles of scientific management*, New York: Harper and Brothers.

Thorndike, E. L. (1920) 'A constant error in psychological ratings', *Journal of Applied Psychology*, 4, no. 1: 25–29.

Tooby, J., and Cosmides, L. (2001). 'Does beauty build adapted minds? Toward an evolutionary theory of aesthetics, fiction, and the arts', *SubStance*, 30, no. 1: 6–27.

Tracer, D. (2003). 'Selfishness and fairness in economic and evolutionary perspective: An experimental economic study in Papua New Guinea', *Current Anthropology*, *44*, no. 3: 432–438.

Trivers, R., Fink, B., Russell, M., McCarty, K., James, B., and Palestis, B. G. (2014). 'Lower body symmetry and running performance in elite Jamaican track and field athletes', *PloS one*, *9*, no. 11: e113106.

Trusler, J. (1833. *The works of William Hogarth*. London: Jones and Co.

Tripsas, M., and Gavetti, G. (2000). 'Capabilities, cognition, and inertia: evidence from digital imaging', *Strategic Management Journal*, 21, no. 10/11: 1147–1161.

Tulving, E., and Arbuckle, T. Y. (1966). 'Input and output interference in short-term associative memory', *Journal of Experimental Psychology*, 72, no. 1:145–151.

University of Pennsylvania School of Medicine. (2006). 'Penn Researchers Calculate How Much the Eye Tells the Brain', *ScienceDaily*, 28 July. Available online: www.sciencedaily.com/releases/2006/07/060726180933.htm (accessed 17 June 2021).

Tyler, C. W. (2000). 'The human expression of symmetry, Art and neuroscience', in *ICUS Symmetry Symposium, Seoul*. Available online: https://icus.org/wp-content/uploads/2015/10/Tyler-Christopher-M.-The-Human-Expression-of-Symmetry-Art-and-Neuroscience.pdf (accessed: 2 October 2020).

van der Linden, S. (2011). 'The science behind dreaming', *Scientific American Mind*, available online: https://www.scientificamerican.com/article/the-science-behind-dreaming/ (accessed 24 June 2021).

Vrtička, P., Andersson, F., Sander, D., and Vuilleumier, P. (2009). 'Memory for friends or foes: the social context of past encounters with faces modulates their subsequent neural traces in the brain', *Social Neuroscience, 4*, no. 5: 384–401.

Walker, R. (2019). *The art of noticing*. New York: Knopf.

Wallis, F. (Ed.) (2010). *Medieval medicine: A reader,* vol. 15. Toronto: University of Toronto Press.

Wansink, B., and J. Sobal (2007). 'Mindless eating: The 200 daily food decisions we overlook', *Environment and Behavior*, 39, no. 1: 106–123.

Weber, M. (2015). 'Bureaucracy', in Waters, T. and D. Waters (Eds.) *Weber's rationalism and modern society*, 73–127. New York: Palgrave MacMillan.

Weick, K. E. (1995). *Sensemaking in organizations*. London: Sage.

Weigall, C. H. (1850). *The art of figure drawing*. Oxford (UK); Oxford University Press.

Wertheimer, M. (1912). 'Experimentelle Studien über das Sehen von Bewegung (Experimental Studies of the Perception of Movement)', *Encyclopaedia Britannica*, 26 May 2020. Available online: https://www.britannica.com/science/Gestalt-psychology (accessed 21 August 2020).

Wertheimer, M., and Riezler, K. (1944). 'Gestalt theory', *Social Research*, 78–99.

Weyl, H. (2015). *Symmetry*. Princeton, NJ: Princeton University Press.

Windhager, S., Schaefer, K., and Fink, B. (2011). 'Geometric morphometrics of male facial shape in relation to physical strength and perceived attractiveness, dominance, and masculinity', *American Journal of Human Biology*, 23, no. 6: 805–814.

Yarbus, A. L. (1967). *Eye movements and vision*. New York: Springer.

Zeki, S. (2011). Splendors and miseries of the brain: Love, creativity, and the quest for human happiness. Hoboken: John Wiley & Sons.

NOTES

1 Pier Giorgio Perotto, the inventor of the P101, describes the idea with these words: 'Between 1962 and 1964, the idea started to take shape in my mind more like a dream than a solution: the dream of a machine that would privilege functional autonomy over speed and power, a machine capable of executing complex calculations while handling the elaboration process autonomously, however under the direct control of a human being. [. . .] I was dreaming of a machine able to learn and execute obediently that would store instructions and data intuitively, and that could be used not only by a few specialists. It had to be affordable and of similar size as other office devices, to which people were already accustomed' (Perotto 2015: 18, our translation).

2 Adriano Olivetti (1901–1960) firmly believed that beauty was an essential key not only for successful products but also for a higher quality of life. He believed that the company needed not only technicians, but also intellectuals, writers and artists who enriched the work with their own knowledge and sensitivity. Olivetti worked deeply to ensure that his vision of beauty and harmony was enacted in all dimensions of the company: in the architecture of the factory, in the organization of work, in the design of products, in the relationship with the territory. In advertising campaigns, he demanded that not only the functionality of the products be emphasized but that equal attention be given to aesthetic beauty.

3 Morieux and Tollman (2014) analyze strategic choices and organizational structures of a sample of large companies and conclude that it is necessary to distinguish between complexity and complication. *Complexity* is measured in terms of the number of challenges that companies are called upon to respond to. Over the period from 1955 to 2010, complexity increased sixfold. *Complication* is measured as the number of organizational mechanisms – structures, procedures, rules and roles – that companies put in place in an effort to deal with complexity. In the same period, the complication increases by a factor of 35. According to the authors, the only chance companies have to escape the complicatedness trap is to pursue a 'smart simplicity' strategy, developing a greater autonomy of individuals and closer cooperation between them.

4 According to data compiled by the Statista Research Department (2021).

5 Digital technologies, while enhancing our experiences, induce much more profound transformations: They create an infosphere in which to live. Luciano Floridi (2010: 10–12) highlights the profound difference between a traditional technology such as a washing machine, which has its own autonomous and defined mode of operation (a closed operating world), and a digital interface such as an app on a mobile phone, which is a gate that invites us to enter cyberspace and negotiates with us about how to use resources there.

6 The title is inspired by the beautiful collection of serendipity exercises proposed by Rob Walker's 2019 book, *The Art of Noticing*.

7 Second Life was a virtual world created in 2003 and thought at the time to be a revolution and a new paradigm for the Internet. While the site is still active, the initial expectations that it was going to change the world were not fulfilled.

8 Researchers at the University of Pennsylvania School of Medicine estimate that the approximately 1,000,000 ganglion cells of human retina can transmit visual data at roughly 10 million bits per second. See the article "Penn researchers calculate how much the eye tells the brain." Published on *ScienceDaily* on 28 July 2006 www.sciencedaily.com /releases/2006/07/060726180933.htm

9 Goldstein and Gigerenzer (2002) propose a model of heuristics that are (a) ecologically rational, (b) founded in human psychological capacities, (c) fast, frugal and "simple enough to operate effectively when time, knowledge, and computational might are limited, (d) precise enough to be modeled computationally, and (e) powerful enough to model both good and poor reasoning" (p. 75).

10 According to Leher (2008), Proust discovered that smell and taste produce intense memories, and that memory is faulty and always changing.

11 See chapter 3 for more on abstraction and minimalistic design.

12 Yarbus' work on eye tracking has been more recently revised and expanded through the use of digital tools able to track and record eye movements (see Tatler et al. 2010 or this web site https://yarbus.eu/references/).

13 *Visual agnosia* is the clinical term for the cognitive disorder of visual perceptual processing. Patients suffering visual agnosia lose their capacity to recognize objects, although their visual systems are functioning (Devinsky et al. 2008: 417).

14 Gestalt theory's key tenet is that 'the whole is greater than its parts'. That is, the attributes of the whole are not deducible from analysis of the parts in isolation. The publication of the psychologist Wertheimer (1912) marks the founding of the Gestalt school. While Gestalt ideas have received empirical support in studies on perception, there is limited or no evidence to show that Gestalt laws and principles have a neuronal counterpart. However, we refer to and apply some of these principles in this book because they have been proved to be very effective at organizing visual information as in image composition (Freeman 2007).

15 Researchers have found that people make an average of 226.7 decisions about food alone (Wansink and Sobal 2007: 106–123).

16 See chapter 6 for the full story on the design of the NEST thermostat.

17 A point that Don Norman makes in his well-known book, *Emotional Design* (2004).

18 While the painting is known as *Girl with a Pearl Earring*, studies have shown that the earring could be actually made of glass and then treated with a special substance to make it look like a pearl. Apparently, this type of jewel was very popular in the Netherlands at the time this painting was made and much less expensive than a pearl of similar size. This observation has been made to confute the hypothesis that Vermeer gave such an expensive present to a young maid, a theory that fostered suspicion of the existence of an affair between the two.

19 Of course, there are other important ways through which we compensate for lack of information and the impossibility of learning everything from direct experience, such as learning from others. Note that even in this case, there is an emotional component. To learn from someone else, we need to trust that person, and this is an emotional decision.

20 'Symmetry, as wide or as narrow as you may define its meaning, is one idea by which man through the ages has tried to comprehend and create order, beauty, and perfection' (Klein 1952: 5).

21 Constantinople, the capital of the Eastern Roman Empire, modern day's Istanbul, fell under Ottoman siege in 1453. The event marked a fundamental change in world history and was a shock for many to its west. Among the other consequences, flocks of Greek scholars and intellectuals found refuge in Italy and contributed to the birth of the Renaissance through rediscovery of ancient Greek language, philosophy and other classic works.

22 Even if Gutenberg printed his first bible in 1455, the significant effects of the invention of print, in terms of book circulation and reduction of purchasing costs of printed books, did not start to be visible until the sixteenth century (Mortimer 2014).

23 At its peak in the late 1980s, Kodak employed almost 150,000 employees worldwide, and its market share in film sales peaked to over 90 percent (*The Economist* 2012). The company was also a leader in budget cameras, where it retained 80 percent of the US market share. Today, both companies still survive, but, after deep restructuring following bankruptcies, have undergone significant downsizing and now focus on specific but small market niches.

24 Kodak executives received a very accurate analysis of how digital technology was going to change the industry as early as 1985, thanks to a report presented by Vince Barabba, a Kodak executive in charge of market intelligence (Barabba 2011). However, the board reacted mildly and slowly. Kodak wasted the opportunity window that its headstart in digital photography had created as early as 1975, when Steven Sasson, a Kodak engineer, invented and perfected one of the first digital cameras. It is also important to remark that these companies' production capabilities were quite different from those needed in the digital camera industry. Polaroid and Kodak were chemical companies and did not have the skills and resources to manufacture electronic widgets.

25 This podcast series contains a great list of design lessons available in direct interviews to entrepreneurs and innovators.

26 Claude Shannon proposed a mathematical theory to quantify the amount of information transmitted over a channel. His theory laid the foundations for the digital transmission of information and contributed to the development of logic circuits that are at the base of modern microprocessors. Shannon's theory relies on a thermodynamic metaphor to treat information transmission similar to energy by introducing the concept of entropy of a message.

27 The Gestalt was a psychology school born in Germany in the first half of the twentieth century. Gestalt psychologists assumed that human perception relies on the existence of cognitive primitives that help us to organize sensorial information based on principles of 'good form'. The word *Gestalt* means form or pattern.

28 Escher plays with this idea in many of his works. In some cases, he uses it in circle, as in *Reptiles* (1943) or in *Waterfall* (1961). In others, forms evolve from other forms through an intense use of tessellation, as in *Day and Night* (1938).

29 See the fascinating concept of human beings as inforgs, interconnected informational organisms, inhabiting the infosphere (Floridi 2010).

30 To appreciate Bosch's mastery and the amazing level of detail in his works, we strongly recommend Fischer's illustrated book in large the format published by Taschen in 2014.

31 Fede Galizia was part of a group of extremely talented female painters active in Italy in the sixteenth century, including Artemisia Gentileschi, Sofonisba Anguissola, Lavinia Fontana, Giovanna Garzoni, Elisabetta Sirani and many others. Their outstanding contribution to baroque painting was obfuscated because of gender discrimination, and their works have been unfairly considered as minor expressions of the Caravaggesque school.

32 Tony Fadell oversaw the development of the Apple iPod and was one of the co-creators of the first generations of iPhones.

33 Augmented reality is instead successful for specialized users and technical applications, such as in medicine. We explain this result with the fact that our ability to process complex information grows with expertise and knowledge of the context in which this extra information is really useful. Generis users, however, may lack both.

34 It is interesting to note that there is no strong evidence that certain facial features in men are generally considered more attractive by women, nor that those features are associated with better health or other forms of evolutionary advantages. The problematic association between attractive physical traits and objective evolutionary advantages is the subject of the critique of evolutionary psychology advanced by Prum (2017), who, following Darwin's less known theory of sexual reproduction, claims that attractive traits are arbitrarily selected by females and then propagated in the next generations through a form of co-evolutionary adaptation. See also Windhager et al. (2011).

35 You can read the full story in the book *How We Decide* (Lehrer 2010).

36 The construction techniques used in Gothic cathedrals are not well known. Architects and workers were typically members of secretive societies in which they were initiated to the art of building under the obligation to not divulge their knowledge. Architects were often anonymous and little is known of their life and training. See Gies and Gies (1994) or Bechmann and Riviere (1981) to learn more.

37 In 2014, the Cooper Hewitt Design Museum hosted an exhibition of human-centred design titled *Beautiful Users*. Pictures of the exhibition's items include dozens of examples of human-centred products, available on the museum website: https://collection.cooperhewitt.org/exhibitions/51669015/page3

38 Frank Lloyd Wright's works are often characterized by the attempt to let the construction emerge from the natural characteristics of the terrain or landscape where it was supposed to be built or by the specific use the construction was supposed to serve. This approach, known as organic architecture, explains the extreme diversity of Wright's building designs, and it is often juxtaposed to the top-down, rationalist architecture proposed by Le Corbusier. We analyze organic architecture in the case study 7.1 available on this book's companion website.

39 The Italian word 'espresso' means express, fast. A modern espresso machine can make coffee in few seconds. The drink can be immediately served at a bar and consumed quickly, thanks to its small size. The whole experience lasts a couple of minutes, which allows for a very quick turnover for the coffee seller. Of course, the brevity of the moment needed to be compensated with the intensity of the experience, so espresso's taste was gradually optimized to become very bold and concentrated.

The history of the invention and perfection of the espresso machine is an interesting innovation tale (Stamp 2012).

40 Nespresso initial patents are, for the most part, expired; that is why today we have compatible pods and machines built by other producers. For a while, however, these patents protected the company from imitation.

41 This convenience did not come without costs. Nespresso had to face sustained criticism about the negative environmental impact of its system due to the excessive production of non-recyclable garbage. The company reacted creating a recycling program through which the exhausted pods can be shipped for free to Nespresso for proper disposal. We are not aware, however, that similar practices have been adopted by imitators and competitors, so the coffee pod business keeps generating a significant amount of unnecessary garbage.

42 A digital version of the picture is available on the site of the auctioneer: https://www.phillips.com/detail/henri-cartierbresson/NY040517/107

43 Interestingly, Daniel Pink demonstrated that functional fixedness increases when problem solvers are offered monetary incentives. Pink's conclusion was that while monetary incentives increase productivity on standard tasks, they work against creativity when individuals are asked to think out of the box.

44 Even if several prototypes were created in the 30s, the production and commercialization of the 2CV started only after World War II. Citroen hid the prototypes in secret locations to prevent the German invaders from stealing the project.

45 A very similar representation can be found in El Greco's portrait of the martyrdom of San Sebastian.

46 See chapter 3 for a reference and examples of Picasso's studies of African Masks.

47 The fascinating story of the creation of the L'Oréal slogan can be read in Malcom Gladwell's article (1999).

48 The Apple ad 'Here's to the Crazy Ones' featured revolutionary geniuses such as Albert Einstein, Bob Dylan, Maria Callas, Pablo Picasso, Martin Luther King, John Lennon, and many others. The spot is freely available on the Internet.

49 Futurists experimented frequently with the idea that speed distorts objects in motion. Speaking of cars, see Luigi Russolo's beautiful painting titled *Dynamism of a Car* (1913).

50 This revolutionary point of view is presented by Prum in his book as 'the Beauty happens' principle. According to this hypothesis, aesthetic preferences in the animal world are typically arbitrary and not associated with specific evolutionary advantages. This hypothesis is harshly criticized by Wallacean Darwinists who typically postulate that beauty is an honest signal associated with superior mating quality and higher chances of survival.

51 Without any scientific basis, Nazi and anti-Semite propaganda, for instance, associated certain physical traits with Jews to support the argument that Jews were ethnically and racially different from other Germans.

52 Fra Mauro was an Italian monk and cartographer who lived in the Republic of Venice in the fifteenth century. The prefix *Fra* is an abbreviation of the Italian word *Fratello*, meaning 'brother', an appellation used for monks. The map created for the king of Portugal has been lost, but a copy is in Venice at the Biblioteca Marciana.

53 Spices were valuable because they were the only food preservatives available at a time in which refrigerators were not available. The Republic of Venice had amassed amazing riches thanks to its monopoly in the control of the spice trade with the East. The emergence of the Ottoman Empire and the war against the European superpowers for the control of the Mediterranean closed the traditional Middle East trade routes and forced Europeans to search for alternative options.

54 De Zurara, a contemporary chronicler, wrote that while the slaves' 'bodies were captive, this was a small matter in comparison with their souls which would have eternal true freedom' (de Zurara 1915). He refers to the slaves with the Portuguese word *almas* (souls). Sometimes, de Zurara calls slaves as *Moors*, a term used to generically refer to Muslims, to imply that it was acceptable to enslave the followers of a wrong faith.

55 A petition called 'Artists against the Eiffel Tower', published by *Le Temps* on 14 February 1887, protested 'against the erection . . . of this useless and monstrous Eiffel Tower . . . dominating Paris like a gigantic black smokestack, crushing under its barbaric bulk Notre Dame, the Tour Saint-Jacques, the Louvre, the Dome of les Invalides, the Arc de Triomphe, all of our humiliated monuments will disappear in this ghastly dream' (Loyrette 1985).

56 Some experts refer to this trend as post-materialism, a trend in which consumerism drives the need to express ourselves through the products we buy, rather than by the actual problems these products help fix (Inglehart 2015).

57 It's interesting to report that sale data of the first release of the device were well below the expectations and seemed to confirm the scepticism of the Walkman program's internal opposition. Luckily, Kozo Oshone, the manager in charge of the Walkman manufacturing, had cautiously limited the number of units by hiding this decision from the CEO. Eventually, though, sales skyrocketed thanks to a new category of buyers, Yuppies, an acronym for Young Urban Professionals, a new emerging group of affluent customers who considered hi-tech gadgets a status symbol. Sony had envisaged the initial target market was teenagers. Instead, teenagers, who ended up liking and buying the Walkman only later, were not the early adopters because teenagers tend to conform. Instead, Yuppies were the minority of early adopters that liked to go against mainstream consumption to affirm their lifestyle and stand out from the crowd.

58 Great chess players develop an ability to recognize structured configurations in a game that help them anticipate their opponents' reactions and draw them into a sequence of choices that will lead to their defeat. Designers can learn this skill to anticipate the moves of their users.

59 In this analysis, we use the concept of visual weight proposed by Arnheim (1965, 1983). In his books Arnheim provides many examples of the application of this method to the analysis of other images and works of art. We recommend our readers look at these examples and try to apply the same approach to the analysis of a design artifacts.

60 For more design lessons from the Three Mile Island accident, see the case study in exercise 4.1 on the book companion web site.

61 A very accurate, yet accessible and emotional account of the series of events that led to the explosion of the Chernobyl's nuclear reactor is masterfully illustrated in the TV series *Chernobyl*. Valery Legasov (played by the actor Jared Harris), the deputy director of the then most important Soviet Institute for Research in Nuclear Energy, in an iconic scene uses a little display and a series of simple index cards to deliver one of the best technical presentations ever.

62 Apple lead designer Jonathan Ive has often referred to Rams as one of his source of inspiration (Kosner 2013).

63 This arbitrary or induced baseline is called an *anchor* and this cognitive bias is called *anchoring* (see Kahneman et al. 1982).

64 Calvino initially wrote the *The Castle of Crossed Destinies* to be included in the volume *Tarot, The Visconti Deck of Bergamo and New York*, published by Franco Maria Ricci, a collection of stories inspired by tarot cards illuminated by Bonifacio Bembo for Milan dukes in the mid-fifteenth century. A few years later, Calvino completed a second text, *The Tavern of Crossed Destinies*, inspired by tarot cards printed in Marseille in 1761 by Nicolas Conver. Both texts appear in *The Castle of Crossed Destinies* book, published in Italian by Einaudi in 1973 (for the English Translation see Calvino, 1979).

65 See Lupton (2017) to learn how to apply narrative models to the design of new products.

66 More examples on the unethical use of product aesthetics, including the Juul and the junk food cases, can be found in Brown (2019).

67 See the company design website for more examples on how Pepsi is using design-driven innovation: http://design.pepsico.com/ and download for free the Design + Innovation book through which Pepsi celebrates design-driven innovation.

ACKNOWLEDGMENTS

This book is the result of several years of work during which we received support, encouragement, ideas, suggestions, and constructive criticism from many colleagues, students, and friends:

Imma Ardito, Carol Aronson Shore, Giovanni Attanasio, Dario Borrelli, Fernando Buarque, Lorella Cannavacciuolo, John Casti, Marinella De Simone, Alberto De Toni, Eileen Figueroa, Gastone Garziera, Glenn Gerstner, Alfonso and Livia Iaccarino, Raphael Jackson, Kevin James, Paolo Legrenzi, Carlo Lipizzi, Mo Mansouri, GianCarlo Michellone, Basilio Monteiro, Katia Passerini, Letizia Piantedosi, Cristina Ponsiglione, José Principe, Zulma Quiñones, José Ramirez Marquez, Alejandro Salado, Giovanni Schiuma, Jia Shen, Barry Shore, Dario Simoncini, Roberto Verganti, Dinesh Verma, Olli Vuolla.

A special thanks goes to the students in our courses 'The Art of Simplicity' (Aalto University, Stevens Institute of Technology), 'Creativity, Innovation, and Entrepreneurship' (St. John's University), and 'Marketing and Branding' (University of Naples Federico II) with whom we have experimented and discussed many of the ideas and materials contained in this book.

We also had the opportunity to share our ideas with participants to several executive programs. Some of these initiatives, such as the one we organized for Telecom Italia, offered us a great occasion to reflect on how to apply our theories and tools to management and complex systems.

Thanks are also due to our editors Faith Marsland, Louise Baird-Smith, Felicity Cummins, and Courtney Coffman for believing in this project and for their support, guidance, and patience. We are grateful to the anonymous reviewers for their suggestions.

Finally, much gratitude to our families for their love and support.

To Matteo, thanks to whom everything makes sense
Luca Iandoli

To Rosalba, for her love and support
Giuseppe Zollo

CREDITS

Figure 4.6 Peter Macdiarmid / Staff, Getty Images
Figure 4.7 Rogers Fund and Gifts of Lucy W. Drexel,
   Theodore M. Davis, Helen Miller Gould,
   Albert Gallatin, Egypt Exploration Fund and
   Egyptian Research Account, by exchange, 1950.
   Metropolitan Museum of Art
Figure 4.8 Author's image
Figure 4.9 Thelmadatter, Wikimedia
Figure 4.10 PhotoPlus Magazine / Contributor, Getty
   Images

Chapter 5

Figure 5.1 and 5.3 Yorck project, By Leonardo da Vinci -
   The Yorck Project (2002) 10.000 Meisterwerke
   der Malerei (DVD-ROM), distributed by
   DIRECTMEDIA Publishing GmbH, Wikimedia
Figure 5.2 Robert Lehman Collection, 1975, The
   Metropolitan Museum of Art
Figure 5.4 SOPA Images / Contributor, Getty Images
Figure 5.5 Smith Collection/Gado / Contributor, Getty
   Images
Figure 5.6 SOPA Images / Contributor, Getty Images;
   VCG / Contributor, Getty Images
Figure 5.7 Jeff Greenberg / Contributor, Getty Images

Chapter 6

Figure 6.1 The Yorck Project (2002) 10.000 Meisterwerke
   der Malerei (DVD-ROM), distributed by
   DIRECTMEDIA Publishing GmbH, Wikimedia
Figure 6.2 www.wga.hu, Wikimedia
Figure 6.3 The Yorck Project (2002) 10.000 Meisterwerke
   der Malerei (DVD-ROM), distributed by
   DIRECTMEDIA Publishing GmbH, Wikimedia
Figure 6.4 The Yorck Project (2002) 10.000 Meisterwerke
   der Malerei (DVD-ROM), distributed by
   DIRECTMEDIA Publishing GmbH, Wikimedia
Figure 6.5 Gift of H.W.A. Deterding, London,
   Rijksmuseum
Figure 6.6 Wikimedia
Figure 6.7 and 6.8 Wikimedia
Figure 6.9 AFP Contributor / Contributor, Getty Images
Figure 6.10 Dennis Murphy, Wikimedia
Figure 6.11A picture alliance / Contributor, Getty Images
Figure 6.11B Raysonho @ Open Grid Scheduler / Grid
   Engine, Wikimedia
Figure 6.11C Nest https://www.flickr.com/photos/nest
   /6264860195/in/photostream/

Figure 6.11D osseous https://www.flickr.com/photos
   /10787737@N02/40358991140
Figure 6.12 Bloomberg / Contributor, Getty Images
Figure 6.13 Steve Schapiro / Contributor, Getty Images

Chapter 7

Figure 7.1 George Heyer / Stringer, Getty Images
Figure 7.2 Bettmann / Contributor, Getty Images
Figure 7.3 and 7.4 Museum of Modern Art, Wikimedia
Figure 7.5 Harvard Art Museum/Fogg Museum,
   Wikimedia
Figure 7.6 Musée d'Orsay, Wikimedia
Figure 7.7A and 7.7B Author's image
Figure 7.8A Joe Shlabotnik https://www.flickr.com
   /photos/joeshlabotnik/2294656527/
Figure 7.8B David Pye, Wikimedia
Figure 7.9 TIMOTHY A. CLARY / Contributor, Getty
   Images
Figure 7.10 Tretyakov Gallery, Moscow, Russia, Wikiart
Figure 7.11 Author's image

Chapter 8

Figure 8.1A Lothar Spurzem, Wikimedia
Figure 8.1B Anadolu Agency / Contributor, Getty
   Images
Figure 8.2 Bequest of Scofield Thayer, 1982, The
   Metropolitan Museum of Art
Figure 8.3 Rogers Fund, 1956, The Metropolitan
   Museum of Art
Figure 8.4 New Orleans Museum of Art, Wikimedia
Figure 8.5 MarenHumburg, Wikimedia
Figure 8.6 The Yorck Project (2002) 10.000 Meisterwerke
   der Malerei (DVD-ROM), distributed by
   DIRECTMEDIA Publishing GmbH, Wikimedia
Figure 8.7 Vatican Museums, Vatican, Wikiart
Figure 8.8 Internet Archive Book Images https://www
   .flickr.com/photos/internetarchivebookimages
   /14578353737/
Figure 8.9A Poster, The Measure of Man (Male and
   Female), 1969 (first published 1959). Designed
   by Alvin Tilley (American, 1914-1993). Designed
   by Henry Dreyfuss Associates (New York, NY,
   USA). Published by Whitney Library of Design
   (USA). Offset lithograph, H x W: 193 x 63.5 cm
   (6 ft. 4 in. × 25 in.). Anonymous lender (se-1627).
   Photo: Matt Flynn. Cooper-Hewitt, Smithsonian
   Design Museum/Art Resource, NY/Scala, Florence

Figure 8.9B Poster, The Measure of Man (Male and Female), 1969 (first published 1959). Designed by Alvin Tilley (American, 1914-1993). Designed by Henry Dreyfuss Associates (New York, NY, USA). Published by Whitney Library of Design (USA). Offset lithograph, H x W: 193 x 63.5 cm (6 ft. 4 in. × 25 in.). Anonymous lender (se-1627). Photo: Matt Flynn. Cooper-Hewitt, Smithsonian Design Museum/Art Resource, NY/Scala, Florence

Figure 8.10 Gilles Mingasson / Contributor, Getty Images

Figure 8.11 Tim Colegrove, Wikimedia

Figure 8.12 Rama & Musée Bolo, Wikimedia

Figure 8.13A DeFacto, Wikimedia

Figure 8.13B Writegeist, Wikimedia

Chapter 9

Figure 9.1 Piero Falchetta, Wikimedia

Figure 9.2 and 9.3 Benh LIEU SONG, Wikimedia

Figure 9.4 Musée National d'Art Moderne, Paris, France, Wikiart

Figure 9.5 1876: bequeathed by Wynn Ellis, Wikimedia

Figure 9.6 Architas, Wikimedia

Figure 9.7 YOSHIKAZU TSUNO / Contributor, Getty Images

Figure 9.8 Jill Freedman / Contributor, Getty Images

Figure 9.9 SOPA Images / Contributor, Getty Images

Figure 9.10 Mario Tama / Staff, Getty Images

Chapter 10

Figure 10.1 and 10.2 The Department of History, United States Military Academy archive copy, Wikimedia

Figure 10.3and 10.4 Photo Josse/Leemage / Contributor, Getty Images

Figure 10.5 Discovered (villa Palombara, Esquilino) collection of Massimo-Lancellotti, Wikimedia

Figure 10.6A Wikimedia

Figure 10.6B PIERRE-PHILIPPE MARCOU / Staff, Getty Images

Figure 10.7 Fine Art / Contributor, Getty Images

Figure 10.8 Cjp24, Wikimedia

Figure 10.9A Wikimedia

Figure 10.9B Dawid SkaleC, Wikimedia

Figure 10.9C Bcos47, Wikimedia

Figure 10.10A Wystan from Ann Arbor, Wikimedia

Figure 10.10B With Associates, Wikimedia

Figure 10.11 The Washington Post / Contributor, Getty Images

Figure 10.12A Louvre Museum, Wikimedia

Figure 10.12B U.S. National Archives and Records Administration, Wikimedia

Chapter 11

Figure 11.1 Beinecke Library: http://brbl-dl.library.yale.edu/vufind/Record/3835917, Wikimedia

Figure 11.2 Author's image

Figure 11.3 Rogers Fund, 1907, The Metropolitan Museum of Art

Figure 11.4 Robert Lehman Collection, 1975, The Metropolitan Museum of Art

Figure 11.5 Sean Zanni / Stringer, Getty Images

INDEX